Praise for

the bees

"Rachel's painfully honest—but also funny and sweet—story of personal pain, tragedy, growth, and self-realization is a must-read. Her ability to point out everyday ways in which women too often cater to their male partners' whims makes this wonderful memoir a necessary book for both men and women."
- **Matt DeMazza**, Publishing Veteran

"This book is incredibly powerful, and I believe it will bring consolation to a lot of people. That someone who has experienced so much trauma can overcome her difficulties. Rachel, I applaud you."
- **Anna-Lisa Reda**, Editor & Industry Specialist

"The Bees is an emotionally evoking and brave memoir that brings a unique insight into how complex PTSD manifests. As a clinical psychologist, Rachel's memoir provides a personal perspective and detailed narrative of how one can work with persistent symptoms in order to live a full and happy life beyond the echoes of trauma. Complete with comprehensive trigger warnings, I recommend this book to survivors and their support system."
- **Nina Erikstad**, Psychologist & Book Reviewer

"I was laughing out loud, even completely alone, which is a rare thing."
- **Diana LeFevre**, Focus Group Participant

"The Bees was an intense, yet beautiful read. More women, and men, need to hear stories like this to even get a fraction of understanding of what some women go through. It's emotionally gripping, eye opening, and really gives a perspective that people need."
- **Teeka Stryker**, Book Illustrator & Book Mentor

"What particularly struck me is Rachel's honesty about her day-to-day difficulties and her day to day work. This is work, but it can be done and life can be good. There are also good people who can help you along that journey."
- **Susan J**, Goodreads Reviews

"I greatly admire the risk, the courage, the commitment, the time, the blood-letting that it took to write The Bees. Stylistically, it's very strong. I particularly admire your sense of the music in the language, your ability to craft the tone and structure of your sentences to suit their meaning. I also admire the tenor of the book, in that it's not in any way arrogant or assertive; it doesn't presume to have the answers; it understands that the questions are more important. The Bees makes you vulnerable, Rachel; and in doing so it makes you strong. I offer my heartfelt congratulations."
- **Christopher Pereira**, my High School English Teacher

"The descriptions of verbal and emotional abuse are extremely accurate and really resonated with me. I've experienced a fraction of that kind of abuse in what I thought was a friendship. I felt heard when reading those sections, because not many people discuss or even realize what happens with that kind of abuse."
-   **Anonymous**, Focus Group Participant

"I think it was helpful that in the prologue you mentioned, right upfront at the beginning of the book, to let the reader know, that you are coming at this from a place of healing. That life was better now. So even when The Bees was dark and having personally gone through a lot of those things [I had] to take mental health breaks just reliving my own trauma reading it, it helped knowing [I would get] to know exactly what steps she took that got her to this place that she then now because that's something that I could apply to my own life. So it was definitely worth it to me; to invest in the book and continue reading."
-   **Anonymous**, Focus Group Participant

The Bees

the bees

a memoir

rachel

suhonos

This book is a narrative non-fiction. The story is written from the perspective of the protagonist, Rachel Suhonos. Other people's perspectives of the same events may differ.

For legal purposes many names and locations have been altered for the privacy or protection of others.

First Edition: November 2023

Manufactured in the United States of America.

Proofreading & Copyediting by Matt DeMazza

Library and Archives Canada

ISBN 978-1-7389673-4-6 (hardcover)
ISBN 978-1-7389673-3-9 (paperback)
ISBN 978-1-7389673-2-2 (e-book)
ISBN 978-1-7389673-1-5 (audiobook)

To my previous self, the woman I was during trauma. You are more than your pain. You will survive. You will become. This is the story I wish I could have read when I felt so alone.

CONTENTS

Prologue

When I started writing this book, I researched other memoirists, especially female authors with similar experiences. I wanted to see how each woman wrote about the hard topics, how much detail they included, and how their character arc developed. I became a book monger, devouring every female memoirist I could find. I would buy a book, finish it in less than a day, and continue that way until I ran out of memoirs I had heard of, or were popular, or had intriguing stories. And through those memoirs I found most women experienced some sort of assault or abuse, yet none of them included how they overcame their trauma.

In fact, other than Alice Sebold's memoir, all others glossed over the sexual assault, domestic violence, or rape. It was a little sidebar, a little "oh yeah, that happened." No deep writing about how abuse impacted their life or how rape changed the way they viewed the world and moved through it; no reconciliation of pain. I felt a little undernourished. While reading about other women's resolution to issues prominently experienced in our gender, I wanted to feel some hope. I wanted some closure and strength coming from these women who lived through what I had survived. I wanted them to tell me, "Hey, I have these scars, and I went through this trauma you're going through. Here, look—I've healed." But there was no healing. In one book, the author casually mentioned, "This is a shadow that hangs off my bedpost and it's just there...." That's it?

I wanted to hear more. I needed them to tell me more. I wanted to read about the unraveling of their essence and how they put themselves back together. That's what I wanted to know because I needed to do it myself. It was like a string on a sweater that kept getting tugged on, leaving me wearing nothing but a sleeve, and I needed to know how to fix it. How does a person keep living and have joy in their life when a man invaded their body? How does anyone trust or fall in love again when the love of their life abused them? *Tell me*. This was what I needed to know.

Sure, I was interested in how they developed their career and the hurdles they overcame as a female actor or whatever. But how did they do that while they were carrying their trauma? How did she act out that creepy misogynistic scene without getting triggered? What do her song lyrics have to do with real pain? Did she hide in the dressing room and cry before any of her comedy shows because she just could not take the glaring from men in the audience? *Because I do not know what to do when I'm frozen in place or hiding in a corner or catching my breath in a bathroom stall.*

Like, stop pushing fresh vegetables on my plate. I don't want to be clean eating I want some raw bloody steak smothered in gravy. Give me the good stuff; give me the meat of your emotions. I don't want to be skin-deep in your story and only see what you want me to see on the surface.

Reach deep inside yourself down to the bowels and dissect your most painful story, lay your trauma on the kitchen table, and then tell me how you survived. How did you crawl out of that ditch? How did you emerge from agony, and how did that journey help you grow into the person you're proud to be?

I think true love is being able to see someone's deepest, darkest shame and fear and loving them even more. Respecting them and loving them for their resilience and their strength from conquering pain every day. The reason I feel the need to tell people about my deepest shame and my greatest fear and my darkest pain is because I want them to *see* me. I'm not looking for a pity party or even empathy. I'm looking for people to see what I've endured, to see my resilience, and to love me even more.

Some of this book was written amid the clutches of last night's hauntings while bony, thorny fingers cinched my lower rib cage; feelings were viscerally palpable and poetically documented. I read the journal entry months later and felt surprised that I was the author. Tears dropped on my backlit keyboard as I scrolled through my manuscript the night before I met with my editors. Sometimes I believed my writing had beautiful moments, and other times I wanted to delete everything I wrote and bury my notes in the backyard. *Such dichotomous thinking, and here I go again, being Hamlet.* To publish or not to publish? To include all my pain or bury it in a box? To expose all my scars or keep some hidden? To protect the ones who hurt me or name them? Let be. *I promise to tell you my story with honesty and vulnerability. I will bare my soul so others can see theirs within these pages.* That is all. Clean. Simple. No politics.

It's only fair for me to start this book with a warning: Some moments will make you cringe, angry, cry, or judge. You may relate to others. If you've experienced any of the things I have—and if you're a woman, chances are that you have—there are potential triggers. I have experienced multiple and compounding traumas. At some point, you'll likely wonder, *how in the hell did all this shit land on one person in such a short time?* Well, I wondered the same thing. It's all true, and in a wildly compact timeline. I will take you along with me down a dark path, and I will ask you to hold on until hope returns and life gets better. You will want to give up—hell knows I wanted to—but please don't. This is a book about trauma, resilience, and healing. Stay with me until the end, where we will cross a bridge into the blissful light of freedom and acceptance.

Trigger Warning: this book covers the following topics:
—Domestic violence: verbal and emotional abuse, physical abuse, sexual abuse
—Traumas of motherhood: traumatic labor, infertility, miscarriage, postpartum depression
—Sexual assault: kidnapping and rape
—Mental-health struggles: Depression, suicidal ideation, postpartum depression, posttraumatic stress disorder

Trigger warnings will be formatted per chapter, noting the pages containing the triggering content. If you forgo reading the triggering pages, you may flip to the back of the book, where there is a definition of triggers as well as a trigger summary. This will briefly explain the content you skipped. Please note that these summaries contain spoilers.

Remember, friends: Always be kind to yourself and respect your boundaries with triggering content. The goal for this book is to help you feel seen and give you hope for healing, not to trigger you and send you into a mental health spiral. If some of the content is too hard to read, take a break, and remember that this book ends with healing.

Lots of love,
Rachel

Chapter 1 – Awakening

"Give me your phone."

"No, why?"

"Because I want to see who's texting you."

"It's none of your business."

"Why won't you show me? What are you hiding? Are you cheating on me?"

"No. I'm texting Cara about breaking up with you."

"Are you serious?"

"Yes."

"Why?"

The spring air lifted my hair as I breezed through the exit onto the airport sidewalk. At the same moment Andrew, my fiancé, appeared at my side and gingerly lifted my luggage and placed it in the back of his car. I slid into my seat as he rounded to the driver's side. This weekend we were going on a road trip to Portland, Oregon. Andrew had made all the arrangements, as usual, and he planned on whisking me away for some romance. We hadn't seen each other in a few weeks. Andrew lived and worked on the U.S. West Coast at a big tech company while I completed my architecture degree in Southwestern Ontario. Every three or four weeks Andrew would fly me across the country to visit him, or he would fly back home to visit family and me.

We drove the three hours to Portland, calm and easy with conversation about our loved ones back home and wedding ideas. Andrew had secured us a room at a five-star hotel downtown, within walking distance to all the main attractions. As always, we held hands the entire drive. Once at the hotel, he took care of checking us in and carrying the bags to our room while I lounged in the lobby and perused the tourism pamphlets.

When Andrew returned, he suggested we go for a walk. We meandered along the river and through the bodegas, bought matching Baja hoodies, and ended up stumbling upon the doughnut shop we wanted to visit. Unconcerned with the long line, we wrapped our arms around each other as I slid into the soothing haven against his chest. Andrew made small talk with other customers and discussed ideas for our weekend tourism. Once in the donut shop, we posed with the giant donut, then carefully chose five to indulge in.

TW:EA//Back in our room, we opened the box to reveal the deliciousness of Voodoo Doughnut. Andrew and I each took photos pretending to take a big bite out of our choices. As soon as the camera dropped, Andrew said with his mouth full, "Are you seriously going to eat that whole thing?" He swallowed, "You don't need that. We're having dinner later."

I looked at him incredulously. "We just waited for

an hour and walked across town. Why do you get to eat yours and I don't?"

"Because I don't look like you."

So *that* was how this weekend was going to be. I left the room and went downstairs to the restaurant bar to have a glass of water. I reviewed our day lamenting about how I quickly removed the sizing tag off my Baja hoodie before handing it to Andrew to purchase. Eventually he joined me, and we had light dinner.

The next morning, we got ready for the day in still air and heavy silence. Sex was not on the table, and for the first time Andrew didn't really push for it—I must have repulsed him. We spent the day walking around and explored Powell's City of Books, sampled beer at Deschutes Brewery, and stopped at a conveyor-belt sushi restaurant for a midafternoon meal.

During lunch I felt hyperaware of the way Andrew counted the sushi rolls I lifted off the belt and onto the table in front of me. He watched me as if I was physically expanding in real time as I ate my food. I tried to choose lighter and smaller rolls I picked a plate of asparagus and cream cheese maki—something dainty and feminine-looking, so he wouldn't notice too much or blast my appetite. Andrew released an exasperated scoff, "Are you seriously having another plate? Gee, why don't you just rest your stomach on the table?!' Giggles erupted from his side of the booth as he delighted in his joke.

My jaw dropped and my face went red-hot as I rapidly looked around to see if anyone had overheard or was making a similar judgement of me. Thank goodness we were the only people in the restaurant, or I may have deflated completely and slid under the table in shame.

"That was really mean," I said to him in an embarrassed voice.

"Oh, come on, it was just a joke," he responded with a nonchalant confidence that made me question if I was overreacting. I ate one roll and pushed the plate to the side. The lump in my throat prevented me from wanting to swallow any more food.//*TW:EA*

Once Andrew paid our bill, we made our way back to the hotel to retrieve his car and start the road trip back to Seattle.

"What you said in the restaurant was really mean Andrew," I said once I finally found my voice again following the shock of his words. He gripped the wheel and stared out the front windshield in silence. "Aren't you going to say you're sorry?" I asked with the expectation of his regular routine of apologetic remorse.

"No, I'm done saying sorry. This is who I am." We pulled off the highway into a scenic path where we had mapped out a stop to take selfie engagement photos for our wedding website.

I always had a hard time picking out my attire whenever I visited Andrew. He wanted me to dress in tight sexy pencil skirts and low-cut tops, and I wanted to cover the body he deemed so unattractive. This day I chose tight white capris and a layered soft pink blouse. I felt like I looked romantic and desirable; my outfit strategically covered my lumps and bumps; tight in some areas and loose and flowy around my midsection. Andrew made it immediately clear he did not agree and made me feel silly for thinking I looked good in the outfit I so carefully chose.

TW:EA//"Why did you wear that? You're dressed like an old lady and your shirt makes you look bigger," he said, my smile fading.

"It's comfortable," was my go-to explanation for when I didn't live up to his expectations. We attempted to take photos as a happily engaged couple, yet joy didn't shine through in any of them. I stood in the middle of a boxing ring not knowing where or when the next punch would land, and I wanted to get back in the car.//*TW:EA*

Was Andrew really going to show no remorse? Was he truly so cold as to not care when he hurt me? Typically, if he hurt my feelings enough for me to tell him, he would apologize and be extra nice for a while. This time was different.

I returned to Canada with a heavy and confused heart. At that time, I lived with my sister, her husband, and my adorable nephew in a calm, warm, and loving home. I stepped off the plane, having emerged from a juxtaposed environment of alert anxiety and sadness.

A few weeks later when Andrew came to Canada for a visit, I told him how he made me feel the entire weekend in Portland; I handed him my last olive branch. He maintained that he was done apologizing. Andrew fantasized out loud about how once we were married, my wardrobe and appetite would not be issues anymore, because he would control the finances, throw out all my sweatpants, and approve any new purchases. He wanted a trophy wife, so I wouldn't have to worry my pretty little head about making any decisions. *Maybe this was not the marriage I wanted. Maybe I deserved something different.*

After this conversation, I knew I should not marry Andrew. But I tried to ignore that voice for the next three months by drowning it out with wedding planning and an engagement party.

"Why? Because I'm not willing to spend the rest of my life with someone who is mean to me. With someone who won't let me have a McFlurry when I want one."

"Oh my God, we can go back and get the McFlurry! Come on, we'll get the keys right now."

"Andrew, it's not just the McFlurry on the way

here. It's all the time. I think we need to call off the wedding and go to therapy if you want this to work."

I partly lied. I had no intention of going to therapy and making it work. I was done. Completely depleted of wanting to try. I had given all my effort through the nearly six years we spent together. I always made the romantic gestures, I mostly traveled to see him, and I always compromised. I was too tired to try anymore. He had used me up completely.

We spent the next day in a sort of trance. We hung out with my family at my parents' house and then had a games night with my brother and sister-in-law at theirs. The mood at games night was somber as everyone had heard the news that we had called off our wedding. We struggled to enjoy the moment and play games and ended up leaving early.

TW:SC//The next morning my parents had left for church and to visit my grandparents, leaving Andrew and me alone at their house. The second we heard the door click closed upstairs, Andrew started pressuring me: "Let's go make love."

"Definitely not."

"Rach, how are we supposed to make this work if we don't physically connect?"

"We don't need to right now."

"I want to be with you. I thought you wanted to work on our relationship."

"I want to be with you too, and I do."

"Don't you love me?"

"Of course I love you."

"Come on, let's just go into the other room. It'll be nice."

"No, Andrew, I don't want to right now." He was going to keep going until he got what he wanted. He always did. I was exhausted and not interested in letting him wear me down even further.

"Rach, please, don't you want to work on us? Don't you want to get married?" I did not want to work on us. I did not want to get married. But I also did not want him to call my bluff before he landed safely across the country from me. I needed us to be at a safe distance before I told him the rest of the truth. //TW:SC

"Fine," I said. I couldn't fight him anymore.

It is weird how sometimes rape is not obvious - even to the person experiencing the assault. It gets minimized, normalized, and you doubt your own memory. You wonder if the pain was warranted or deserved. You wonder if he was violent enough to be considered rape. If you said no loud enough to claim assault.

Was it rape? What to call it? Sex with Andrew was certainly not something I always wanted to participate in. By the last year of our relationship, providing my body for him to get off was an expectation of our relationship. He had me so conditioned to comply, there wasn't much fighting anymore. *What do you call that? Slavery?* Because I learned to avoid pain by faking orgasm. I learned how to get him off me by saying the right words. I learned to escape reality by focusing on the ceiling[ii]. I learned how to survive by normalizing it all.

If I was talking dirty and not fighting back, how could I see it as rape?

Andrew raped me. He raped me when I said no a dozen times and finally gave in. He raped me when he threatened to find another woman if I didn't put out. He raped me when I was too tired to fight him. He raped me in the middle of my sleep. He held me down while he overstimulated me as I cried in pain. He held me back as I tried to push him away. He grabbed my hair as I tried to catch my breath. And he kissed me as tears rolled over the sides of my face.

It took years before I recognized that Andrew sexually abused me in our relationship. I have since learned that sex is not consensual if you convince or pressure someone. That is coercive rape. The Sexual Assault and Prevention Awareness Centre describes sexual coercion as "a tactic used by perpetrators to intimidate, trick or force someone to have sex with them *without* physical force. Coercion is an issue of power and control. A perpetrator who uses coercive tactics knows his victim neither wants nor enjoys this sexual interaction." Furthermore, if your partner is too drunk or tired to be an active participant, it is rape. Consent is when both partners are enthusiastically involved. Involved not because of guilt, pressure, or obligation, but for mutual connection and pleasure.

TW:SC/ Andrew led me to the spare room that had a mattress on the floor. I laid on my back and stared at the ceiling. I was not even going to pretend I enjoyed this. I was done pretending, and I was done being the body he used to get off. I focused on the ceiling as he raped me and disassociated as I repeated this mantra to myself: "He will never fucking do this again. I will never let him touch me again." *//TW:SC*

As Andrew walked away from the car and I watched him disappear into London Airport Terminal, a sense of relief washed over my body and calmed my frayed nerves. *How did we get here?* I was sure we didn't start this way.

Chapter 2 – Beginnings

Andrew and I knew of each other throughout high school. I was the girl often mentioned in the announcements for excelling at sports, and he was the boy who joined the upper year in math because of his intellect. My last year of high school, I did a victory-lap year. I had skipped grade one and therefore progressed a year ahead of my age group. I elected to stay back to have more time at home, to build my art portfolio for architecture school applications, and to compete in sports again.

When Andrew and I met, I was president of the athletic and recycling clubs and a member of student council and the yoga club. I competed at high levels in wrestling and soccer, placing at provincials and going to nationals. I was highly social and able to enjoy many circles in my grade. I was at the top of my class academically, played piano and painted, taught swimming lessons and coached soccer, and I looked gorgeous. Yet, like many teenagers battling hormones and angst, I did not realize what a catch I was, and I turned into a sweaty speechless wreck whenever a boy turned his attention toward me.

Andrew was incredibly smart, played trombone in the school jazz band as well as piano and guitar, had a positive relationship with all the teachers, taught seniors how to use computers, and hung around with some great intellectual friends. Andrew was, however, incredibly nerdy-looking, and at five-foot-eleven and a hundred and ten pound, a brisk wind could seemingly blow him across the parking lot. He wasn't ugly but was not classically handsome.

Our lives intersected in Mr. Laxon's grade-twelve physics class. Andrew and Mr. Laxon had a great rapport and would chat throughout the period. Andrew's brilliant confidence and easygoing nature piqued my interest. He seemingly breezed through physics while I had to try a bit harder. I chose to sit behind him and would often bring baked goods to class so Andrew, our lab partners, and I could have a picnic and flirt. I would tap him on the shoulder and ask him to show me how to solve a problem even though I knew the answer. I played down my intelligence so I could get more attention from him.

As the winter formal approached, I hoped he would ask me to go as his date, but much to my dismay he asked another girl from his friend group. I felt disappointed but quickly changed my frame of mind to go with my girlfriends and rip up the dance floor. I showed up to our high school gym in a great mood and feeling very sexy in my royal blue dress. Turns out I caught Andrew's eye; I was a firecracker and he wanted to be near me. Andrew and his date spent very little time together that night; she disappeared to be with friends, and he was drawn to me.

We flirted and danced and laughed much of the evening. Andrew convinced me to join him at the afterparty. Drinks were all around with an atmosphere of easy laughter and young fun. I enjoyed the party sober and ended up driving back and forth into town, acting as the designated driver. I headed home much later than my parents had expected and had not told them of my change of plans, which resulted in being grounded from the privilege of using the car for two months.

Later, my girlfriend asked Andrew why he had asked Sara to the dance instead of me, and he replied that I "was too muscular for him." She scoffed and we both agreed me being so fit and confident intimidated him. As much as I outwardly acted like he left me unaffected, this marked the beginning of the decline of my already fragile teenage self-esteem—and we weren't even dating yet. Andrew's insecurity in his own body image immediately transferred to mine and I worried I looked too manly.

Instead of seeing that Andrew was intimidated—an issue with his self-esteem rather than my confidence—I felt like I was too intimidating, so I shrunk myself. *Now I know that if a man is intimidated by me, I'm not too much to handle—I just need a stronger man.*

"Dear Woman,
Sometimes you'll just be too much woman.
Too smart,
Too beautiful,
Too strong.
Too much of something that makes a man feel like less of a man,
Which will make you feel like you have to be less of a woman.

17

The biggest mistake you can make
Is removing jewels from your crown
To make it easier for a man to carry.
When this happens, I need you to understand
You do not need a smaller crown—
You need a man with bigger hands."

— Michael Reid

After the semiformal, Andrew gave me his old flip phone and helped me set up a cell plan and SIM card. He wanted to be able to text me more often, which I thought was incredibly sweet. I felt desired. All through December and January, we texted in the most dramatically cheesy way infatuated teenagers do. We used pet names like cuppycake, pumpkin, and sweetiepie.

On January 1, 2009, I was still grounded, so my parents drove me to my first date with Andrew. They even stayed at Coffee Cultures and enjoyed a latte at another table. We had the most awkward yet adorable first date ever. I hid behind my big scarf, and we giggled at each other for over an hour as we sipped our tea and coffee. Andrew brushed off the fact my parents sat twenty feet away, and we had a great time. Reimagining this date from my parents' perspective is bittersweet.

Throughout January, Andrew and I went on dates during spare period or after school. We went to McDonald's and fed each other melted cinnamon buns, and we walked through Elgin Mall. One day we went to Pinafore Park so he could help me take some photos to add to my architecture portfolio. Needless to say, we ended up flirting and climbing on the children's play equipment while taking completely useless photos of each other doing silly things.

On one of our drives through town, the song "I'll

Be" by Edwin McCain came on the radio. I remember turning up the volume and telling Andrew that if anyone ever sang me that song, I would probably love them forever. Another time, as we hung out at his house while his parents worked, Andrew played the guitar and sang to me "Wonderwall" by Oasis and "Your Body Is a Wonderland" by John Mayer, and we kissed for the first time.

I felt incredibly shy and nervous because I had only ever pecked a boy before. Andrew and I were making out and he started using his tongue to French kiss me. I felt uncomfortable and started to giggle. Andrew immediately felt embarrassed before I explained to him that I was unprepared and felt awkward because of my inexperience, not that I thought he was a bad kisser. He seemed to understand and apologized for making me feel uncomfortable.

As Valentine's Day approached, we agreed to do "ten things I like about you." I made a creative booklet with the help of one of my girlfriends as we giggled in my parents' den.

Before Valentine's Day arrived, however, I celebrated my eighteenth birthday on Wednesday, February 11. Andrew drove to Strathroy and bought lattes for my parents. He then gave me my birthday gift: a DVD of him playing and singing the song I mentioned in the car weeks earlier, a Brad Paisley CD, and tickets to go see Brad Paisley in concert on Friday in Hamilton. He blew me away.

He kept his school-night visit short, yet our make-out session on the front porch was anything but. Andrew intended to show me and my parents how wonderful and romantic he could be, and I didn't bat an eye or question any of it. In retrospect I can identify this period of our relationship as "love-bombing," whereby Andrew orchestrated grand spectacles of love and attention, which cemented in my brain a perception of reality where Andrew, at his core, was a kind, thoughtful and romantic human. Later in the relationship, when he began calling me chunky and giggling, I brushed it off as 'boys will be boys' because he'd been kind otherwise.

On the way home that night, Andrew spun out in the snow and got stuck in a ditch. His car flew under a fence into the farmers field, just missing being entangled in the cattle wires. The next morning, I did not receive a good-morning text from him and felt concerned. At school he did not show up at his locker in the morning or at second period. He didn't text me, but he had messaged his friends, which is how I heard of his accident. My concern overshadowed the question of where I sat on his totem pole of priority, and I jumped into matron mode. Once Andrew woke up from his late morning sleep-in, he and I texted back and forth, professing our feelings for each other.

That evening Andrew and I both attended the school Valentine's dance. We spent the night watching each other across the gym when we danced with our own groups of friends, and coyly finding ways to be near each other on the dance floor. We slow-danced with goosebumps and clammy palms to Lonestar's "Amazed" and laughingly twirled to "I Gotta Feeling" by the Black-Eyed Peas.

Friday evening, Andrew drove us in his car from the school parking lot to Hamilton for the Brad Paisley concert. Andrew did not enjoy country music, so I found it extra romantic that he'd bought the tickets and gone with me. We held hands the entire way, his car shaking from the mud in the wheel wells from the accident. During the concert I was too shy to feel comfortable standing, dancing, or singing, so we sat in the back row holding hands and gazing at each other with smitten eyes and sweaty teenage palms.

On the way home, Andrew concernedly asked if I had truly enjoyed myself. I definitely had. We held hands the entire way home, even as I drifted to sleep. Back at the school parking lot, we kissed and said our sweet goodbyes until the next day.

Saturday evening, I drove in the snow to Andrew's house and parked my car at the end of his long driveway that dipped into the forest grove valley. Andrew met me at the top in his parents' beat-up old black Chevy truck to drive down the treacherous lane. When we entered the house, I briefly met his parents before they sweetly scurried up the stairs to give us some privacy.

As I sat on the worn loveseat, Andrew played me a DVD of him playing and singing "You and Me" by Lifehouse on the guitar. I gave him my booklet and he gave me a heart-shaped cake and his typed-out list of *eleven* things he *loved* about me. The last item on the list was that I would say yes when he asked me to be his girlfriend. (Honestly, I thought we already were a couple.) I said "of course," and we went outside to gaze at the stars.

We kissed and slow danced as we gazed into each other's eyes, wrapped up in the cold. This was my fairy-tale beginning of a teenage romance as high school sweethearts and soulmates—or so I thought. Andrew then drove me in his parents' manual transmission pickup truck back up the long, muddy lane to the top of the hill where my car sat parked; this became the first of many long goodbyes we had in his truck at the top of his driveway. We lingered and kissed and stared deeply into each other's eyes, never wanting to part. Eventually, of course, we did, and I would drive the fifty minutes home to my parents' house before my eleven p.m. curfew.

Throughout our relationship, whenever Andrew said unkind words or pushed my boundaries, I returned to this night and played his songs. I thought I knew who he was and who he could be, and if I just behaved differently, he would sing me songs again and buy me flowers. Instead of seeing him as the problem, I started seeing myself the way he spoke to me.

When we returned to school on Monday, I faced the challenge of public displays of affection. I had never held Andrew's hand at school or kissed him amongst my peers. I felt very awkward and uncomfortable with locker talk and walking between class holding hands. I imagined that each student in the hall watched and judged every flushed and sweaty step. I felt like I kissed wrong and that I looked as awkward as I felt (*I did*).

All my girlfriends were confused as to why I began dating Andrew, as well as everyone on my wrestling team. I had previously dated jocks. I somewhat knew I might have been out of Andrew's league at the time, yet he gave me the impression he was out of mine—especially intellectually—and the insecure teenage part of me believed him. Because what he thought was paramount to me at the time. It did not matter how much I impressed other people unless I impressed him.

My wrestling teammates and coaches lovingly teased me about my relationship with Andrew. Occasionally, the crew would wonder if we had started having sex yet. I put an end to the discussion by saying Andrew would have to cure cancer before I would be ready to lose my Catholic virginity before marriage. Still, the jokes would roll, and they began calling Andrew by their preferred nickname, "Sexbot3000," and would check in every once in a while to see if he had cured cancer yet. Ironically, the school yearbook's "Most Likely To..." section listed Andrew as the most likely to cure cancer.

Andrew said he loved me a month later in the school parking lot by his truck before I left on a family trip to Florida during March break. I did not feel ready to say it yet, so I kissed him dramatically before getting in my car and peeling out. Before we reached the States, I texted Andrew apologizing and saying I was not ready to say those words yet, and he acted kind and understanding about it. I waited to find out which university Andrew had chosen before I reciprocated in June, telling him I loved him too. I refused to say my first *I love you* if we were going our separate ways for university in the fall of 2009.

The week following my breakup with Andrew five autumns later, I felt surprised at how I moved through my days so normally and so ... undevastated. I did not hesitate or waste time in real or perceived mourning. I was ready to start taking back my life and my autonomy. I felt free to do as I pleased, so I made a take-back list. I dated Andrew for six years, so I figured I deserved to give myself six gifts for the pain I endured.

The first one I gave myself was a pair of sweatpants—the biggest and baggiest I could find in Walmart. Then I bought a pair of pink-and-gold Ray Ban sunglasses; something girly. Next was a case of Moosehead beer and a new cell phone with a new number and a plan I would be managing myself. For my fifth gift I went to a charity gala for SASC (Sexual Assault Support Center), and there I bid on the silent auction, winning an iPod speaker. Finally, last and most impactful, was the gift of allowing myself the liberty to find and explore my sexuality: I began hooking up with one of my soccer teammates.

Wes and I were teammates and friends for months

before we started hooking up with each other. I knew him as a kind and genuine person who had a positive outlook on life. Initially I did not find myself attracted to him. I was focused on planning my wedding and engagement party with Andrew, not meeting new men. I showed off my engagement ring to teammates and annoyingly gushed about my fiancé.

Wes said he saw me as a positive spirit and someone who would be fun to be friends with. At the end of the summer season, I decided to put together a team for the fall season. Wes joined. A few weeks separated the seasons, and in that time Wes grew out his hair and beard and came back looking like a goddamn model. At least, that was the way I felt. Things *stirrrred*.

During our second season of soccer together, our team began having beers in the parking lot after games, which migrated to the pub down the street as the weather grew colder. One night during the warmer weather, we drank beers standing under the back hatch of Wes's Pathfinder when I noticed Wes lighting up a cigarette.

"You smoke?" I asked in a surprised and trying-not-to-sound-judgemental tone.

"Yep," said Wes.

"Oh, okay, I didn't know that."

Wes must have noticed smoking cigarettes was not my jam because he never smoked in front of me again, even though at the time he smoked a pack a week. *That's hot.* Our friendship grew over nachos and pitchers with our teammates. Conversations started getting more personal and open. My team knew about some of my trauma, and my relationship struggles as I ramped up to separate from Andrew.

I had planned to break up with him before Christmas, but ended up doing so much earlier, because he wanted to look at my phone. I texted Cara about breaking up with him. I also sent texts to Wes; nothing inappropriate, but I knew Andrew would lose it.

Once Andrew and I broke up, I wasted no time letting Wes know. At our first opportunity, we got together. The first time I went to his house we both acted awkward, trying to keep it cool. Wes called from the couch, "Come on in," when I rang the doorbell. As I let myself in, I saw the side of his classic hockey sweater peeking out of the upper level of the stair-split townhouse. I timidly said, "Hello?" Wes pretended like he didn't realize I had arrived and jumped up off the couch to come down and greet me.

We both knew what I came for and wasted no time. Everything with Wes was comfortable and easy: kissing, stripping, intimacy, and trust. We enjoyed each other until four a.m., and in the morning, Wes left early for work and I slept until ten a.m. before heading to school. Quickly we fell into step with each other.

After soccer-night beers, we would head back to Wes's place and have incredible sex. I felt liberated, beautiful, and desired by Wes. After a sweaty game of soccer, we would be driving in his SUV to his house, and he would gaze over at me with twinkling eyes and talk about how gorgeous I looked. I always felt embarrassed and shocked because I did not look my best. I was stinky and sweaty with my hair slicked back in a tight high ponytail and my breasts squished against my chest, hidden under an oversized men's jersey.

Yet as much as I felt unflattering in my state, Wes's attraction to me never changed with my outfit or my hairstyle or even my hygiene. He wanted to be with me and kiss me and have great sex with me after soccer before we even took a shower. Wes's unconditional attraction to me led me to finally believe I was an attractive woman. With him, I felt invincible, sexy, and uninhibited.

One time, as Wes pampered me with kisses and attention, I slowed him down and warned him I was still finishing my menstrual cycle. Without skipping a beat, he said, "So, I'll get a towel."

I was confused. "You mean, you *want* to have sex with me even though I'm on my period? Aren't you grossed out?"

"Why would I be grossed out? It's natural." Well, this is a *man*, I thought to myself. This brought forth a comparison to my previous relationship.

Andrew picked me up from the hairdresser, where I was getting my style adjusted to suit his liking: long bleach-blond bombshell. It was the first time we had seen each other in four months since Andrew had moved out west for his internship. We'd spent the summer of 2012 separated after an attempted breakup. We had both gone through a difficult semester apart and looked forward to some comfortable and familiar companionship in each other. I felt incredibly nervous, because I wanted Andrew to desire me and woo me back into his arms. So, I freshened my hair and wore some tight pants.

He acted distant and played hard to get. I guess we were not on the same page; in my mind, he needed to win me back. He probably sensed my desperation and knew he did not need to try at all. On the drive back to my parents' house, Andrew was ready to jump back in … to bed with me. His lust made me feel desired, so I suggested we head down a dirt sideroad to the back of a farmer's field and park the car for some nooky before our arrival.

As we drove, we caressed each other and began undressing. The car barely shifted into park before we had our doors open and were getting out of the car to meet each other in front. Andrew had me the way he wanted:

fast and pressed against the dirty hood. We quickly scrambled to clean up and head back on the road so my parents wouldn't be suspicious.

"Rachel?"

"Yeah, honey?"

"Are you on your period?"

TW:EA//"No, it finished yesterday." I felt panic rising in my chest as I approached Andrew on the driver's side of the car. He stood there clenching his belt with one hand and reaching for wipes with the other. He began dry heaving.

"Ahh, you're disgusting!' Andrew spat at me as he shoved me away from him. I stumbled and fell, landing on my hands and knees in the dirt field.

He coughed and spat and dry-heaved. "You clean this up! It's your mess!' he yelled as he threw disposable wipes at me. With my shoulders up protecting my neck, I quickly and dutifully cleaned Andrew up, crouching in front of him with fear of a blow to the head. As I dabbed up the minimal blotches, he heaved and gagged like he had a bucket of blood dumped on him. *Carrie handled it better than he did.* I had never seen Andrew lose his temper so physically before. My face burned with shame as he scolded me for my idiocy and my repulsive female attributes. *What a petulant boy.*

Didn't I know I was on my period? Was I that dumb I did not know how to count days or look as I wiped? Didn't I know how repulsive and disgusting dirty period blood was? I should have known better. I should have waited an extra day and just given Andrew a blow job instead. I would *never* make that mistake again.*//TW:EA*

After the first time Wes and I had sex while I was on my period, a visceral fear hit me in the back of my head at the end. My chest began to flutter, and I started to have a strong feeling my body was in immediate danger. My spidey-senses allowed me to feel every bit of air in the room, so I could feel it shift if someone took a swing at me. I cringed, anticipating a blow from behind.

I felt the need to plead for my safety and feared Wes would turn on a dime and hurt me once he saw the blood. I explained to Wes I felt embarrassed and needed him to keep his eyes closed until I cleaned everything up. He was confused but did not question or pressure me. I scurried to the bathroom and quickly returned with a warm, wet washcloth. I tenderly and thoroughly cleaned Wes, and then returned to the bathroom to clean myself and put on pad-lined underwear.

When I returned to the room, Wes asked, "Is everything okay? You know I could have cleaned myself up. It's not a big deal, it's natural and I expected it seeing as I was the one who suggested we have sex anyway." He spoke with genuine kindness and confusion as to why I acted the way I did. *He probably thought I was a little crazy.*

My earlier fear and embarrassment were *not* caused by this wonderful man sitting in bed beside me. I knew he would never hurt me, and I knew I could trust Wes with my pain just as I knew I could trust him with my body. I felt compelled to explain myself to Wes, and so I did. In our safe and trusting relationship, I broke the seal of silence about how Andrew treated me in private. Wes was the first person I told the truth to about Andrew—and Wes hated Andrew for me, because I couldn't.

When I started sleeping with Wes, I was not looking to find a partner or jump into another relationship. I wanted the freedom of a no-strings-attached relationship because I knew I needed some time to build myself as an individual. There was an exhilaration to the way Wes and I connected with each other and snuck around together as we kept our friends with benefits relationship a secret.

For the first time in years, I felt confident, desired, and safe. I became liberated and empowered by my singledom. For the first time in six years, I felt strong and free. Free in the absence of Andrew's repression and strong for leaving and being single. Wes and I pushed our boundaries with when and where we were willing to please each other. Bathrooms at events, in the parking lot at lunch, even in a booth at a bar. We became wildly enchanted and enjoyed exploring each other.

Wes and I soon found ourselves committing acts of love outside the parameters of the friends-with-benefits pact we had. Wes would make me breakfast in bed and I would bring him tea and lozenges for his sore throat. I soon found myself feeling the urge to blurt out the words, "I love you' as they teetered on the tip of my tongue. Wes was just too easy to fall for. I did not mean to have a relationship so soon after Andrew, but I quickly found myself falling deeper and deeper for Wes. We needed to decide if we wanted to break off our benefits and remain friends or become a couple.

Wes and I had two simple rules we decided on when we made our benefits pact: tell each other if we hooked up with another person and have open and honest communication. For me to feel safe and uninhibited, I needed Wes to be honest with me always and to feel like I could be open and vulnerable with him. For us to enthusiastically enjoy sex together, we needed to feel free to communicate during sex about our needs and after sex about our experience. This in turn led to long, deep conversations about our interests and passions and led to a wonderful friendship and connection.

I strongly considered if a relationship was a wise decision so soon after breaking up with my fiancé. I knew

I had healing to do, but because I was so caught up living in the moment, I rarely took time to sit and process the loss of my planned future. When I did stop and try to reflect on Andrew and what went wrong or right, I was met with a blank brain.

As hard as I tried, I could not conjure any memories on command. My body and brain blocked my ability to retrieve memories, likely because it protected me from raw trauma. In the first three years after breaking up with Andrew, the only way I could recollect something was when an event, song, or conversation triggered a memory.

After much internal deliberation, I came to the conclusion I was not ready for a relationship, and it would not be wise to jump in with Wes. Logically, beginning a new relationship so soon after such a difficult one where I'd lost my sense of self and my strength was not a good idea. I decided to date him anyway. Why? Well, quite honestly, I had a sense he was rare human being.

I knew his soul, I knew his kindness, and as much as I knew I could have left him behind and one day be in a very fulfilling relationship, I did not want to regret leaving someone so rare because of timing. Timing was not a good enough reason for me to miss out on Wes. I looked for reg flags and didn't find them. I was learning to listen and lean into my gut, because ignoring it for six years hadn't worked well. My gut was telling me to run toward Wes. Every day since that decision, I have never doubted that Wes, now my husband, is indeed rare, beautiful, and the best human for me to spend my life with.

Andrew and I returned to our respective seats in the car to continue the drive to my parents' house, and I sat stiffly still as I took shallow breaths with a lump in my throat. We drove in silence, the air too thick to speak, and the tension too high to hold hands. When Andrew started to slow and pull onto the shoulder, I felt panic and fear rise from my stomach. He got out the car and disappeared into a ditch for a moment before re-emerging with a fistful of wildflowers. He handed them to me and said, "Well, you've always wanted me to pick you flowers."

Five minutes later, we entered my parents' home in each other's arms, wearing megawatt smiles. "Look! Andrew *picked* me flowers. Isn't that sweet and romantic?" I gushed to my mom. She snapped a photo with Andrew's arm around me as I faked happiness, gripping the flowers in my hand. In my body I felt confused, cornered and trapped, portraying the illusion of love while questioning my feelings of hurt and discomfort. The juxtaposition of anger and disgust with romance and outward smiles made me feel off balance. Was I losing my mind? What was real? Did Andrew truly love me?

Now I know this stark contrast created cognitive dissonance in my brain. Cognitive dissonance occurs when the brain and body experience extreme stress from holding two contradictory beliefs or worldviews, like *Andrew is a protective and romantic man* and *Andrew is abusive.*

When a person experiences cognitive dissonance in a relationship, their brain keeps flip-flopping between *He loves me forever and always* to *He can't be bothered to talk to me*; from *I'm the most beautiful woman in the world* to *I disgust him*; from *I feel so happy and loved* to *I feel so incredibly lonely and empty*; from *He protects me from others* to *He abuses me.* The fantasy felt more comfortable than the truth, so I held on to the good parts and minimized and denied the bad parts.

I thought I loved Andrew. He was my first relationship and the person who fit the bill for "marrying right." But years later, I can clearly see I was in love with the *idea* of Andrew—not his soul, but the man I conjured in my imagination, stringing all the hints of light through the years with fraying yarn. I loved the idea of who he could be as a husband or father, but not who he was as a human, and my lofty ideas of who he could *become* would never be realized, because they were not grounded in reality.

Chapter 3 – Finding Real Love

After a few months with Wes, we decided to be in a committed relationship. We started the new year with the most incredible first date. On January 10, 2015, Wes drove us up to Toronto in his rusty gray Pathfinder accented with strips of duct tape and rusty rims. We pulled up to Le Germain—a five-star hotel—with a squeal and a manual-transmission jerk. Yes, we would like to use the valet service: please follow our quick set of instructions so the car doesn't self-immolate while you park.

I felt incredibly awkward walking into the hotel with my mall-bought clothes and Adidas sports duffle in what seemed like a sea of designer clothes and gold-wheeled suitcases. I moseyed around the fancy lobby while Wes breezily chatted with the clerk as he checked us in at the front desk. His ability to charmingly strike up a conversation with any person, even in foreign situations, was incredibly attractive and comforting.

Our hotel room filled with light and the bed felt like sleeping in a cloud. Moments after we set down our bags, a knock followed us at the door: champagne and chocolate-covered strawberries. Wes pulled out all the stops to impress me, and I felt luxurious basking in his pursuance. Soon we headed out to the basketball game across the street at the Air Canada Centre. I bought a Raptors tank top that let some of my bright pink strappy bra peek out the sides – *two can play this game Wes.*

Wes and I could barely keep our eyes and hands off each other the entire game. He wanted to get under my shirt, and I enjoyed making him wait. Following the game, we walked the midnight streets under the glow of the city lights to find a place to eat, settling at a Texas Grill.

After a quick bite we hurried back to the hotel room. Wes wanted to jump in bed, but I had more tantalizing ideas in mind. I sat him in a chair and strip-danced for him. I wanted to enjoy his anticipation a little bit longer. Moments into my tease I struggled with intrusive thoughts barging into my brain. One moment I felt sexy and connected to Wes, and the next I frantically shoved memories back into boxes; echoes of dancing for Andrew, trips to hotels with him, and being nervous with expectations—to look a certain way, to act a certain way, to dress a certain way, and to be ultra sexual all weekend like his vacation prostitute. *Focus.*

This man in front of you is not Andrew. You're not dancing because he expects you to. You are safe. You chose this. You are in control, not him. You were enjoying this, remember? Look how handsome and kind he is. You are safe. You're okay. You're with Wes. I got on Wes's lap and allowed his smell, touch, and kiss ground me back to that room and time. And that's where I stayed the rest of the night: in the present, loving

Wes.

Only now do I know that what I was intuitively doing was grounding myself using my five senses. After therapy, I know grounding is a taught and learned technique, but in the moment I was just following my gut on how to survive. I am so lucky that I intuitively knew how to survive those instances and didn't turn to numbing techniques.

A couple weeks later, I couldn't hold back anymore and needed to tell Wes how I felt. One night in bed as I stared at the ceiling, I said to him, "Okay, I'm going to say something, and I don't expect you to respond or anything, I just need to say it 'cause it's true…. I love you."

Eternal screaming silence. *Kidding. I actually meant it when I said I didn't need him to say it back. I felt fully confident that he felt the same and respected his time and space.* Wes responded with something sweet enough that I don't remember any embarrassment, but not sweet enough that I remember what he sweetly said. *So pretty neutral. Nice work, hun.*

But patience can only go so far. I could see it in his eyes and hear it in his voice that he loved me back. So *why* wouldn't he say it? A few weeks later, right before Valentine's Day, I asked him, "I know you love me, I can see it in the way you look at me, so why won't you just say it?"

"I don't know, I'm just not ready yet," he said. I responded with smirky silence until he capitulated. "Okay, you're right, *I fucking love you.*" I knew it!

A couple days later, we went to Blackshop for a double date on Valentine's Day. Wes's ball-hockey friend pointed out that we seemed like a couple very much in love, to which Wes confidently replied, "We are."

Unfortunately, my family acted furious and judgmental about our relationship. They judged how I dropped Andrew weeks after our engagement party and months into wedding planning. They judged how I quickly skipped to another man who was ten years older than me. They scoffed when I tried to explain why I left Andrew saying that I "didn't need to villainize him just because I broke up with him." And they rebuffed me when I insinuated the relationship contained abuse. While I knew they might feel as if they'd lost Andrew, who had become a part of our family, I didn't anticipate this level of volatility.

I felt abandoned and unsupported in a time of need. I chose freedom and love, and in return my family treated me like I had completely fucked up my life and their imagined future for me. They were not on board with Wes, and they were not kind to me about my decisions. So, I decided to distance myself from them until they were ready to accept my choices and have a reasonable conversation with me. I had to stand completely on my own two feet and protect myself, because no one came around to catch me. Abuse did not fit the narrative my family held about my relationship with Andrew.

Fall 2014 was not the first time I had broken up with Andrew. I had done so twice before and attempted again a year earlier as he prepared to move out West. (In total, I attempted to break up with Andrew four times before successfully ending our relationship, which according to RAINN is below the average of seven attempts to end a domestic violence relationship.) He visited me in Cambridge a lot that summer, because he had nothing else going on; he graduated from college and impatiently waited for his permanent job to start. Before he left, my parents came up to visit and we all ate dinner at a Thai place in downtown Galt. We sat at a table on the right side of the entrance by the bank of windows, Andrew and I on the booth side, my parents in chairs opposite us.

As we were discussing Andrew's drive out to the coast, my mom looked at me in an unforgettable way and said, "You're planning on breaking up with Andrew, aren't you?" The question was rhetorical. She knew. I *was* planning on breaking up with him, but she'd caught me so off guard that I didn't have a lie prepared, so all I could mumble was, "I don't know," as Andrew's eyes burned into the side my face. TW:EA//My parents scoffed.

"Why would you do that?" she asked, incredulously. I thought to myself, *Because I felt insecure about him going across the country; he'd cheated on me last time, although they didn't know that.* Then they tag-teamed while telling me something that are still burned into my brain:

"You're an idiot, why would you do that?"

"Andrew handles you so well; I don't know how he does it."

"No one else will put up with you and your depression."

"He stays so calm when you're so unreasonable."

"I would lose it if I were him."

"You're not going to find another person as good for you as Andrew is."//,'TW:EA

Mic drop. My cheeks flushed and burned with shame. I believed them.

It infuriates me now looking back that not only had they said it, and in front of Andrew, but that *I fucking believed them.* The rest of the conversation centered around how Andrew and I could carry on our long-distance relationship. My parents did what they thought was best for me and tried to be helpful, but they made me feel trapped and completely unlovable. This kept me in the relationship with Andrew for more than another year. *Parenting of adult children 101: don't meddle in their relationships.*

I often thought that my family loved Andrew more than they loved me, and it didn't just come from insecurity. It came from words like these. It came from scoffs and eye rolls and huffy walks from the room. From groans and uttered moments of abandonment. Cold shoulders and lack of understanding.

When I dated Andrew, I felt at odds with my family. In front of them, Andrew always acted kind, calm, and reassuring. He checked all the boxes my mom had drilled into us growing up: He was financially stable and capable; he practiced the same religion, he was committed to me, and he believed that family was priority number one. He employed sarcasm and got along with my family's witty banter, and he helped manage me to the standards they held for me.

While I was with Andrew, I lived on a roller coaster of emotions. But my family was unaware of Andrew's abuse. They only saw an emotionally unhinged young woman. They saw a woman who cried for seemingly no reason at all, couldn't manage her emotions, couldn't handle additional stress, and was anxious, depressed, emotionally unregulated, and unreasonable. Conversely, they saw a calm, reassuring presence in Andrew. A rock for my emotions to rage against as he calmly took it and settled my waters. *This was the image Andrew built over time: the more he abused me, the more unregulated I became, and the calmer he grew in front of others, because he knew he had the control.*

But at least my family's presence gave me the strength to snap back at Andrew when he demeaned me for what I ate or how I acted in front of them. I could confidently say to him, "I don't appreciate that" or "Don't talk to me like that" when they were around. But they felt this was uncalled for because Andrew was doing his best with me. They assumed my emotional highs and lows were integral parts of my personality. But I felt they made me deeply flawed, and that my parents were ashamed of me.

I always felt extremely misunderstood and isolated because I lived in this alternate universe that no one seemed to be aware of. They were all wrapped up in Andrew being this perfect humanitarian who courted me with love and stability. There was no back-talking Andrew or trying to tell my family about any of his wrongdoings, because they always saw me as a pain in the ass. So, they gave Andrew all the slack, even if he slipped up and said something completely rude in front of them, like when he called my sister a bitch on the MS Bike Tour. He got all their understanding and empathy, because he had to manage me.

And they were happy I was not something they had to take care of. I was off their plate and in Andrew's arms, which worked great for them but was absolutely insulting to me, even though you know the circumstances. The part that hurt me the most was that they viewed me as a problem instead of seeing that I was struggling.

According to *Psychology Today*, abusers don't just charm the person they are dating; they also charm everyone in their inner circle, so if anything goes down, they come out looking good. Andrew absolutely charmed my family until they basically believed he was the Lord Savior his goddamn self. Just visiting earth in order to take care of their daughter who was off the wall. They also saw me jump at Andrew with excitement, flinging myself into his arms, and making out with him in front of the group. They thought I was head over heels in love with him. *But I was just on edge.* There was no middle ground—just flying or falling.

When Andrew and I had our final breakup, I thought I would be completely shattered if my depression and anxiety went away and didn't come back, because it would mean that the love of my life caused me the most pain. Months rolled into each other, and I didn't have any depression or suicidal thoughts, both of which were common when I was dating Andrew. Still, I planned on waiting another year before ending my antidepressant and antianxiety medications.

When I realized that being away from Andrew meant I wasn't going to relapse into depression, I felt surprised by my lack of emotional reaction to the realization. I thought my heart would be shattered. I thought I would be devastated that our relationship was not the love fest I so wanted it to be. Instead, I felt like I received clarity and calm. I felt relieved I was not this "broken human" destined to battle depression, suicidal ideation, and anxiety for the rest of my life. I was not permanently depressed or an emotional roller coaster or the kind of person who'd be "lucky just to have a partner." I had depression because of a situation I survived, because of abuse and trauma I endured.

There is no single incident that marks the beginning of the abuse or a crossed line. My relationship with Andrew was more of an erosion of my soul and sense of self over time. I may be able to recollect a particular insult or moment of aggression that really stuck with me, but for each moment I can clearly remember, I know there are twenty more somewhere hidden in my memory, because they were repetitive or I was immune to the shock. Every day, Andrew employed multiple moments of control, coercion, manipulation, abuse, and insult. But each day also surfaced a moment of relief or kindness I chose to cling to.

I was steeped in Andrew. He lived throughout my entire body. I craved and needed his voice to calm down—

even if he said mean or insensitive things, just hearing his voice on the phone gave me happiness. I needed his attention. I needed him more than I needed to be a human. And I was often left longing for the intense intimacy we shared. I knew no future relationship would have the same interdependency, because I wanted them to be healthy. Without the lows, the highs were not as mighty—and I missed that.

I knew his insults emerged from his intense insecurities. Black words of bile bubbled up from his darkest secrets of white male fragility and held me against the ground like sticky black tar engulfing my shoes and creeping up my shins as the years went by. He would distract me with his silky voice and strummed guitar as the tar climbed toward my back, a promise ring here, a lovely bracelet there, a bunch of flowers and a look of love.

I began to notice the tar immobilizing me, so he stepped up his game with flights and expensive meals, a diamond ring, and wedding plans. But the darkness rose too quickly; it choked me a little too soon before we wed. I noticed it at my neck, and I finally felt like this tar was not worth the checklist or my parents' approval. I knew my decision months before I gained the courage to make it. I was not going to marry Andrew.

Before I could leave him, I needed to be ready to stop carrying my family's expectations and live for my true self. I needed to not care if my parents agreed with me or supported my decision. My breakup and subsequent life choices were the emancipation of Young Rachel, which began the transformation of me becoming the strong woman I am today.

Only once the blackness receded did I realize I was a bird who could soar and sing! I may have bits of tarry trauma clinging to my feathers, but this bird has been soaring since I escaped, and I have no plans on coming back down from the sky. Once I shed his dark cloak from my heart, I could feel the wind again and breathe the fresh air filling my lungs for the first time in years.

I never realized the weight he had on my chest, the repression that weighed me down and prevented me from fully breathing in or out, like I was always holding my breath, waiting for the next moment of devastation, or unable to breathe in from the aftermath of the blow. There was something new every day—something more or less hurtful, but something nonetheless.

When I left him, I sprinted so that his grip could not reach me and manipulate me back into his arms. I catapulted free into the light sky; I found my wings, and I was not going to be chained, caged, or covered in the tar of his inadequacy again. *I will never allow my feathers to be clipped now that I have discovered what it feels like to fly.*

Wes and I continued to grow and explore our relationship. We spent every moment possible with each other in our bubble of love. We cooked dinner by candlelight with a glass of wine. We built couch-cushion forts and watched old films. We shared our morning work commutes, we were each other's wedding dates, we coached Timbit's soccer on Saturdays, and played soccer together multiple days of the week. We shared baskets of Morty's chicken wings, coolers of chilled cider and beer, and the duvet on our double bed.

I introduced Wes to my godparents, who witnessed a big change in my demeanor with him. They said I seemed calmer and more content than they'd ever seen. Their observation spoke volumes: I *was* able to settle into myself with Wes. I felt safe enough to be vulnerable and free enough to grow into my own person. I didn't feel the need to overemphasize the "perfection" of our relationship, because there was nothing to hide. Our dynamic was healthy and balanced, and we both felt *content* together.

We spent the next few months getting to know each other on a deeper level and enjoying our time as a couple. I was so smitten with Wes that I wanted to give him a birthday party like he'd had never had. I planned his thirty-fifth for months, inviting all his friends and family, and I booked the patio on the top floor of my apartment building for Canada Day.

I gathered photos and stories about Wes to make him a scrapbook of memories. To do this I corresponded with his mom, in British Columbia, gathered his friends for a story session, and even drove to Hamilton to meet his dad and stepmom. I enjoyed getting to know Wes's family and friends and hearing all their loving stories about him.

Wes was astounded by the party and the album. I pulled off my grand gesture and Wes absolutely felt the love I had for him. Though everything went smoothly in the execution, since Wes hadn't yet opened up to me about any of his familial struggles, I was unaware that his parents shouldn't be together…or near alcohol. The evening went very well but ended up finishing in disaster when Wes attempted to get his mother in a taxi back to her lodging.

TW:PA & A//She was quite inebriated, refused to get in the cab, and slapped Wes. He walked away and came upstairs to watch the fireworks with me. I urged him to find her to confiscate her keys, and he went back to the lobby and walked around the building – unable to find her. When Wes returned to watch the fireworks on the rooftop, he reassured me that his mother would likely sleep in her car. She ended up driving under the influence. The police subsequently arrested her, and she spent the night in jail.

The next day, Wes and I had lunch with his mother before she headed back to British Columbia. She made it clear she felt her DUI was my fault as I hosted the party. Wes and I reminded her that we cut her off from drinking and got her a cab as soon as she seemed over her limit. She didn't seem to remember much about the previous night, including slapping Wes. The whole experience was...enlightening. I got quite the crash course on Wes's family dynamics and history that weekend, and I was thoroughly disappointed.//TW:PA & A

I had dreamed of having in-laws who adored me and appreciated my generosity. I wanted siblings who treated me without the baggage of our childhood influencing our relationship. I wanted to have a second family full of love and connection. I knew if I chose Wes, I would not be getting this, and instead would be managing toxic relationships, painful childhood memories and mediating alcoholism. I told Wes I would need some time to decide if this was a deal-breaker for me, because as the saying goes, you marry the whole family.

It took less than a day for me to shake off any doubt. Wes was different than his family; he moved forward from his past and didn't repeat the cycle of addiction and abuse. I knew his soul, and he was pure of heart and incredibly kind. The entire fiber of my being told me Wes was worth his family dysfunction. This wasn't based on statistics or scientific evidence or sound logic. My decision came from an ethereal sense that Wes was the exception to the rule and he was worthy of the rest of my life.

Outsiders told me I'd made a very risky decision, and I would have to agree with them. But I also know that the only opinions that matter are those of the people in the relationship. I learned to listen to myself and brush off what others thought. In my recovery from Andrew, I learned to unapologetically listen to my gut, because I hadn't before. Now it's seven years later, and I am so happy I did!

As the end of the summer approached, so did my semester of school abroad in Rome. Wes and I would be embarking on a new, long-distance stage of our relationship. Both of us had previous negative outcomes from surviving long-distance relationships, so we were both anxious about the idea. As a farewell, Wes flew with me to Europe, and we backpacked through Norway and Scotland for ten days before parting ways to different countries. Wes had never been on a plane across the ocean before, and I have never been on a trip that I had completely researched and organized myself. We were tackling a lot of scary firsts together, and it put our relationship to the test.

Let me paint a picture for you: Imagine bright green grass, clear blue water, sunny skies, and a nice temperature of twenty-two degrees Celsius without humidity. The mountains were a bit chillier (about fifteen degrees), but it was perfect weather for hiking and biking. We'd hoped for beautiful scenery, perfect temperature, lots of photo opportunities, and an all-around smooth trip. But what we got was dirt, sweat, no showers, peeing in the grass, running out of gas, sleeping in a wood shed, cold, hail, rain, flooding, breaking into a cabin for shelter, puking on a mountain, forgetting shoes, losing car keys, getting tickets, and nothing going to plan. We had a lot of fun though!

Our entire trip through Norway and Scotland was filled with struggle and disappointment. Every day we learned and adapted alongside each other. But as much as we faced adversity, we still had fun and never fought. We took things in stride and addressed problems united. As Wes and I boarded our separate flights going in opposite directions, we individually came to the same conclusion: We were certain we wanted to spend the rest of our lives together.

But a few weeks into my semester in Rome, our relationship began to falter. Wes had told me about his ex-girlfriend cheating on him during her semester abroad. This similar situation, he said, resurfaced old feelings, and he began to put up walls to protect himself. I could feel his struggle, and even though I had left him cute notes and sentimental gifts and continued to call and send photos, Wes was pulling away from me. I sensed we needed to physically reconnect to last the rest of the semester, so I bought Wes a round-trip flight to visit me for a week.

The trip was everything we needed in that moment, closing the gap our physical distance had created. We spent the week exploring all the sights Rome had to offer in the most romantic way possible. We embodied the romance of Rome: Wes bought me flowers from a street peddler, we had wine and cheese on the steps of the Vatican at sunset, and we made out on street corners in the pouring rain, laughing and splashing each other in puddles.

Above and beyond the romance, we sipped wine over deeper conversations of the future and how to survive the remainder of my time in Rome. Most importantly, Wes and I decided we were ready to start trying for children. Wes was thirty-five and knew he wanted to spend his life with me, and he wanted to have children before he turned forty. I was ten years younger but had been looking forward to having children since childhood.

This was the man I wanted as a life partner, and I was ready for the next step, whether it be moving in, getting engaged, or having children. Neither of us were hung up on doing anything in a particular order. We figured we would try for a few months at least before we would succeed in getting pregnant, and we sure didn't mind practicing.

The trip ended in bittersweet fashion as Wes and I had reconciled our struggles and were on a positive trajectory in our relationship, but also had to part again for almost two months. We planned to meet up at the end of my semester in Turkey for another trip before returning to Canada. The rest of the long-distance phase of our relationship felt like a struggle we were in control of. It was hard but manageable now that we had a purpose.

When we reunited in Turkey, then Egypt in December, we toed the line to abide cultural expectations. We could barely contain our passion. We once kissed on a romantic evening carriage ride in Egypt, and the tour guide reprimanded us, saying that if we did it again we could be in serious trouble because of the strict laws.

Overall, this trip went much smoother than our first one. I had taken all our lessons learned from the first trip and applied them to the planning of this one. Because of the currency exchange, Wes and I were able to stay at nice hotels in Turkey and Egypt. We could afford a tour guide in Cairo and on the Nile cruise. All the people we encountered were incredibly kind, and in return we used most of our spending money giving generous tips.

In public we wore rings so we could do things like hold hands and take photos touching each other. In private we made up for lost time, and by the end of our two-week trip, I became pregnant with our first child.

About a year after our first date, Wes and I discovered we were expecting a baby. Even though we consciously made the decision to start trying, we felt caught off-guard that I had gotten pregnant on the *first* try. We both agreed we were ready to have a baby and start the journey to parenthood, but we certainly thought we would have more time before being successful.

We immediately went into overdrive to prepare for our baby. I searched for, applied to, and started a new job in Kitchener within two weeks. Soon it became clear that Wes and I needed to find an apartment of our own that we could turn into a family home. By the beginning of February, we had a new place rented and ready to move into.

We had a month of overlap between our two rentals and spent much of that time cleaning, painting, and preparing our new home. We purchased our first big item together, a $1,600 gray sectional for our living room, then bought our first bed for $200 on Kijiji. Moving in together came easy, and we lived in sort of a whimsical dance. We both contributed to the home in our own ways. We worked well together cleaning, painting kitchen cupboards, and - preparing breakfast smoothies, burritos, and sandwiches in batches.

I struggled to ask Wes for help with my overwhelming pregnancy symptoms. I had heavy morning sickness, back pain, then the dreaded PUPPP (pruritic urticarial papules and plaques of pregnancy—an incredibly itchy rash that covered my body and infiltrated my muscles.

Now that I was in a stable, loving relationship, I needed to learn how to ask Wes for help instead of always trying to take care of everything myself, as I'd had to when I left Andrew. I landed in a stable loving relationship and I needed to learn how to let Wes in to help me because I didn't need to hold everything together on my own anymore. I would learn to be clear and direct and not expect Wes to know what I needed and how to help me. Guessing games were too uncertain and emotional.

On May 1, 2017, I became fed up with waiting for Wes to ask me to marry him. The ring had been in the house for *two weeks*, and I was unable to comprehend Wes's level of patience. If I had been the one with the ring, I don't think I could have waited a day to orchestrate the proposal of the year, but my lovely Wes, on the other hand, was paralyzed in self-doubt on how to best execute popping the question.

Just as I had to push him to profess his love for me in the beginning, I inadvertently did the same with our engagement. I didn't want an over-the-top engagement; I only needed a genuine expression of commitment and love. So, one night when Wes and I had had a very minor argument, I stayed up late and worked on an assignment instead of going to bed and snuggling.

Once Wes had gone downstairs to bed I silently tiptoed to his backpack by the front door and retrieved the ring box from its hiding spot in the front inside pocket. I ogled the shiny rose-gold-and-diamond halo in the dim hallway light before slipping the ring on my finger. I returned to the faded red Ikea couch in the back room to continue working on my assignment.

As I typed away, enjoying the glistening of the ring on my unengaged finger, I heard a noise. Unable to sleep, Wes came upstairs. I quickly removed the ring and hid it under the blanket on my lap. Wes came into the room and started explaining how he couldn't sleep without me and never wanted to again, when he came to the realization that all that really mattered was being with me and not making a big, emphatic proposal in public.

Wes asked me to wait a second and walked toward the place where he had been hiding the ring. I listened with acute awareness, cringing at Wes's impending realization that I had been secretly wearing it at night. As he ruffled through his backpack to open an empty box, I could feel his panic before he breathlessly re-entered the room.

"Rachel, please tell me—"

I sheepishly held up the ring looking down to avoid eye contact.

"Thank God!' Wes exclaimed, then looked at me with amused bewilderment and asked, "You knew the ring was here?"

"Of course! Why do you think I was so anxious for you to just ask me already." Wes laughed with exasperation as he pulled me into his arms.

Then he got down on one knee and said a whole bunch of cute romantic words along the lines of not wanting to wait any longer to be engaged and realizing how much he wanted to be my husband. The answer came easy and followed with a feeling of calm gratitude. I felt incredibly happy and content with my low-key intimate proposal because it came naturally from a place of love.

Chapter 4 – From Woman to "Mother"

I experienced incredible physical and mental changes during my first pregnancy as I transitioned into motherhood. From the moment I found out I was carrying a child, I began to fall in love. I adored reading about the baby's growth and development each week and comparing my darling to different-sized fruit. I watched hours upon hours of the same YouTube video where an entire pregnancy from sperm to birth was depicted in three-dimensional graphic representation to a symphony orchestra, crying hormonal tears of awe, wonder, joy, and elation.

I frequented websites like The Bump and Baby Center to read about the current week of pregnancy I was in, watch the What to Expect video, and read about the next two weeks for something to look forward to. I had anticipated becoming a mother my entire life, and now I had the privilege of embarking on this life-making journey. I often found myself crying tears of joy and feeling deep gratitude from the whole beautiful process I felt lucky to be a part of.

And then immediately after I would cry tears of loneliness while I grieved my lost dream of my family being excited and highly invested. I had hoped for family text chains of baby's growth, a family-planned diaper party, and the general family love and support that my siblings received. Rather, I experienced the now-familiar pattern of opposition and abandonment by my family for getting pregnant out of wedlock and living with my boyfriend before marriage. They saw my "condition" as a problem instead of a cause for celebration. I mourned the loss of the excitement I expected from my parents and siblings.

I understand from a logical perspective why they reacted the way they did. I'd seemingly jumped from Andrew, who they saw as my savior, to a rebound relationship with a man a decade older, in Wes. I then traveled with him—which my family saw as rebellion—before getting pregnant out of wedlock, all within a year. While I experienced these moments, I knew Wes and I had progressed rather quickly—probably too quickly—but I *was pregnant*. After the shock passed, Wes and I looked forward to our future and started enjoying the moment because this was the only time we were going to become parents for the first time.

I wanted my family to greet the news with grace and enthusiasm. Eventually, they begrudgingly accepted the fact of my pregnancy and partnership, but Wes and I still had to throw ourselves a celebration, because no one else set up a baby shower or diaper party. We did a backyard babies, beers, and barbecue party with all our friends and family invited to come celebrate and give advice. We had a wonderful turnout of fifty-six people and a very fun afternoon, our downtown Kitchener backyard looking like a scene from *My Big Fat Greek Wedding*.

Along with all the positive emotions of becoming a parent, a lot a physical changes and hormonal shifts impacted me at many levels. My morning sickness was more of an all-day sickness where I often threw up multiple times a day. At work I had to manage my nausea so I could complete my final co-op placement for school. I often found myself in the first-aid closet, vomiting in a bucket. When I could, I'd take a catnap on the cot at lunch, because staying awake all day was nearly impossible.

On days where I threw up more than twice, I would head home for the day and generally sleep through the afternoon. I experienced my calmest digestive hours in the early evening, which was when Wes would be my knight in shining armor and fetch whatever my heart desired. This pregnancy, I craved BLT sandwiches, cookie-dough Blizzards, and chicken and spring-roll Vietnamese vermicelli. Wes often went across town to satisfy my cravings, never hesitating for a moment.

One of the more troubling symptoms, to me, was how my vulva changed—*hear me out*. No one talks about this! I had to look it up on the internet to know if I was just special or if this was really a thing. Seemingly overnight my labia felt puffy. I hated it. My downstairs felt uncomfortable and *in the way*, like I needed to rearrange things all the time. I learned this occurs due to a higher level of blood flow in the pelvic region because, well, the baby needs it. This can also cause the vulva to look more purple or blue. So, I was like, *Great; now I have a flappy bubble-gum vulva!* So, I would sometimes twerk in the kitchen, singing, "Shake that Laffy Taffy," because *when else does an opportunity like this come around?*

And there's some good news: It's not permanent, and the extra blood flow does have perks. Big-O perks. For months I had the privilege of a quickie actually resulting in an orgasm, which was very unexpected, because I felt like a whale and was too tired to have a three-hour sexcapade.

Another symptom that doesn't get enough attention isn't the change in breast size, but how your nipples are constantly hard (which can be very embarrassing). *Seriously, they could cut diamonds.* I remember one day in particular my boss seemed very awkward and looked at the ceiling or over my shoulder. Later, I saw myself in the bathroom mirror and flushed with a gasp.

My mom had bought me maternity clothes for my birthday, and I wore a comfy nursing bralette and maternity top for the first time. I guess I didn't look in the mirror when I left my apartment that morning, because my breast pads and nipples showed through my blouse, making me appear as if I had perky pancake nipples resembling a target or the fembots in *Austin Powers*. I wanted to cry with embarrassment, instead I wore my coat the rest of the day and returned the maternity shirt later in the week.

My morning sickness lasted two weeks later than the baby books indicated, finally beginning to fade at fourteen weeks. As the anatomy scan approached at eighteen weeks, I began experiencing anxiety about the baby's sex. Pregnancy seemed to bring up hauntings of the past: nightmares about being held down, flashes of being assaulted, fear of the dark, and ghost sensations of unwanted touch. I felt hopelessly wrecked, not knowing how I could raise a daughter in this world of sexual harassment and assault. I prayed and hoped for a boy. I was not mentally ready to carry the burden of parenting a girl or raising a daughter in a sexist world when I still managed sexual trauma myself.

My already-dwindling sleep and mounting anxiety mounted before it completely disappeared with the news that I would mother a baby boy. Wes and I promised each other we would keep the sex of the baby as our little secret. *Our secret lasted less than a day, people.* Wes broke the pact. He was in the locker room before a hockey game and couldn't hold back his excitement Since the cat was out of the bag, we abandoned the idea of keeping a secret. Soon the whole family knew and began suggesting names. We bounced between Sebastian (my uncle's suggestion) and Michael (the name of Wes's late father), but soon my dad started referring to my belly as Sebastian, and the name became set in stone. We were going to have a baby boy named Sebastian Peter.

After I successfully completed my final co-op placement at the firm, I had one last semester at the University of Waterloo School of Architecture to complete my professional degree. I severely underestimated the impact pregnancy would have on my work. I felt as if all the blood abandoned my brain to tend to the baby. My mushy mom brain slogged through texts and emails, requiring several readings before anything would sink in. Learning progressed much slower, and my body couldn't handle the long hours at the computer I was accustomed to when working on design studio. I had a learning curve on how to properly pace myself for projects so I didn't get too sore. Procrastination was no longer an option this semester. In fact, I aspired to finish papers and projects as early as possible in case I had pregnancy complications or went into labor early.

Above my new physical limitations at school, I also faced judgment from my classmates and professors. I often felt treated as less than or, much worse, as trailer trash.

Group meetings were made last minute so I couldn't attend, and I received the scraps of the project. In all fairness, I was definitely a slow waddler. By the end of the semester my group complained to the professor about my availability and tried to get me kicked out. I ended up completing my own individual assignment and receiving a better grade than they did. I may have had pregnancy brain, but I did not lose my work ethic and experience.

Early in the semester, I began having intense joint stiffness and pain. I would play a soccer game and drive home without any stretching. As I sat in the car my muscles seized, and Wes would have to hoist me out of the car and up the steps before taking off my socks and shoes and helping me into the shower. This was too much. I ended my tenure on the soccer team and hung up my cleats until I recovered after baby.

Even after I stopped playing sports, the pain continued to worsen. I mentioned the pain at every midwife appointment, and each time she dismissed my symptoms as normal pregnancy discomfort. Well, pregnancy was not my "normal" and neither was this pain. Without the assistance of my medical team, Wes and I became determined to find a solution to my body aches. We tried different pillow arrangements and sleeping in a recliner and a gravity chair before finally finding an unlikely solution in a partly deflated air mattress. I went from barely being able to get out of bed and being sore all day to rolling off the mattress like a ninja and walking around without any problems.

When the weather began to heat up in June and July, I began to as well. My complexion adopted a persistent flushed hue of pink, and I always looked damp with perspiration. One outdoor lecture in particular, I wasn't sure if I had peed my pants, my water had broken, or if I was truly *that* sweaty (I was). The professor turned to me and asked how I was handling the thirty-seven-degree heat, and I responded in a whisper that I thought I might actually be melting. She opened her mouth to speak when a young tart cut in and said everyone felt hot. *Well, not everyone is two humans in one sweaty sausage casing, Tracy.* I think the prof and I both pulled a muscle holding back an eyeroll. As you would expect, she gave me the blessing to cut out early. I sped home with the windows down and placed frozen bags of vegetables all over my body as I splayed on the couch in front of our window air-conditioning unit.

My pregnancy quickly became a comedy of errors. Acid reflux playfully jumped up my throat, often causing me to swallow a mouthful of bile. Zantac and fruity Tums became mainstays of my purse. At thirty-two weeks, a rash began to develop in my stretch marks before quickly spreading across my body and extending from my neck down to my heels. My stretch marks looked painfully purple with red splotches, and my legs rippled with lumps and bumps of red The itch was all-consuming and insufferable, like poison ivy and eczema made a baby on steroids. If I allowed myself to scratch, I would tear my skin apart to the point of drawing blood and damaging my muscles. After much research I resolved to resist itching all together and find ways to calm the burning desire to rip my skin off.

After being dismissed yet again by my midwife, I went to the hospital for an evaluation. They diagnosed the rash as PUPPP, an allergic reaction my body had to the baby. They said I could expect the rash to stay until I gave birth and that it very rarely remained for months after the birth of the baby. PUPPP was a condition more typically found in first pregnancies with a boy or multiples. The doctor wrote me a note for more flexibility for deadlines and exams in my final weeks of school.

I spent the last six weeks of architecture school managing my condition and gritting my teeth through the grueling completion of final essays and my design studio project. I moved in with my parents so I could use their large bathtub since our apartment only had a shower. I spent upwards of eight hours a day in a cold oat-fermented bath, soothing the itch filtering through my skin and into my muscles. During those hours, chilled and pruned, I would endlessly scour the internet to find any and all suggestions for calming the itch of PUPPP.

At the beginning, I would soak a cloth in cold aloe-vera water and place it on the rash to calm the itch. Next, I moved to trying different topical creams: PUPPP cream, aloe vera, Aveeno, eczema cream, even toothpaste. I tried homeopathic remedies and old wives' tales—we even bought special volcanic-ash mud. One blog I read swore by drinking a liter of tomato juice per day. Although I don't mind a good Caesar, drinking that much tomato juice made me gag. I would plug my nose and chug tomato juice while trying not to vomit. This amplified my already-fierce heartburn, so I also popped Tums like a candy addict.

After a week of no improvement, I moved on to other ideas. I tried thirty-two different recommendations from countless blogs and comments I read on the internet. My mom, who had returned to her generous and helpful self, would go to the store at all hours and fetch or stock up on anything I needed, even obscure items at health-food stores down a backcountry road.

I desperately yearned for the itch to leave me. The best solution I found was the cold oatmeal bath. The bath would soothe me for the duration of my soak plus about an extra hour after. I clawed my way to the finish line of my final semester of architecture school writing essays in the tub, reclining in my maternity bra and undies with toothpaste slathered on my stomach while working on my design panels, and agonizing with bloated ankles over my mesh-contoured topography with papier maché and cardstock-plexi model. Wes and my mom helped as much as they could with layering papier maché and fetching materials, but there was only so much they could assist with.

When I wasn't researching PUPPP, writing an essay, or making notes for my design studio, I spent time loving Sebastian. I adored his movements as he rolled across my belly. I would sing to him, talk to him, and even cry to him. Whenever I needed love or reassurance, he would kick or roll, and I would remember my purpose. I would lie in the tub watching my toes, squishing the oat-filled nylon stocking, and feeling his tiny hiccups rhythmically annoying the crap out of me. Honestly, I originally thought my baby had OCD and just tapped in threes inside my belly. Once I read that the taps were in fact hiccups, I felt so silly for thinking otherwise.

Nights inched along in incredibly lonely, aching increments. I would stay in the oat bath until I slipped under the water with exhaustion before pulling myself up and out to pat my skin dry. I'd then slide between cool, dry sheets for an hour or two of solid sleep. The moment my itch returned, I would wake up and slather my body in Aveeno oatmeal moisturizer or the doctor-prescribed PUPPP cream, hoping for more rest. I averaged between two and four hours of sleep per night for the last eight weeks of pregnancy. By the time my due date approached, my mind felt trapped in a prison of anguish from the relentless, torturesome itch and sleep deprivation; I became desperate to escape my body. I needed the baby out so the suffering would stop.

Wes would make the ninety-minute drive to spend time with me Tuesday, Thursday, and on weekends. For hours he would sit on the toilet or a stool in the humid bathroom as we chatted, watched videos, and researched PUPPP on our phones. My lack of sleep made me nauseated, and as I felt the urge to vomit one day, I was unable to get my big-bellied body up and out of the bath on time. As I leaned over the edge to throw up in the toilet, my weak pelvic floor released urine. Soon I climbed out of the soupy tub and drained the water, feeling completely dejected and betrayed by my body. I felt so humiliated by the episode that all that was left to do was laugh about it. It was peak pregnancy to throw up in a compromising situation and pee in the process.

Leading up to giving birth, different fears ran through my mind. One emerged from a childhood memory when I was six or seven years old, hanging out at my grandma's on a typical Sunday after Church. All my aunts and uncles sat around the kitchen table or leaned against counters, sipping coffee and grazing on slices of gouda cheese or brown-sugar coffee cake. Sometimes I hung around the adults on laps of comfort and snacked while trying to understand grown-up conversations about politics and family dynamics. This Sunday, one of my uncles made a joke about a woman's vagina postpartum being like throwing a hot dog down a hallway.

When the men heard this "joke," their laughter filled the room and the women shrunk to fit in the remaining space. In this profound moment, I witnessed men's bravado and insult of women take over the room and the degradation of my aunts without opposition. All the men who influenced me in my life agreed a woman's vagina turned into this undesirable thing after birth—a thing they compared to throwing a hot dog down a hallway.

I am not going to dissect how that impacted me regarding my perceived value and worth as a woman, but I do know this sentiment terrified me up until I had sex the first time after I had my son. That's when I realized *that shit goes right back*. One of my girlfriends after reading this huffed and said, "Whenever I hear something like this, I just ask the men if their butthole hangs wide open for eternity after they poop. Works every time." I think my pop came out my nose!

The comedian Jo Koy agrees. If you haven't seen his special yet, please put down this book and go watch *Jo Koy: Live from Seattle*. My favorite skit is about twelve minutes from the end, when he talks about watching his then-wife give birth to their child. He started by telling the women in the crowd that they needed to be more graphic with their exes who were not paying child support.

"Why do I want extra money? Because those kids ripped my pussy apart. Ripped. Ripped. Ripped it. Ripped." He laughed as he used his hands to demonstrate what it looked like when his ex gave birth to their son. Then, explaining the elasticity of the vagina, says, *"It doesn't stay like that. I don't want you to think it's ripped and stays like that. That's the cool thing about the vagina. It comes back together. It's fucking…it's like a Transformer. It's like Pussimus Prime."* That explanation sounded pretty badass. Women have incredibly resilient anatomy.

This was when I realized my vagina can do whatever the fuck it wants and still be worthy; it's still a wonderful magical thing my husband should be damn appreciative of. Every time I heard people, especially television doctors, saying that women (sorry not women, *wives*), needed to do their Kegels, they reminded me of this fallacy. I never associated Kegels with helping my pelvic floor or my personal health. No, Kegels were always assumed, at least to me, to keep my vagina in shape for my husband. Not once did someone ever warn me that I needed to do certain stretches or exercises to keep my pelvic floor strong for *myself* so my bladder didn't fall out of my vagina or I didn't get urinary incontinence. *Spoiler alert: both happened.*

TW:SI//When I drove back and forth to Kitchener for my prenatal appointments, I would recline my seat as much as possible so my belly wouldn't rest on my legs and create a heat-induced itching frenzy. If I drove myself, my white-knuckled grip on the steering wheel resulted from having to physically restrain myself from swerving into the concrete barrier or oncoming traffic. I constantly fought an internal battle between the desire to escape the pain and survive. I felt like a character in the movie *The Happening*, defending my life against the lure of suicide.

A week before my due date, I soaked in the tub as Wes rested his arms on the ledge while he sat on the floor. In my oat-fermented tomb, I burst into tears, admitting I was dangling by a thread and didn't know how much longer I could continue. The itch agonized my soul, and the lack of sleep left my body unbearably anguished. I felt ready to give up on life. Wes looked deep into my eyes and felt my pain. He knew I said these words heavy with intent.//TW:SI

The next morning, we drove back to Kitchener together, and Wes set an appointment with my midwife to discuss induction options. The midwife agreed and did an evaluation of my cervix which hurt like hell and brought on a contraction. *Holy fuck!* On the way home I held Wes's hand and informed him I had decided I was not giving birth anymore. He chuckled at the ridiculousness of it. Expressionless, I looked at him and said, "I'm serious; that shit hurt in there, and that was likely one percent of what labor will feel like. I don't wanna do it!' He smiled and pointed out I didn't really have a choice. *Pfffff, fine!*

I continued, "Well, if I'm going to push a baby out—"

"*When*," said Wes.

"Okay, *when* I push the baby out, I get all the things." I proceeded to negotiate a freezer full of ice cream for a month, massages on demand for a month, and a spa day. Wes felt that was completely reasonable considering the pain I'd endured throughout my pregnancy. Now looking back, I totally could have asked for more.

My cervix needed to be prepped before medical induction, and I was booked for a balloon insert the following day, "ripening" my cervix for induction the next day. On Wednesday, I returned to the hospital to have the balloon removed. For a cervix to be favorable for labor, there must be a certain level of dilation, effacement (thinning), and softness as well as proper positioning. These elements are scored based on their progression, and the numbers added up indicate how imminent labor is or how successful an induction may be. My Bishop score was around eight, which allowed the midwife to add me to the list of nonmedically indicated inductions. Wes and I were told to go and enjoy lunch and to expect a call to come back later in the afternoon. The call never came because my induction kept getting bumped by more-pressing medical issues.

That week I stayed at our apartment in Kitchener without the crutch of my oatmeal bath. I survived with Aveeno, aloe vera, cold showers, and dips in the local pool. We waited and waited without a call or update. Wes would check in with the midwife once a day to ensure I remained on the list and to find out how far I'd progressed in the queue. September is one of the busiest months for childbirth, which contributed to the induction delay. In other words, my condition was not worthy of prioritization.

Four days later, on Saturday, Wes and I walked into London hospital to see if I could get on the induction list there as well. The nurse evaluated my condition and scrutinized my lack of visible rash. Due to my obsessive bathing in oats, the red-and-purple bumps had dissipated on my skin but the intense desire to scratch my rash-riddled muscle fibers remained. I looked bat-shit crazy talking about my PUPPP diagnosis with flattened bumps and calmed skin. For once my staunch discipline did not assist me. The OB-GYN came in to speak with me, and I cried while explaining the struggle with my condition and the rapid decline of my mental health. I felt so desperate to escape my body, I was willing to give up on life. The doctor calmly responded to my pain with news that my baby's vitals and growth were good, so there was nothing they were willing to do.

In that moment the doctor made it perfectly clear that my mental well-being as a human was insignificant now that I was pregnant. Baby was not just more important; he was the only person who mattered. I was no longer an individual human, but a mother—a vessel for another life. My identity, health, and personhood erased by my role. I asked incredulously what I'd have to do to be taken seriously, pointing out the injustice. Did I have to threaten to stab my stomach, or would the doctors wait until I actually lost my mind and self-harm before they took action?

"Well, are you going to stab your stomach?" the

doctor asked.

"No, of course not," I replied.

She left the room and allowed the nurse back in to explain my release. I would not be added to their induction list, and the nurse gave me tips on how I could "relax" until birth. *Fucking great.*

Wes helped me walk down to the car, and we drove back to Kitchener feeling incredibly abandoned and dejected. Sadness evolved into determination, and by the time Wes and I entered Kitchener, we had decided we would spend the night doing all the tricks in the book to get this baby out. I was sleepless anyway, so we figured we might as well suffer through this together. After arriving home, we queued up some stand-up comedy films, grabbed snacks, and set up the breast pump.

Although smugly smiling creepy older men and wise, winking women advised that sex could help induce labor and wind up with hubby getting laid (win-win), I was not entertaining it. I joked that I didn't need Sebastian coming out with a semen-soaked head. I was a prickly, rash-addled whale, waiting to pass my mucus plug and release a floodgate of water. Yes, that's what it's called: *a mucus plug.* Who wants to put their penis in the same place a mucus plug waits to emerge? Also, my cervix was four centimeters dilated, which meant the common fear of poking the baby during sex was *actually possible* considering the midwife touched Sebastian's head during a recent digital exam. I had *so* many reasons sex was off the table.

To induce labor, we alternated between the breast pump, relaxing, and Wes giving me a shoulder massage. By two a.m., I was getting *real* contractions whenever Wes massaged my shoulders. Hallelujah, and praise the Lord! I could see the light at the end of the tunnel. The end was near!

Chapter 5 – The Trauma of Motherhood

Trigger Warning:
This chapter contains obstetrical violence and post-partum depression throughout.
Please be kind to yourself and respect your personal limits. If you would like to
forgo these triggering scenes you may read a summary on page 322.

Leading up to my first experience giving birth I focused on frantically finishing my degree and bullying my way through PUPPP. I didn't take time to mentally prepare myself for labor or visualize the days that followed birth. I had spent so much time researching PUPP remedies that I forgot to research pain management, the process and recovery from labor, or newborn babies. I survived moment by moment. As you can tell by the state of my pregnancy, this isn't going to get better. Because in obsessing over the termination of PUPPP, I just tried to make it to the finish line of pregnancy. What I failed to goddamn realize was that giving birth was not the fucking finish line—it was the *starting* line. So, needless to say, my pregnancy was a setup for epic failure and pain. *This isn't ending well, let's be honest.*

Let's learn from this together as a team so future

pregnancies in the world don't end up with these kinds of births and new-parenting experiences. Because as shitty and traumatic as my experience was, it does not have to be this way. There are some things we can prepare for in order to create a better outcome, and there are absolutely moments that are unpreventable, like emergency health scares and all that kind of stuff.

But I'm not talking about those, I'm talking about mentally and physically preparing yourself for birth and learning what life will look like after birth. I did none of that shit, and I was fucked.

Thinking that I was finishing when I gave birth— oh, honey, pregnancy was the warmup! So, let's pause and learn from this situation. Buckle up, people, because this shit is going to get worse.

On September 4, 2016, we went to the hospital at eight a.m. for contractions lasting thirty seconds every four to six minutes. We knew it was a bit early in labor to go in, but we were new to this process and wanted to be there earlier rather than later. The doctor evaluated my cervix at the same dilation as the Wednesday earlier in the week: four centimeters. The nurse advised us to try walking around the hospital to help speed up labor, but after two hours of dry underwear, they sent us home until labor progressed more.

On the drive home, Wes went over some bumpy train tracks, which jerked my contractions into hyper speed. Suddenly I had one-minute contractions every two to three minutes. We breathed and counted for a bit at home before getting back in the car to head to the hospital once again. The doctor immediately brought me into a delivery room.

Since I was on the list for induction, my care had been transferred to the hospital OB-GYN. My secondary midwife still came to assist me in a nonmedical role. Honestly, she was a wallflower after the first five minutes. TW:OV//She set me up with a warm bath, which was very helpful in reducing the severity of contractions, but soon a nurse bullied me out of the tub so they could strap me up with wires to monitor the baby's heartrate.//TW:OV I spent hours pacing the room in my bubble of pain. Pain so deep I could no longer see or properly breathe. I was experiencing back labor, meaning Sebastian was facing the wrong direction and pressing against my sacrum. Wes would brace himself against the wall with his foot and push with his entire force on my lower back to help reduce the pressure as I braced on the hospital bed.

After fifteen hours of labor, I got over my fear of a huge needle entering my spine and opted for the epidural as my contractions began to overlap each other. Little did I know that I was in transition. If I had done the proper research or had better support from hospital staff, I would have known I was near the end. Instead of slowing labor with an epidural, I probably could have started pushing.

The nurses tried to get an IV into my left arm. After two nurses, warming blankets, and multiple pokes, the anesthesiologist succeeded. The epidural turned out to be a catheter inserted into my spine, not a needle! I relinquished control over my body and relaxed in a false sense of security as labor contractions melted down to my toes and exited my body. I felt so relieved that when the OB came in and asked if they could show the resident how to evaluate dilation, I enthusiastically replied with, "Sure! Hell, bring in your aunt and uncle, I feel amazing!'

The OB checked my cervix, broke my water, and left us to rest. Three hours later, a nurse checked in on us, and I was fully dilated. Soon the whole team filed in and buzzed around the room, setting up tools on trays and stacks of cleaning supplies. Nurses lifted my heavy legs into stirrups and turned on the baby's warming light. Wes stood by my head and held my hand while my mom and the midwife each had one of my legs.

I felt absolutely nothing below my breasts. Nurses tried to coach me on how to properly push the baby out, but I had no clue which muscles I was using. I was guessing how to push and was likely pushing wrong. With each contraction and push I threw-up in a tiny bean-shaped cardboard bowl. First, I pooped on the table, then I pushed out a baby—*magical.*

Sebastian Peter Suhonos was born on Sunday, September 4, 2016, at nine twenty-one p.m. He weighed eight pounds, five ounces, and measured twenty-one inches long.

TW:PPD//As a new mom with my first child, I struggled incredibly adjusting to motherhood, caring for a child with colic, and battling postpartum depression. I remember asking my mom how she coped and dealt with having five children who each suffered from colic. "Have you never felt like you might implode if you didn't get the baby off you? Have you never had to walk away to another room because you envisioned yourself chucking the baby at the wall?"//TW:PPD

My mom looked shocked, and though this was not the solidarity I had hoped for, she replied, "Never. I just felt sad because the baby was sad. Sometimes I cried with the baby because we were both so exhausted. But that's just how it was. That was life." And like that I felt completely betrayed, alone, and like a terrible human. But looking back, I can say my mother was an anomaly. She was so incredibly tough when she was given the shit end of the stick. She took it in stride and never let hardship snag her and hold her back.

I've since read countless articles in which women spoke of their transition to motherhood: adjustment and regret, mental anguish and resentment, exhaustion, and sadness. These were raw stories of the hidden side of motherhood, and I hadn't been exposed to any of them. My mother spoke of difficult times but made them feel like they were breezy and worth it. That, paired with mainstream media projecting the idea of eternally happy parents, left me totally and utterly unprepared for the negative aspects of motherhood.

I expected to feel a rush of happiness and exponentially growing love when I first saw and held my baby. I did not. *Apparently, this is not unique, yet it is not talked about, because women are shamed for not immediately feeling a motherly connection. It's supposed to be natural and easy to love your child—right?* Wrong. For me, and for countless others, it took time.

When the doctor held the baby up in front of me, I was mostly shocked with the awesome reality that I had created a human within my body. There was also this disconnect; I didn't *feel* the baby come out of my body. I didn't experience the rush of hormones when my body was released from the pain, because I felt nothing. As they handed Sebastian to me, I was anesthetized and thus deprived of feeling. Where was this overwhelming rush of love that would bring me to tears of happiness? Nowhere.

TW:OV//I knew I had to push out the placenta at some point, so when the nurse brought Sebastian to be weighed and cleared, I asked the doctor when I should gear up for the last couple of pushes. He told me that it wasn't necessary as he pulled at something between my legs, and I believed him. *Impatient fucker.//TW:OV*

At the weighing station my baby screamed in fear from the painfully cold and blinding medical lights. I motioned for my boyfriend to join him. When Wes started speaking to Sebastian he immediately calmed down and cocked his head towards the sound of his father's voice. Soon baby boy was snuggly wrapped in a blanket and returned to my arms.

Sebastian was introduced to me with my legs splayed in stirrups as I was being stitched up and losing blood. The nurse placed him in my arms along with the weight of societal expectations of maternal intuition piled on my chest. I held him from obligation and expectation, but really, I was STILL IN LABOR. *Give a woman some damn time before shoving a tiny fragile human onto her tit.* I was at the tail end of eight weeks of PUPPP and nineteen hours of labor—I needed a goddam minute to recover first. I felt weak and very hot, so I told my mom, "I think I'm going to drop the baby."

"No, you're not; don't worry," she said as if I was being ridiculous. Wes looked at my face and gestured to my mother. I started losing my grip and drifting out of consciousness. My mother saw and grabbed Sebastian while Wes called the nurse over.

Immediately there was a flurry of action, and two nurses came over with another IV and inserted a line into my right arm. Someone mopped up blood on the floor, and rags upon rags of blood were being tossed into a biomedical bin. The doctor was not talking to anyone; he was focused. I was just trying to stay conscious when my arm with the new IV felt incredibly heavy.

And that's when my dad walked in—whoops! Someone got him a little early. He caught a glimpse of my grizzly vaj—and I mean grizzly in both ways, like a grizzly bear and a murder scene. Maybe you could also say a bleeding beaver. There's a lot of fun ways to describe it, but I don't think he had a lot of fun getting PTSD from that shit. My Dad spun right back around and went down to the lobby, traumatized by the sight of it all.

"Wes, my arm feels funny," I groggily said to him. He looked at my arm, into which the IV had been hastily inserted, and it looked like I had elephantiasis. He called one of the nurses and said, "Is it supposed to get bigger?" The nurse quickly came and removed the needle. I was too dehydrated at this point for them to get an easy line in me, so they focused on other tasks at hand. TW:OV//The doctor took over an hour to stich me up. I had extensive tearing and had lost over a liter of blood. Partly, I'm sure, because the OB was too impatient for me to push the placenta and had tugged on it. *Fucking asshole. That's my body you're messing up.*

We spent the night in the hospital exhausted from the lead-up and process of labor. The next morning Wes, Sebastian, and I left and returned to our family home before noon. To say I was ready to go home with a baby would be a flat-out lie, but I refused to stay in that hospital another hour. Because throughout the night and the following morning, I had nurses coming in and demanding they see a successful breastfeeding latch at least five times before I went home

They weren't gentle and caring; they were brusque and condescending. *Um, excuse me, but I've been a mother for less than a goddamn day and was still largely recovering. No one masters a brand-new skill on the first try.* Not being able to get a successful latch on demand wasn't predictive of my future success as a mother, yet these nurses seemed to imply my ineptitude. I was too tired for this breast-is-best mantra.//TW:OV

So, we signed the papers acknowledging that I was leaving against medical advice and went back to the silence of our apartment, which soon ended with the arrival of my sister and her children with Tim Hortons coffee and Timbits. Then my mom and dad visited every few days for weeks. My younger brother came with his boyfriend and a few other times by himself to snuggle his newest nephew. My other sister came with her husband and held Sebastian cross-legged on our couch with pizza in hand. My older brother visited with gifts, my cousins came with cupcakes, and friends dropped in to smell soft baby skin and nuzzle wispy hair.

Any previous trepidations about how, when, and with whom I had made this gorgeous little boy were forgotten as hearts melted with tiny fingers gripping one of theirs. As usual, people dropped by to see the baby—not mom. I didn't mind at the time. I had learned what a martyr was growing up and inherited it. So, now, when I visit a newborn, I make a point of spending time with the mom and taking care of her needs. I praise her strength and build her up with compliments in the face of insecurity. Rather than asking to hold the baby, I ask what needs to be cleaned or cooked. I drop off food and spoil older kids so Mom can enjoy some quiet with the baby and feel relief that her elders are being loved. I think we could all use more of that in North America.

Adjusting to life back home came as more than a shock to our relationship and our schedule. Wes largely took care of my recovery, and I focused on caring for Sebastian. When the doctors discharged me, they didn't tell me how much blood I'd lost or that I'd had extensive tearing, nor was I given recovery instructions—other than to not carry the baby around the house or do stairs for a while. I found out those details when I later requested my medical records.

Settled at home, I claimed a station on the couch in my pad-lined diaper and nursing bra. Wes assisted me on my journeys to and from the toilet. Wes took care of everything else for me. Our child only touched a surface other than our chests when we changed or cleaned him. We did skin-to-skin like it was Sebastian's lifeline—not only because of the benefits, but because we were both so anxious about being parents, we couldn't put him down.

The midwife came for a house visit our second day home and showed me some breastfeeding tricks. My breasts had exploded from a DD to a J, and I was at a loss for how to maneuver a baby around those honkers. She suggested a football hold and physically assisted me with getting Sebastian into the proper position. Thank the lord! She explained large-breasted women have difficulty with any other hold. This explained a lot, because growing up I had only ever witnessed my aunts or women in public breastfeeding with a cross-chest hold, and that was not working for me at all.

The football hold was the best skin-to-skin loving experience for Sebastian. He was so tiny, and my breast was so large it literally covered his entire body. He would wrap his tiny little arms and hands around my boob and still not be able to connect his fingers. To say I had back problems during the months I nursed is a huge understatement!

Next, I hesitantly asked the midwife if she would check me down there because *something* was going on. She didn't hesitate. I placed a towel on the couch under my bum and removed my diaper so she could take a quick peek.

TW:OV//"Oh!" She exclaimed. "Did you know you had an episiotomy?"

"Um, no," I responded, dumfounded. In fact, I had specifically asked that I not receive one, preferring to tear naturally. I felt completely violated and traumatized. The midwife went on to explain how to care for the stiches and keep the area clean. She suggested using a sitz bath to soothe and cleanse, as well as a peri bottle each time I urinated.

She continued to finish the items on her visitation list: weigh the baby, count fingers and toes, etc. I only partly moved along with her as I mentally processed my medical news. Wes helped ensure I had proper sitz baths, and I ended up physically healing incredibly well and quickly. But my mental health took a huge hit. I hadn't realized I needed to police my own body during delivery. I thought I could trust my care providers to listen to me and get my informed consent before hacking at my vagina. But babies are business and businesses must keep running, right?//TW:OV

During my first week of physical recovery the most painful and disturbing aspect was my first post-partum poop. *Hear me out.* I had never even heard of this, nor considered it in preparing for the period after giving birth. Apparently, this is yet another very common thing women only talk about with other women who have gone through the same thing. What?! Where is the solidarity with women preparing women for labor and motherhood? So many women in my life could have said something about any of these symptoms: cracked bleeding nipples, the flood of breastmilk, hair falling out in chunks, meconium poop, nasty umbilical cord stump, constipation, and hemorrhoids! And they could've given me tools to prevent or intercept these symptoms.

Let me tell you, being constipated and having brick-hard poop when your perineum is being held together with stiches is terrifying. It is worse than labor. In the show *Working Moms* one character says if she didn't use her finger to hook out her PPP (post-partum poop), it would probably still be up there. Yes, it can be that bad! No amount of stool softener and prune juice helped once I was as that point.

I am now the friend, your friend, who is spreading the word to start taking a laxative when you go into labor. The epidural, pain killers, and even the pressure your intestines endure during labor cause constipation. Low hydration as your body adjusts to breastfeeding exacerbates symptoms, and if you don't take laxatives from the onset of labor, you're practically screwed. Particularly if you end up requiring stitches. Trust me when I say that unnecessarily soft poop is much preferred to constipation after labor.

Here's some more friendly advice: Nipples are not used to that much consistent suction, and they will hurt like a motherfucker for a while. Some women experience no pain. Yay for them, but many women do, and it doesn't mean you're doing anything wrong. Coat your nips with lanolin after your first feeding; if that's not cutting it, ask your doctor or midwife for Newman's Ointment. Stock up on breast pads and get a Haakaa to catch the flood of milk. It's handy to have a little stash of frozen breastmilk on hand if possible. Don't stress about newborn hunger; colostrum is filling, and their tummy is only the size of a strawberry. Bring Vaseline to the hospital and put it on baby's diaper area. It prevents the meconium poop from sticking. Ugh that nasty umbilical cord stump; don't fiddle with it, just keep it dry. Get your beautiful undercarriage a toilet-bowl sitz bath and herbs. When you finish pounding out a baby your vulva feels a bit battered for a while. A sitz bath can help you heal very quickly and assists with hemorrhoids.

Also, it's not just the baby that will need diapers. Yup you guessed it. You get to lounge in style—in a bloody diaper—for the first couple weeks of tending a newborn.

This is also helpful for your slips of incontinence. *Still want kids? I don't blame you. Good luck!*

Moving on.

Near the end of the first week of motherhood, Wes guided me downstairs to our basement bedroom to sleep together as a family. And by sleep, I mean lying in bed watching our child, because we were too wired to sleep.

Sebastian had colic from day two. He didn't go through this two-week "calm-new-baby period" like people of the internet claim. The first night in our family bed, I remember him crawling up my chest crying so he could scream in my ear. Our days-old baby was so distraught, he gathered the strength to literally army-crawl up my chest to scream right into mommy's ear. How did he know where to crawl to? Something was wrong. We panicked.

We tried everything to make Sebastian feel better. We changed his diaper, we changed his clothes, I breastfed him, we formula fed him, we rocked him, sang to him, held him in countless different positions, walked with him, sat with him, wrapped him up, and dressed him down. Still, we held our screaming, shaking, red-faced tiny baby in the dark quiet of the night.

TW:PPD//I felt like a failure.

A pure motherhood failure. I was not able to comfort my child. I couldn't figure it out. What kind of mother can't figure out what's bothering their child? What kind of mother can't calm their child's cries? We called the midwife and woke her up. She assured us that if we had done everything and checked all his basic needs, there was nothing else we could do—Sebastian just needed to adjust. It didn't feel like he was just adjusting. Not all babies scream like this, or there would be no second or third children in this world.

Wes and I made it through the night, but Sebastian's crying only increased in length and intensity as he grew. At the peak of his colic. he started complaining at around ten a.m. It steadily increased in volume and persistence until peaking around seven p.m. He then screamed for about an hour before slowly quieting down, until he fell asleep around eleven. Now, he did take thirty-minute naps here and there during the day, probably from sheer exhaustion, but he would instantly wake up if I ever put him down. The only other quiet moments were during breastfeeding. I had no breaks during the first four months.

Wes did his best while he was home, carrying Sebastian around and doing nightly bottle-feeds after the first month. *I am not at all diminishing how wonderful my parenting partner is*, but when Wes held our crying, screaming baby at night, I was completely unable to relax. I felt slightly less helpless holding Sebastian than I did watching Wes try to soothe him. At night, when Wes bottle-fed, I pumped. Sebastian never slept more than two hours until he was thirteen months old. Which of course means that Wes and I did not sleep for more than a two-hour stretch for thirteen months

We. Were. Exhausted.

I was bitter. I was bitter that everyone I seemed to talk to had a child who started sleeping eight hours after two months. I was bitter that no one I knew had a child with colic. I was bitter that I only saw women immediately loving their newborn while I was not blessed with that experience. I was bitter and traumatized that I was mistreated by the medical system.

I regretted becoming a mom.

I lamented that I forever had stretch marks, I forever had a flap of skin on my stomach, and I now peed my pants if I jumped, ran, lunged, sneezed, or coughed. I was bitter that my boyfriend's body didn't go through shit to bring a baby into the world and that he could play sports just the same as before.

I suffered postpartum depression, and no one hearing my story would ask why. I didn't care to shower or get dressed. I didn't want visitors, because I didn't want to move from my corner seat on the couch or wear something more than a blanket. I did the bare minimum at home with regards to cleaning and housekeeping. I looked at Wes and felt nothing. I held our baby and felt nothing. I looked at myself and cringed. I was not worthy of this child. I was not worthy of my boyfriend. I felt like I was waiting for Wes to throw up his hands and walk out. This was not what he signed up for. I was no longer the person he thought he was getting out of this deal.

I struggled through the days that felt like weeks, and the weeks that felt like months or even years. There were days where Wes had to come home from work at ten a.m., because I was so completely overwhelmed and knew I couldn't be alone with our child. There were evenings where Wes walked in from work, and I handed him the baby as I walked out of the house without a word.

I was barely surviving.

At Christmas we spent a week or so at my parents' house, surrounded by my family. One evening as I hunched over the kitchen table with my hands holding up my heavy head and greasy hair slicked back between my fingers, barely keeping myself from crying, my mom came and sat across from me. Wes walked up and down the hall jiggling our baby as screams grew louder and softer, louder and softer.

My mom asked me, "What could be so wrong?"

"I just can't handle this anymore," I barely squeaked out.

"You have a healthy baby. Can't you just focus on that?" she offered as an intended helpful bit of advice. She didn't realize I didn't feel anything for my baby. She would have been mortified to find that out, because she never experienced it or fathomed it.

I didn't know how to respond. This must have been the hundredth time people had diminished my pain as a new mother, because "at least the baby was healthy." As if one person's health supersedes another's if it's a child and their mother.//TW:PPD

I started to open my mouth when my sister jumped in. "She just doesn't like being a mom right now. That's okay. Not everyone likes being a mom all the time."

"I did," my shocked mother indignantly replied, as if this were a new concept to her.

"Well, that's very nice for you, but Rachel is very clearly struggling right now, and I can't blame her."

Wow, my hero sister. Thank you! I couldn't say it at the time, because I was barely hanging on, but thank you, sister. I did *not* like being a mom, and I had serious doubts I ever would—which was crushing to me, because I had looked forward to being a mother since the second grade.

I knew I had an awesome mother growing up, and I wanted to be just like her. She was the reason I always responded with "I want to be a mom when I grow up' if anyone asked. She was the reason I had an hour-long debate with another student in architecture school about being a stay-at-home mother, which ended with a mic-drop accusation that I was getting a hollow degree as the bridge between high school and housewife. Even as an adult I looked at my mother and hoped one day I could be at her level. *She doesn't always give the best advice or say the right things, but literally no one in the world does. She does her best, and her best is pretty damn impressive—especially considering the home she came from, which you'll hear about later in the book.*

Needless to say, Sebastian was in the process of self-weaning and soon would not breastfeed anymore. I pumped until my milk dried up, which was about the same time Sebastian's colic dissipated at four months old. This marked the point where my mental health began an upswing—finally! I can't say if it was because his colic disappeared or if the hormones related to breastfeeding adjusted or both. But I started the road to recovery, and I was finally able to say I fell head-over-heels in love with Sebastian when he was about six months old.

But my mental health didn't have a continual upswing, nor did I feel completely happy and normal until Sebastian was about two-and-a-half. This was not because of postpartum depression though; it was just a clusterfuck of a few years.

"Good night sweetie," said my mother.

"Night-night, I love you," I replied.

"I love you too."

"I love you three!"

"I love you four."

"I love you more!" I was sure of it.

"I love you most," she smiled.

"I love you mostest," I bragged.

"I definitely love you more," said my mom with certainty. But I didn't believe her. It was impossible for her to love me more. She was my entire world. My all-encompassing safe zone, the beginning and end of my love. Decades later when I became a mother and fell in love with my firstborn, I called her one night and finally said, "You're right."

"About what?" she asked.

Ryan Reynolds once said on a talk show, while explaining how much he loved his wife and children, that he would use his wife, the love of his life, as a physical shield to save his children if he had to. He said it in his classic comedic fashion, but the point shining through was how his love for his children was paramount and overshadowed everything else. He explained that he thought he'd gotten to the apex of love when he found his wife, his "one," but that when he had his children, he loved them infinitely more than he had ever loved anyone or anything before.

"You do love me more than I love you, because I know how much I love Sebastian and I don't love you that much." She smiled through the phone with happiness as her daughter finally understood her love for her and her sacrifices as a mother. And I did, *I do. Because before you love your child, you don't realize how deeply and infinitely your love can grow. I love my children more than any other person and all other love I've felt in my life.*

Chapter 6 – Legacy of a Mother

Trigger Warning:
This chapter contains: body image issues (pages 89-92) and sexual coercion (page 100). Please be kind to yourself and respect your personal limits. If you would like to forgo these triggering scenes you may read a summary on page 322.

Immediately after I started feeling all the love for Sebastian, I felt strong enough to push myself in other areas of my life, such as completing my project-management certificate and playing soccer. In a game in February, I quickly changed directions and lunged. Something dropped inside me, and I felt a bulge in my vaginal canal. I waddled out of the game and days later went to the doctor to learn I had suffered a bladder prolapse. Great, my body had betrayed me.

I spent seven months waiting for an appointment with an OBGYN to evaluate the prolapse. I didn't play soccer or do any high-impact sports. During those months I felt stressed with every bowel movement because I was worried that if I pushed too hard, my bladder would fall into the toilet bowl. I know that sounds dramatic, but that's the headspace I was in. Physical activity helps level my overactive ADHD brain, and sitting still made my imagination run wild. I felt defeated. I was finally ready to start getting fit and feeling my athletic self again before this happened.

In the end, the doctor said my prolapse was very minor and that sports would help strengthen my pelvic floor and lessen symptoms. I took the green light and joined two soccer teams the next day.

When Wes and I became parents, we anticipated settling down with kids and waiting until they grew before we traveled again.

That lasted a month.

When Sebastian was nine months old, we went on a much-needed trip to Croatia and Greece. We brought along my cousin Edwin, Sebastian's godfather, as a "parental assistant" so we could ease into traveling with a child, and so Wes and I could have some time reconnecting as a couple.

I desperately needed to feel like a woman and a wife again, so I was really looking forward to the trip. I hoped it would cure my burnout and help me feel rejuvenated and unburdened by motherhood. I was also secretly hoping the relaxation would help Wes and I in our journey to getting pregnant with our second child, which we'd started trying to do as soon as I healed from Sebastian's birth. Why does everyone always suggest to couples trying to get pregnant that "not stressing" and "going on vacation" will do the trick? *Super helpful advice.*

The rug was pulled out from under me when I got a severe double ear infection on the trip. Three days in, pus and blood seeped from both ears. Wes was surprisingly less than sympathetic, saying an ear infection was no big deal and that I was overreacting. I guess he forgot what it feels like.

Croatia and Greece are both mountainous countries, and driving up and down was torturous. I first went to the hospital in Korcula on a Croatian Island, and they dismissed my symptoms as swimmer's ear and wrote me a prescription. The ear drops did *not* work. The pain worsened and extended from my ears down into my neck, jaw, and teeth, keeping me up most of the night and causing me to feel nauseated.

Wes and I ended up going to the hospital again a couple of days later in Dubrovnik at five a.m. as Edwin slept at the Airbnb with Sebastian. The entire experience at the hospital felt eerily similar to the beginning of a horror film. The wall paint, floor tile, and drop ceiling were all white, except for footprint smudges illuminated by flickering fluorescent lights, and the bathroom had blood smeared along the floor and up the wall. The examination room was equipped with stainless steel tables and trays with white clothes under stainless steel tools—all manual items and decade-old technology resembling a bunker in the show *Lost*.

The doctor used his cellphone light in lieu of a flashlight to see in my ear as he tugged me around so roughly that I had to bite back tears. He recommended we see the ear, nose, and throat specialist in the building up the hill. This building also had the horror-film motif; it felt completely abandoned, and none of the rooms were locked or lit. A hospital without people felt unfathomable, but apparently, they only provide non-emergent health assistance from nine a.m. to five p.m. in Croatia. We waited in an empty corridor lined with ghostly chairs until nine in the morning, when the specialist arrived at work.

The doctor vacuumed the pus and blood out of my ears and was alarmed at the state of the infection. He prescribed heavy painkillers, nasal spray, ear drops, and heavy oral antibiotics. In broken English he explained that I had a "very severe middle-ear infection; very, very severe," and he strongly recommended no elevation changes as they would cause "tremendous pain and likely an eardrum rupture." But I had a flight to catch to Greece.

I rested a bit in the Airbnb while Wes walked around town with Sebastian and Edwin to get breakfast and fill my prescriptions, then we were off to the airport. The plane ride was a level of pain that left me rocking in my seat with my head on my knees before my eardrum eventually ruptured and released the pressure. I lost much of my hearing and became practically deaf for two days, and my ears vibrated like broken speakers for months. I woke up every three hours to ensure I always had a dose of pain killers, and by the fourth day of antibiotics I was starting to feel better. We had five out of seventeen days left in our trip.

Wes and I did our best to take advantage of the last five days, even though my ears still ached. We went out to dinner together once and had a cobb salad as an appetizer, which had almost a half-jar of mayonnaise on top and made us both feel sick, but we did enjoy walking around the town holding hands. We mostly hung out as a family so I could spend time with Sebastian, as he sorely missed his healthy mama. Needless to say, I did not get the reconnection with Wes nor the relaxation I desperately wanted. And we didn't have any sex, so no chance for baby number two. The trip felt like a bust to me, and I was sorely disappointed with how it turned out.

A week after we returned, I had an appointment with my doctor. He confirmed one of my ear drums had ruptured but was healing well. I still had fluid in both ears, but I would heal up nicely. After I showed him the prescriptions I received, he was shocked at the potency of antibiotic, one he said they didn't even use it in Canada. To me, this just confirmed the seriousness of my infection, because it still took over five days to clear up, even with that antibiotic. In a way I felt validated I wasn't being dramatic about my pain, but I also felt bitter, because I really needed that damn trip and put a lot of hope into having a positive vacation.

During the rest of my maternity leave, I fought my burnout by walking seven or more kilometers, pushing a napping Sebastian in the stroller a few times a week. I connected with my sisters, and we shared the burden of motherhood while watching our children play or teaming up for excursions to the zoo or Marineland. But the majority of the time I was very isolated with an nontalking child among child-free friends. I visited the corner café down the block so often that the ladies who worked there would walk with Sebastian or carry him around so I could sip my cappuccino in a moment of peace.

Just over a month later, on a random Thursday at about eleven p.m., I received a phone call from my dad. I felt a bit annoyed that he'd called so late considering that he knew how little we slept, with Sebastian waking up every two hours. I answered the phone with a tone I immediately regretted. My mom had done a routine cosmetic surgery earlier that day and had not yet come out of the anesthetic. My parents had not told us about the surgery, so this came as a complete surprise.

TW:BI//My mom had struggled with her body image my entire life. At a young age I found photos with her face blacked out with permanent marker and asked her why, she said she didn't like the way she looked in that photo and I didn't understand how. In grade six she had me take naked photos of her, as she pointed out her "problem areas" asking me to photograph her cellulite and rolls. She kept those photos in her wallet to remind herself how disgusting she was so she wouldn't snack or slip-up on her current diet – or just so she could be miserable.

The summer before grade eleven my sisters, younger brother, mom, and I all did the "lemonade diet" a magazine said Beyonce did for *Dream Girls*. The diet consisted of not eating anything for two weeks and just drinking lemonade with cayenne pepper. For many years my mom did weight watchers and included us as we counted calories – eating cardboard crackers with light cream cheese and salsa – *as children*.

This body-image obsession infected the whole family with dysphoria. My sisters would challenge each other with weird food restrictions and once only ate clementines and carrots for the forty days of Lent (except for Sunday cheat days). Excessive exercising paired with food restriction was an issue my sisters and I faced at different times and varying degrees. I was once down to 8% body fat and had my soccer coach tell me I needed to eat in front of him before I started practice – I negotiated him down to a Powerade which I knew was zero calories.

I used to know the calorie content of every fruit and vegetable by heart. I would order the side-salad and side-chili at Wendy's because the caloric intake of the chili was less than the dressing that came with the salad. I would eat that meal of less than 300 calories between school wrestling practice and club wrestling practice, and I would also work out during my spare period running on the treadmill holding my discman flat on my hand so the CD wouldn't skip as the treadmill jiggled.

This toxic culture of body image issues is something I have fought and continue to fight every day. I am learning to love my body. Honestly, my children help me with that. I refuse to speak negatively about my body in front of them, or restrict food, or label food as good or bad. I run to feel fit and not to lose weight, and I play soccer to be social and because I enjoy it. My daughter loves my tiger marks and squishy belly so much I am learning to accept it and love it because she finds so much comfort in my soft squishiness. I am rebranding my cellulite as cute dimples, and my jiggles as joy.

As a young child I thought my mom and my aunts were the most beautiful women in the world: they way the glowed when they smiled, or lightened the room with their laughter. Their softness and hugability was one of the most beautiful things about the mothers in my life. That's what I want for my kids. Soft, big, squishy hugs.

My mom tried every diet available, and she even had a personal trainer for a while. Doctors and nutritionists always assumed she snacked and didn't follow the diet plan; she was lazy or incompetent, but she was the most determined and disciplined person I knew and never had a cheat day. No matter what she tried, the weight never came off. Her constant swollen feet and ankles were dismissed as a weight issue by doctors.

A few years earlier, she had a lap band inserted and was finally able to lose some weight. As much as the lap band helped her lose weight, it was not a cure-all solution. She still had difficulty with her swollen ankles and feet, and her weight would fluctuate between appointments depending on how much fluid had been removed from or added to the band. She had many troubles with her lap band, including an infection of the port and device, so she'd had it removed about a year prior. The weight started returning slowly.

This surgery that my dad was telling me about was a more permanent one: a gastric sleeve, where up to eighty-five percent of the stomach is removed, leaving it with the ability to hold only sixty to ninety milliliters of food at a time. This forces the recipient to eat little bits slowly or risk vomiting. *I know, it sounds like a terrible ordeal just to be thin.*//TW:BI The clinic stapled the seam of my mom's stomach closed, and since she previously had such a troublesome lap band for so long she had a very weak stomach lining. The doctor placed one of the staples along a particularly weak and vulnerable part of her stomach. Once they closed her up, that staple tore her stomach and she began to bleed internally.

Her blood pressure tanked and she was not emerging from her anesthesia. The nurses palpated her stomach, but because she, like me, had extra skin from babies, her stomach just filled with blood and never felt firm. Eventually the clinic rushed her to the nearest hospital, which, luckily for us, was the top trauma hospital in Toronto. This was when my dad called all five of their children.

At first, I was unsure of how to react, so I called my sister. She told me I needed to leave immediately and head to the hospital; we had to be there for dad if mom died. *If mom died.* Mom might die tonight. I numbly spoke with Wes and he encouraged me to go. I fumbled in the dark of our room to get dressed and silently gathered a few things into my purse: laptop, charger, phone, car keys, wallet.

Wes gave me a hug that felt hollow in my state; nothing would comfort me until I knew my mom was alive. The drive to Toronto from Kitchener felt surreal. I stopped at a Tim Hortons rest stop on the way, not because I needed coffee, but because I needed some comfort. I needed something to ground me and pull me out of my trauma response. I felt the urge to tell the employee at the drive-through window, "My mom might die tonight," but instead I paid and found my way back onto the 401 eastbound, feeling a suffocating fog of fear.

As I continued my drive, I kept yearning for comfort and had a deep urge to get in contact with my ex-fiancé. He was previously a source of great comfort to me, and I thought he would be able to quell all my fears. This thought embarrassed me, because I knew it was wrong and illogical. We had broken up three years prior and I was living with and engaged to the wonderful father of my child. I was incredibly happy and healthy in my partnership, yet for some reason unknown to me at the time, I felt drawn to Andrew and craved the comfort he once brought to me, the fix-everything-in-the-world-and-protect-you-with-my-encircled-arms kind of omnipotence. *Yeah, I know right? I bet you're all thinking,* Gross, Rachel! Move on from that dickhead. *That's how I felt too!*

A few days after my mom's surgery, I sheepishly asked Wes if it would be okay if I contacted Andrew. I explained that I had no clue why I wanted to, but I felt the need to tell him about my mother. Wes acted incredibly strong and patient, and kindly did to not respond negatively to my absurd request. I contacted Andrew through Facebook messenger and explained the entire saga of my mother's incident. Through the entire conversation with him, I felt timid and confused, not wanting to give Wes or Andrew the wrong idea, and not knowing why I was even contacting him at all. I was responding to the trauma of my mother's sudden health complications, not understanding my own urges. Sometimes silence can be deafening when falling through the void left by things unsaid. Andrew's responses fell flat, and I didn't receive the comfort I yearned for. His power had dissipated, and I felt foolish for contacting him.

Now I know my urge to be comforted by Andrew

had developed from six years of trauma bonding, when I felt unsupported and isolated from friends and family, and Andrew was my main source of support as well as my abuser. He was the person I turned to for comfort, even if he was the one who'd caused me pain. And because he controlled my time, my body, and even my emotions, he had the divine ability to make me feel completely frenzied or completely calm. After years of separation and being in a healthy relationship, those strong emotions I used to have with Andrew had faded, and no one besides myself could bring me that kind of comfort anymore.

I was the second person to arrive at the hospital, and soon all five of my parents' children stood there talking, and waiting to hear about what we certainly thought would be our mother's death. When the doctor emerged at three a.m., he didn't ask us to go with him to a private room—a good sign. We had a tiny sense of relief, but quickly understood Mom wasn't close to being out of the woods. She had been left to bleed for too long and had lost sixty percent of her blood. It was unfathomable how she survived. She was incredibly lucky the surgeons were able to save her.

My family felt relieved enough to go to my sister's house in Brampton to get some sleep. But was no way in hell I was going anywhere. At four a.m., I went down to the ICU with my family, and they all gave mom a kiss before leaving. I got comfortable in the chair beside her and reached over to her bed to hold her weightless hand, delicately covered by tissue-paper skin. She felt empty.

This was not the strong woman I always knew. My mom was no longer immortal. She was suddenly very precious and vulnerable. I never really thought my mom could die. It was never a tangible reality before this moment. Sure, I'd had bad dreams, or would imagine the pain I would feel as I watched the movie *Stepmom*. But whenever I thought of my mother dying, it was always theoretical and without devastation.

I watched the computer track her oxygen and blood pressure levels. I gazed at her and all the tubes penetrating her arms and face. The hum of the blood pressure cuff broke the repetitive beeping of the monitor and almost inaudibly shallow sound of my mother's breath. Blood pressure 80/60, heart rate 130. The monitor began to flash and beep, and a nurse came in to hook up a new IV bag.

Mom was not waking up any time soon, so I turned on my laptop for a welcomed distraction—a movie, perhaps. I looked through my downloaded films and picked something lighthearted and mindless. I half-watched the movie and half-watched my mom and all her monitors.

Shift change for nurses occurred at about seven a.m. I listened to the handoff and learned as much as I could about my mom's condition and prospects. It was not looking good. Maybe my siblings and dad made a mistake going to Joanna's house to sleep; this may be her last day.

The days in the ICU held my entire family in a state of shock. After four days of touch-and-go, the staff began to remove some tubes. Mom went from cloudy, yellow eyes and half-consciousness to being able to hoarsely speak in short sentences and make eye contact. She could sit upright and drink water from a sponge. As soon as she became stable enough, they transferred her to another floor.

During her recovery, they discovered new and old pulmonary embolisms and deep-vein thrombosis in her legs. The doctor prescribed blood-thinner injections among other prescriptions. Mom remained in the hospital for only four more days before heading home—a premature release that felt way too soon for us all. She was not better yet. *Please keep her under doctor's supervision until she's not skeletal anymore.*

A week later my mother urinated pure blood. She had a one-in-a-million complication with her blood thinners that produced a bladder bleed. The first time she went to the hospital with my father, they dismissed the severity of her condition and told her she was merely experiencing a UTI. *Excuse me?* A woman who just escaped death was peeing pure blood, and all they did was prescribe an antibiotic and send her home? My parents had a combination of old-school respect for authority and denial.

I immediately understood my mother could not withstand another setback, so I drove to their house and informed my mother that either I would be taking her to the hospital or an ambulance would. My dad seemed to snap out of the denial and agree with me. At Strathroy Hospital, I prepared myself to challenge the doctors until we received proper care and an accurate diagnosis. The on-call doctor, thankfully, took my mother's condition very seriously and did a thorough investigation. Mom was admitted immediately, so they could monitor her as they lessened her blood thinners to stop the bleed and flush her bladder. Once she stopped bleeding, they would allow her to return home and continue with a new blood-thinning medication.

Two days later I returned to visit my mom in the hospital to bring her flowers and family photos. When I walked into the room and saw her lying on her gurney, deflated, my heart sank. She had lost so much weight so rapidly that her skin drooped onto the bed and pooled beside her, a real-life Dali painting and a persistent reminder that time with my mother was now uncertain. I felt her sliding through my fingers like a slippery oil-painted clock on the side of a cliff.

It brought me back to an earlier moment in life when I returned after a three-month exchange program abroad, and my mom had gone on a rapid-weight-loss program. I got off the plane and wrapped my arms around her. And I'm not sure if it's the maturity I gained on my three-month exchange abroad, or just her weight-loss, but instead of hugging this comfy warm woman whom I remembered not being able to encircle as a child, I could easily wrap my arms around a person who seems so much smaller - too small - and no longer larger than life. This was one of the first moments I recognized her as a human beyond her role as my mother.

Because as my mother she could be a revelation— at least while I was young. I had always seen my mom as the martyr who lived for others at the expense of herself. Always tired. Always overworked and underappreciated. Yet always incredibly strong and somehow able to hold our family together, work, nurture a marriage, and maintain a household. She was the superhero of moms. An impossible standard to live up to yet always humble, never once thinking of herself as extraordinary.

She lived the life of ten women in one. She was a board member of our local credit union, church and school volunteer, nightly chauffeur to five children and their extracurriculars, chef, house cleaner, party planner, and family accountant. She always filled a social and activity calendar, and in the summer she had an incentive program for the kids that included different school subjects and day trips. My mom built two successful businesses, got a second degree when I was in grade eight, and started a new career when I was in high school.

When I was younger I also saw my mother as weak,

because she always seemed at her wit's end, never standing up for herself. But as I matured, my perspective changed, and as a parent I have gained a new kind of respect for my mother. She was an unstoppable force, a woman to be revered. She went above and beyond all our physical, intellectual, and educational needs. But you can't teach what you don't know, and that's the way it was when it came to our emotional needs. She parented with all the loving attention she could muster while she was experiencing her own emotional storm. She was surviving her own childhood traumas, relationship difficulties, and deep-seated insecurities. So much so that she almost died trying to be skinny.

For the next seven months I called my mother every night and spoke with her in long conversations. I felt like I could pick up the phone any minute and be told that she'd died. We spoke about what she wanted at her funeral: how she wanted to be dressed, that she wanted her boobs to look great, and how she wanted her eyes to open when people knelt on the kneeler (I *think* she was kidding). Definitely open-casket. Definitely have someone sing "Ave Maria" and "On Eagle's Wings." We spoke about mundane things, conversations that would meander through stories of the past or worries of the present. I even asked her to write me a letter for my wedding day in case she died, but she refused multiple times, saying she was not going to die. *Well, you* weren't *going to die, but now NO ONE KNOWS anymore.*

I had experienced loss before when my Opa and my Grandpa died, and the year after high school, three of my classmates were killed in two separate car accidents. But my mom's near-death was the event that truly convinced me that I needed to seize the day. *Carpe diem, which I live now more and more honestly each day.* I try to say yes to every request and opportunity possible, and I work to sear every sweet moment into my brain, not knowing if it might be the last.

I let my parents spoil the crap out of my children and don't worry too much about them eating sugar or going to bed late. They're at Grandma and Grandpa's—that's how it's supposed to be. We're so lucky they have grandparents to spoil them.

I also try and live in the moment with the people who strain my heart. Appreciate them when they are kind and good and give them grace when they are hurtful and wrong. It's a work in progress, but I feel there is not enough time in life to hold a grudge or to lose time with someone important. *To those who think I* am *holding a grudge: Setting boundaries with toxic people is not the same thing; it's stopping patterns of negativity.*

Right before my birthday in February we found out my mom's blood clots had resolved in her lungs, and the scarring left behind was quite minimal. She was in the clear. But I still kept an eye on the scythe that sat in the corner for a couple of months though, just in case the reaper was coming back to claim it. *Not today, Satan!*

On the tail end of my mother's initial recovery was the #metoo movement. I was binge watching *Big Little Lies* at the time, and like many others became breathless when Celeste's husband abused her. He was abusive in the mainstream-media type of way, a Jekyll-and-Hyde of physical abuse that left bruises needing powdered makeup. Yet it also showed the complexities of abusive relationships in which the abuser is loving at times and there are moments of light and laughter between bouts of violence and fear. It showed how the abused person isn't always a wilting flower who doesn't rage against the machine and the strength a person can exude by staying *and* by leaving.

TW:SC//One scene in particular raised the hair on my neck and stopped my breath in the middle of my throat. The man had previously raped the woman in the middle of a physical abuse episode. He later pressured her for sex, and the anxiety was palpable. He wanted her to have another baby and continue to be a housewife, but she was not interested. After much prodding, he finally laid back in defeat, ending the conversation on a sour note.

She paused before switching on a smile and climbing on top of him flirtatiously to initiate sex. I cringed as I recognized the scene as coercion. I recognized her obligation to keep the peace out of fear of anger the following day or later in the evening. I recognized the emotional manipulation and guilt which made her succumb to his manipulation. I recognized this as sexually abusive; as rape. And I saw myself—for the first time—as a victim of sexual coercion in my relationship with Andrew.

Not once during the six years Andrew and I dated or the three years since I broke up with him had I considered that I'd been sexually abused. Even at this point my only memories of sex were during the last year of our relationship, when he had already conditioned me to be his orgasm maid. Like the woman in the scene above: If one hadn't known about the previous rape, this may have seemed like a woman changing her mind and wanting sex from her handsome husband. And that's what left me confused and questioning myself. How did I get to the point of not physically fighting back? *Whyyyyy can't I remember?//TW:SC*

I needed to stop watching the news and raging on Facebook about straight white male rapists like Brett Kavanaugh and Brock Turner suffering no consequences and receiving sympathy from people in power. I needed to stop watching triggering shows like *Law & Order: SVU* and *Big Little Lies*. Exposure therapy clearly was not working. The #metoo movement was a wonderful way for women to have their fifteen minutes of fame, and then have America vote in Donald Trump over Hillary Clinton, because they are even more sexist than they are racist.

I know some people truly believed that Hillary ran a child sex ring in the basement of a pizza shop. But *most* people didn't. Yet they voted for someone who was proven to sexually assault women and bragged about it on a recording. *Where is the hope? Why are we bringing more children into this world?*

Unromantically, I believe we have more children because we hope to the younger generation will fix our fuck-ups. Romantically, I believe it's because children bring love and hope. They enter the world with a new perspective, and they bring light and evolution. I believe each generation strives to be better than the one before. There are phenomenal young leaders that ferociously fight for what is right. They have the energy and resilience to push further than us old, tired biddies. They'll do better than us, like we're doing better than our parents, who did better than theirs.

Chapter 7 – The Struggle of Fertility

Trigger Warning:
This chapter contains: miscarriage (pages 108-109) and emotional abuse
(pages 117-118). Please be kind to yourself and respect your personal limits.
If you would like to forgo these triggering scenes you may read a summary
on pages 322-323.

Wes and I hoped to have four children in as many years, before Wes turned forty in 2020. We started having sex to practice making baby number two in October 2016. I hoped my fertility mimicked my great grandmother, who had eight children in a row without ever getting her period, or my other great grandmother, who had sixteen children in eighteen years, or my grandmother, who had six children in a similarly short time period. My mother had eleven pregnancies and five births in eight years. Since we got pregnant on the first try with Sebastian, I hoped we would get pregnant as easily the second time. Even though Wes and I desperately wanted a big family, we struggled with secondary infertility.

I got my first menstrual cycle following Sebastian's birth in February 2017. I was ecstatic to know I had begun ovulating again and therefore had a chance of getting pregnant. I didn't get my period again until June. During those five months I kept having false pregnancy symptoms: nausea, headaches, cramping. I convinced myself my period was late because I was pregnant. I bought a container of one hundred dipsticks to test for the pregnancy hormone HCG so I wouldn't waste so much money on pregnancy tests.

I honestly became addicted to testing my urine. I struggled to limit myself to one pregnancy test strip per day. *Per day*. They continually came back negative. *Of course they did*. With each negative result I became more and more melancholy, bitter, and hopeless.

I was so desperate for a sibling for Sebastian, I was actually experiencing nausea and tender breasts despite not being pregnant. My body kept betraying me, and I kept feeling like a failure. We tried all the natural ways, listened to people unhelpfully telling us to just relax, and even had strangers comment on how we should give Sebastian a sibling. *Seriously, complete strangers in a café*. After my menstrual cycle in June, I decided I would start birth control if I did not become pregnant by mid-August—which I didn't. Occasionally, I would question the validity of the cheap test strips, because I was so sure I was pregnant. So, I would go and get an expensive pregnancy test from the store just in case the cheap ones were faulty, only to be met with the same defeat.

I started taking the pill at the end of August for two cycles before stopping in hopes that the birth control regulated my cycle, making ovulation and pregnancy more likely. On December 5, 2017 at eleven p.m., I took a pregnancy test and went downstairs to lie down, refusing to look at the result, because I was sick of seeing only one line. The plan was for Wes to check the result and eventually join me in bed.

I could tell by the way he moved through the house that we finally had a positive! Wes entered the room trying hide his joy, saying, "I think we should just look at this one together."

"Okay!' I played along. We both scurried up the stairs and Wes grabbed the test off the counter and we turned it over together. We shrieked and jumped up and down in the kitchen, holding on to each other while laughing, crying, and shaking with joy. After fourteen months of negative tests, we had a positive!

Within thirty seconds, we'd called all our parents and told them the great news. Even though I was only two months into my job following maternity leave, I felt too excited to keep my pregnancy a secret. By the time I was six weeks pregnant, the entire office knew, as well as my siblings, cousins, friends, neighbors, and the lovely ladies who worked at the café down the street. We had waited long enough to get pregnant and we were not going to wait a second longer to bask in our joy by sharing the news with others.

I booked our first ultrasound after the holidays at ten weeks' gestation. I always booked a dating ultrasound, just so I could see our little munchkin as soon as possible. As Wes and I watched the black-and-white screen, we gushed over our tiny little ten-week-old bean with its fluttering heartbeat. We printed ultrasound photos and hung them on our fridge, and I pinned them in my office cubicle. I would gush as I told my coworkers that I could already tell our baby had the best personality ever (half-joking, of course).

Wes and I went to Niagara Falls the following weekend to celebrate the anniversary of our first date. I glowed with excitement and enjoyed wearing my maternity clothes again, already uncomfortable in my regular clothes despite being only weeks into my second pregnancy. We had to take our special steak dinner as takeout, so I could be sick in our hotel room and take a nap before finally eating at eleven p.m. I enjoyed my morning sickness, because I relished in experiencing *real* symptoms after having so many false pregnancy symptoms the year prior. We buzzed with happiness the entire weekend.

A week after the ultrasound, I finally got a call from the midwife, who was supposed to tell me the due date. I answered excitedly and she asked if I was in a place to talk. I totally missed her tone and cue and answered happily, "Of course!" as I sat at my desk in my cubicle.

She went on to talk about two cysts found on the umbilical cord and fluid found in the baby's chest. She said both could go away and mean nothing, or it could be something more serious. She said I should have another ultrasound in three weeks and not to do my own research on the internet. I was in shock, never expecting news like this. I just wanted to know our baby's due date.

I texted my husband and asked him to call as soon as possible about the ultrasound results. When the phone rang and as his voice broke my trance my breath caught in my throat; I couldn't speak. Eventually, and with many pauses and great effort to control my voice and breathing, I was able to give him the news. Wes was in denial. He assured me everything was all right and, just like the midwife said, everything could be fine and dandy on the next ultrasound.

The next three weeks waiting for the ultrasound was a type of hell I wouldn't wish on another soul. Friends and family tried to keep everything positive, but I did my research on the symptoms (just like the midwife told me not to), and I knew the chances were not good. I read pages and pages of published medical studies and data analysis.

Fluid in the chest at that gestational age had an eighty-five percent chance of being Turner Syndrome, which would mean that our baby was a girl and that she had an abnormality with her sex chromosome. She would have a one percent chance of not being stillborn, and if she was brought into the world alive, she would live with many health complications.

Cysts on the umbilical cord were likely to resolve themselves by the next ultrasound. But if they were still present in second trimester, it pointed to either Trisomy 13 or 18, meaning that our little baby would be in pain their entire life. Our baby would only have a five percent chance of being born alive and if they were, would have only a ten percent chance of living longer than a year.

My husband refused to think the outcome would be anything but positive and did not want to speak about the possibility of losing our baby. Friends and family tried to console me and advised me to stay positive and not stress out, because stress hurts the baby—*give me a break*. I hoped with my entire being that everything would be resolved by the next ultrasound and that we wouldn't have to make any difficult choices regarding the health and life of our very wanted and wished-for child. But I was also trying to be realistic and mentally prepare myself for the likelihood we would be undergoing some sort of medical intervention.

> My bones began to *rattle*.
> My body began to quiver and shake.
> I clattered with despair
> as I spoke
> on the phone to my sister,
> sitting at the dining room table

under a dimmed chandelier
and my back to a wall of
black windows.

My heart shook,
my voice quivered.
My body jerked
with trauma
as I explained how our baby
had fluid in its chest
and two cysts on the umbilical cord.

TW:M //Six days before the ultrasound, my body started to feel different, and I intuitively knew the baby had passed away. My morning sickness started to disappear, and my stomach felt as if it was getting smaller and less hard. Days ago, I couldn't sleep on my stomach, but now I could.

At our friend's child's first birthday party, we sat on a couch in a room mostly full of strangers. Our friend, knowing full well of our situation, breezily asked how the pregnancy was going. I was bewildered that she would ask such an insensitive question among strangers knowing that we were distraught with worry and sadness. So, I looked her straight in the eyes and said, "The baby's probably dead." The room went awkwardly silent and no one knew how to react. I just stood up and went to another room and spent the rest of the party in a corner with a girlfriend, talking about the baby.

Slowly, the ultrasound appointment crept closer, and we went into the procedure room with hope and fear. I came prepared for a long ultrasound, taking all the measurements of the baby to see if they had any markers for genetic abnormalities. After about five minutes the ultrasound technician said that I could use the bathroom while she got my husband. Again, I knew the baby had passed away.

When I came back into the room, Wes asked me if we were going to see the heartbeat. I looked across the room at him and explained how the baby had likely passed away. He was in shock and disbelief, totally unprepared for this outcome. I sat on the table and called my mom to tell her the news. The technician soon reappeared and said the midwife was on the phone. I answered, knowing what was about to happen. She explained that there had been a missed miscarriage and that the baby had passed away about a week earlier. She referred me to the abortion clinic at the hospital to assist with the miscarriage as it was not occurring naturally.//TW:M

Wes and I left the ultrasound office, numb. We asked for a photo before we went home—our baby was still beautiful with a great personality, just a little squished in my collapsing uterus.

Wes and I spent the afternoon crying together and snuggling on the couch. I contacted human resources and reported the days I would be missing. I received many phone calls from concerned family and friends. When we picked up our son from daycare, we tried to have the most normal evening possible, and we still went out with my cousin to sushi as previously planned, telling him the bad news at the end of dinner so as not to ruin the evening.

The next day I stayed home and moped around the house. Wes went to work but ended up coming back at lunchtime. We were absolutely devastated. Wes was mostly sad, and I was mostly scared. I was scared to start miscarrying and to see the baby, and I was scared to get a dilation and curettage, better known as a D&C. Four days after the ultrasound the midwife booked me into the abortion clinic at seven a.m.

The days in between stretched time in the worst kind of way. Each trip to the washroom filled me with the fear that the rush of blood would begin or that I would lose my lemon-sized baby in the toilet. One day I went to work as a distraction. I spoke to the women, tried not to cry too much, and emailed my boss to let him know the news and that I would be taking a few days off. He responded with *k*. That was it, a simple lower-case letter. He then later informed me that my days off would be unpaid. No empathy. No concern. *What in the actual fuck?* The entire office knew I was pregnant nine weeks ago and celebrated as I received a pregnant-snowman tree ornament from my secret Santa. He had children of his own. This was a loss that a human should understand as devastating, yet he responded with *k*.

The next day Wes and I left Sebastian with my sister and headed to the abortion clinic at the hospital. I felt completely awkward asking for directions to get there and wanted to tell everyone that this was not a choice I made or wanted. I wanted people to know this was tragic to me and that I was not okay.

Sitting in the waiting room, I looked around at the couples and women with their moms and wondered what kind of pain they were in. Who had lost their baby, like me, and who had to make the most difficult choice of her life? Some people may think there would be some feeling of resentment to women terminating healthy pregnancies while I lost mine. No. Not at all. Reasons for abortion, mental or physical, are valid for women's health. Just because I lost a very wanted and longed-for baby does not mean a woman should be forced to keep an unwanted and unplanned pregnancy. *That's not how it works.*

Once the OB called me in to her office, we went

over my options: a chemically induced labor, where I would give birth to my deceased baby at home, or a D&C. *Who the fuck would not choose a D&C? Option number one sounds insanely traumatic and painful.* Yet for some reason she tried to sway me toward the red pill. *Yeah, nope, please direct me to pre-op.*

Unable to eat or drink while I waited for my upcoming surgery, the nurse eventually put me on an IV drip for dehydration. I spent much of the day alone as my husband went home to tend to our toddler. The woman on the other side of the curtain was probably the worst person I could have been placed beside. She was pregnant with her third child, and she was there for an infected knee, which was infected from IV drug use. She used every drug in the world other than birth control and had no intention of getting sober for this pregnancy—"'cause I didn't for my last two!"

She kept moaning in pain to get more medication, and every time she complained, hot anger ran through my blood. So, I turned my headphones on to drown her out. How was it possible or fair that this reckless woman brought three babies to term while harming them with drugs, and I, who so badly desired a healthy baby, suffered a loss? I cranked up the volume on my headphones to the max. Thoughts like these were not constructive or helpful. *That woman had a much worse life than I. For fuck's sake, Rachel, she lived on the street. How do you think she likely got pregnant? Let her have all the drugs.*

I waited in pre-op until it closed, at ten p.m. Then I waited on a gurney in the hall for another ninety minutes before I finally went into surgery at eleven-thirty p.m. That's sixteen and a half hours that I'd been in the hospital waiting for a procedure I was led to believe was booked for seven a.m. I was the last person to go into surgery that night and almost had to wait four more days if the OB didn't show up in the next five minutes, because they only performed abortions on Tuesdays and Fridays. My surgery was considered elective, unnecessary, and a woman's issue, so they moved me to the end of the list. *Classic.*

When I was wheeled into the room I tried to keep my sanity and fear under control by making jokes. "Everything is fine as long as you don't say, 'Do you want to play a game?'" I said, referencing the movie *Saw.* The nurses chuckled, and soon I woke up groggily in post-op. I could hear the moaning woman getting rolled out of the room from her knee surgery. The nurses reviewed her chart and said, "Holy cow, she got pumped full of pain meds—I hope she doesn't code!" They must have thought I was still out, because when I mumbled, "She's fine, she's a drug addict," they started whispering a little quieter.

A half-hour later, feeling quite numb, I cleaned up and dressed to leave the hospital. One nurse wiped the iodine from my thighs and mentioned that the male nurses always slop it all over the place, while the other nurse fed me water. They helped me get into some netted hospital underwear and put on my comfy clothes. They debriefed me about recovering and advised me not to go get a burrito even though I was ravenous, explaining that I could get very sick and advising that I stick to soda crackers until the morning. Wes wheeled me to the car and helped me in.

When Wes and I got home at one-thirty a.m., my dad sprung up from the couch and grumpily barked at my mom, "Maria, it's late, we're going home. I'll meet you in the car." (Thinking it's always about him is typical of my father.) I rolled my eyes at my dad and reminded him the day was traumatic for me, not him, and he should be a little more supportive and concerned for his daughter. He sighed, knowing I was completely right but not wanting to admit it, and gave me a hug and kiss before heading out the door. My mom hugged me and ignored him and gently spoke to me about my day. She updated me on our son, then said she would see me in two days for my birthday before hugging and kissing me again at the door.

Wes and I stayed up a bit later as I munched on soda crackers and sipped on water. My legs felt itchy from the iodine, but I was told to keep dry for twenty-four hours to avoid infection, so I waited until the next day to shower. We went downstairs to the darkness of our room and snuggled in our family bed with our perfect beautiful son. I felt exhausted and slept like a rock, relieved to be through the fear and to not be carrying our dead baby inside me anymore—which was a weirdly awful feeling of not wanting to let go, but also irksome to carry a decaying fetus).

I spent much of the next day, which would've marked fifteen weeks of pregnancy, on the couch, depressed, uncomfortable, and woozy. My cousin came over to help take care of Sebastian and prepare food for my twenty-sixth birthday party the next day. Edwin completely cleaned the kitchen and cooked a bunch of food *because he was my village.*

At around seven p.m. my wooziness began to dissipate, so I took a long shower and washed away all the blood and iodine—and cried about the fact I was washing away blood and iodine. Both my husband and cousin periodically checked on me. I finally emerged, and Wes encouraged me to go out to dinner with Edwin, which I did. Dinner was an out-of-body experience, especially when I had my first alcoholic drink in months, another clear indication I was no longer growing a baby. After dinner I let Edwin pay, which I usually never did. I was just too tired and empty to fight it. We went back to my house, and I went to bed exhausted.

The next day my family came over for my birthday: two parents, two godparents, ten siblings, two cousins, and six screaming children under age four. They came with love, loud laughter, and a large, beautiful edible arrangement, a sympathy gift arranged by my older sister. I had wanted everyone there, but I felt too overwhelmed, exhausted, and emotional to be social.

I cried in the basement for most of the morning and eventually came upstairs for lunch and cake. I avoided eye contact and conversation. I often retreated to my bedroom in tears. I thought family visiting would be nice, but I realized I just wanted them to be near me without having to interact with them.

By the end of the day, I was ready for silence and to be alone again. I took two more days off work and binge-watched *Scandal* while eating birthday cupcakes.

The following month I dragged myself out of bed to go to work, hated every minute at my desk, cried in the bathroom stall, cried sitting in front of my computer, and cried on the way home. During the day, I often had the feeling of a raw uterus—a reasonable feeling considering a baby had just been scraped out of mine. The residual cramps and pain were a constant physical reminder that I was empty and my baby had died. The fear of blood as I wiped remained and my heartrate increased each time I entered my work bathroom stall.

This loss was not something I could run from or fight against. I felt paralyzed. At home I laid on the couch all night and avoided parenting. I stopped cooking, cleaning, and doing household chores. I only showered and groomed enough not to get fired, and I hardly faked enthusiasm and happiness when my child ran to spend time with me. I sulked on the couch until Wes put

Sebastian to bed, then I binge-watched Netflix and ate junk food until I finally fell asleep. I was miserable.

After a month of just surviving, I had a string of horrible days at work. On the drive home one Wednesday night, I tearfully asked my husband if I could quit my job even though I didn't have a new one lined up. He didn't take long to say yes. because I'm sure he hoped, just as I did, that quitting this job would help me start my journey back to happiness.

The next day I cleaned my desk, my computer, and wrapped up all my projects, planning to quit on Monday. My boss had a word with me, trying to get me to do part of his job without the pay, and I'd had enough. I texted Wes and asked if I could quit that day and if he would pick me up. He replied that he was ready when I was. So, I wrote a resignation letter and notified Tina in Human Resources. I then gave the letter to my boss, and he was shocked.

He asked why, and I had a list of reasons, including his brusque "k" email response. We sat in the conference room with Tina, and I went through my list and the exit interview, poised and professional. I surprised myself by remaining calm and not crying. Then I walked out of the building, already feeling free. I spent the next day at home with no pressures or responsibilities. A new chapter began and I already felt markedly better.

I immediately planned many projects, so I could smother my sadness. I renovated the Sebastian's playroom, applied to new jobs like a madwoman, and planned the shit out of our upcoming wedding and honeymoon. I kept so busy running around doing errands that I lost enough baby weight and cupcake weight to fit into my wedding dress again. I was so worried I would have a skinny dress, a maternity dress, and a fat dress! Thank goodness I could cancel the maternity dress and slim down to avoid the fat dress.

I ended up getting eight interviews in three weeks and two promises of job offers. I only ended up receiving one job offer and planned to start the new job when I returned from our honeymoon.

Though Wes and I had been engaged for two years we didn't do any wedding planning in the first year of engagement. My parents withdrew their financial contribution, which my four siblings had received and which I had counted on since being told about it at a young age. They did so because I moved in with Wes before we got married. They chose this as the reason, because they knew they would look bad if they blamed it on me having a child out of wedlock. But in reality, two of their other children also lived with their spouse before marriage and received wedding money.

Without this contribution from my parents, Wes and I just couldn't fathom spending all that money on one day, because we would rather travel. Then, at Valentine's dinner, Wes offhandedly suggested we just get married while traveling. We had struck gold! This was the solution to our internal battles. Two birds, one stone, which also reflected how Wes and I enjoyed our relationship: saying yes to adventure and trying new things.

We immediately knew the country we should be married in was Italy because, well, *Italy*, but also because we had a connection to the country from when Wes visited me in Rome. Italy was where we made the decision to take the next step in our relationship and start trying for kids. And the food. The wine. The landscape. The architecture. The whole country just made us both swoon with romance.

We tentatively floated the idea to my family and received a hesitant response. No one was enthusiastic about the idea, and some said no. I shouldn't have posed it to my parents as if they had a vote—they lost that when they withdrew their financial support. And when we sent out our save-the-dates for an Italian wedding, all hell broke loose.

My older brother and his wife handled the situation perfectly. They didn't feel comfortable traveling outside of Canada with young children. They sent a thoughtful email regretting their absence, promising to support in any way they could, and celebrating upon our return. Though I was disappointed I understood their position and respected the way they presented their response with love. With each exciting planning milestone, my sister-in-law enthusiastically ogled villas, invitations, décor, and dresses. She complimented everything down to the font style. Though they were not at the wedding in person I felt supported and loved leading up to and following the big day.

TW:EA//On the other hand, my younger brother, sisters, and parents absolutely sucked. They didn't want to hear about my wedding at all, and if it came up, it was in an argument. They tried to bully me into changing my mind. They dangled the prospect of attending until three months before the wedding, when finally my remaining siblings said they would not be attending for various reasons—but really because they were pissed I *chose a location over them*. My mom whispered to me that she and my dad would end up going but to not talk with him about it.//TW:EA

To be clear, Wes and I paid for everyone's accommodations for five to seven nights. We set up welcome baskets on each person's bed with enough food and drink for breakfast and a snack, we paid for a winery tour, had an extravagant dinner with enough leftovers to last the remaining days, and we organized two days of caravan tours people could join. We aimed to make the trip as affordable as possible for loved ones and offered to pay for people's flights, which some accepted.

Guests bought round-trip flights for between $450 and $700. And we also wanted all of our guests who took the time and spent the money to fly to Italy to feel appreciated. Ten percent of our budget was spent on gifts. We felt very grateful for the attendance of all forty guests. *I write this to emphasize that Wes and I did our best to accommodate our guests and express our gratitude to those who flew to Italy.*

TW:EA//My siblings' and parents' refusal to attend wasn't financially based—not only because we generously offered to pay for so much, but also because they were all financially in good standing. My sisters claimed they didn't feel comfortable traveling with their children, then went to the Bahamas with their families eight months later. My family vehemently claimed they were all against destination weddings, but two attended those of friends.

Their attitude around and leading up to the wedding was the most hurtful part. If everyone could have taken a page from my older brother's book, we could have saved a lot of tears and heartache. I wish they could have been happy for me and celebrated with me.

My parents wanted no part in the planning and always scoffed when I tried to bring something up, though sometimes my mom reluctantly half-listened to my excited chatter as she took a break from lesson-planning. This hurt—even more so because I had a direct comparison. I had previously gone through planning a wedding with my abusive ex, and my parents showed enthusiastic interest in each location, photographer, and color swatch. I knew what it was like to plan a wedding that was paid for and highly anticipated with love and excitement.//TW:EA

You know what though? Everything worked out the way it was meant to. Had my parents paid for our wedding, it would have been in the same church and with very similar traditions to my siblings, and my mom would have been overbearing and controlling on the day of the wedding (like she was at my reception when we returned). I got to channel all my planning passion and creativity into each part of our wedding From the font on the invitations to the personalized poems in people's welcome baskets, and from the laser-cut place names to the fairy-lit wine bottles. From the photos of loved ones lining the aisle and behind the altar to the handpicked flowers circling the sign remembering Wes's dad and stepmom, and from the love songs played during dinner to the vows we wrote. The entire day was completely thought through and sentimentally constructed. It was perfect.

The people that ended up coming to our wedding were not necessarily the ones we thought would come, but they were the ones who were meant to be there. Our group of friends and family in Italy were all kind and fun people. The day went calmly and beautifully without any drama or people trying to change things I designed. We just enjoyed our planned and self-financed dream wedding.

This may sound like a cliché, but I had been planning my wedding since I was a young girl drawing pictures of white dresses. When I felt stressed or bored throughout university, I would fully plan different weddings in different locations at different budgets. I knew all the going rates for photography, catering, dresses and so forth. So, when it came to planning a wedding in a foreign country, I was up for the challenge.

For the same cost of a wedding at home with a hundred and twenty guests, we could host forty in Italy.

Along with accommodations, winery tour, wedding meal, and wedding attire, we flew out a chef and event-coordinator couple, photographers, and videographers. Luckily, we were able to pay these unique people with only travel expenses, which helped us gain amazing talent for a budget price.

I planned minimal and effective décor that I could fit in one suitcase: microphone, wireless speaker, tulle, printed photos of loved ones, memory board, tubes of bubbles, stationery, cork fairy-lights, two forty-foot strings of lights, laser-cut place names and hearts, and battery-powered tealights. My dress traveled as free carry-on (everyone loves to see a wedding dress travel).

On the morning of our wedding, we all congregated in one of the kitchens and had pastries, fruit, and espresso while Wes gave everyone a pep talk. Then the wedding party and helpers walked down the driveway to set up and decorate the ceremony space. We used chairs from the villa and lined the aisle with tulle and black-and-white photos pinned to twine, as well as pinned photos to the wrought-iron gate behind the altar. We set up a podium, tested the speakers, and did a quick rehearsal. Then friends finished placing itineraries on chairs with bubble tubes while I went back to the villa for the beauty regime.

The groom's and bride's crews got ready in separate buildings. The chef brought in platters of sandwiches, but I was too nervous to be hungry and tried to stay somewhat on schedule. My cousin did my hair, I did my own makeup, and my mom laced up my dress. My dad helped me out of the villa and I gave gifts to my friends and family before walking down the back path in bare feet to where I would begin my walk down the aisle.

The ceremony went without a hitch and was

absolutely divine. Everyone who is special to Wes and I played a role: some gave readings or blessings, some stood by my side, others were officiants. We ended by dancing up the aisle and driveway and back to the villas, where prosecco and paperwork waited for us. We all cheered, took photos, then drove to the winery for a tour, tasting, and lots of photographs.

We returned to the villa for a phenomenal family-style dinner on one long rustic table lit by stringed lights, tealights, and fairy-lit wine bottles. Our chef presented us with two types of fresh pizza topped with ingredients such as prosciutto, arugula, and buffalo mozzarella. Next came two types of pasta, then two types of meat, and finally a huge array of special pastries. In between courses we would turn the music up (all songs submitted by invitees as their love songs), and if a song from a present guest came on, we encouraged them to dance.

One of the most iconic moments of the wedding experience was when the song "Can't Help Falling in Love" by Elvis Presley came on, and someone flicked off the lights. People picked up tealights and waved them back and forth as everyone sang along, and Wes and I danced with Sebastian in our arms. The entire day was meant to celebrate love—not just ours, but everyone who came in person and was there in spirit.

The evening ended with Wes and I sitting in our honeymoon suite hot tub while my parents—yes, they'd ultimately decided to come—slept with Sebastian elsewhere. My husband removed all eight hundred bobby-pins from my hair as we went over the day and exclaimed to each other how well our plans unfolded. We felt so incredibly grateful for the people who came and the people we hired, because everything went so perfectly. We cried while remembering sweet, happy, and loving moments and felt blessed to be surrounded by the right people.

The next day Wes and I led the driving caravan tour to Siena, Pienza, and Montepulciano. The whole day was an exhausting blast. Traveling in a big group from town to town was a fun challenge, and we were able to hang out with people and have experiences we couldn't have planned. This marked a wonderful beginning to the rest of our trip, which was our honeymoon±—with Sebastian.

We visited gorgeous landscapes in Tuscany, Umbria, and Cinque Terre. We enjoyed our food and family siestas, and reconnected with love. As much as I wanted to enjoy the wine and cappuccinos, my body was telling me *No, thanks.* So, I listened, knowing in my heart what it meant, but too scared to mention it until it was proven with pink lines. We wandered Roman streets at night while musicians played and Romani danced to rhythmic drums. Italy was where love surrounded us and where we felt at home. This was the only place that made sense to us. It's where I learned, where we loved, and where we one day hope to live.

Chapter 8 – Not Again

Trigger Warning:
This chapter contains: scenes of miscarriage throughout.
Please be kind to yourself and respect your personal limits. If you would like to
forgo these triggering scenes you may read a summary on page 323.

Our first week back from our honeymoon was one of the most eventful weeks of my life. On Monday I started at a new job, my sister-in-law gave birth to my newest niece on Tuesday, Wednesday we bought our first family car and my first car ever, and on Thursday we confirmed I was pregnant for the third time.

I had felt pregnant for over a week and knew the test would come back positive. But when the test showed two little pink lines my heart did not jump with excitement or happiness, it sunk with worry. I felt pregnant, and now I knew I was pregnant, but something was amiss. Regardless, we waited less than a day to excitedly tell our parents, siblings, and close friends about our honeymoon baby.

Two days later we had our wedding reception, an event at which I very much needed a drink, but was unable to take one. An event where I could have really used an ibuprofen for my throbbing, pounding earache, but was unable to get some relief. I felt miserable.

Two weeks later, at our annual family camping weekend, I showed up prepared for a good time but feeling despondent. I brought all sorts of activities and toys for the kids: We collected and painted rocks; we played in the sand and climbed the dunes, watching my adorable little niece sing that she was the "king of the castle, and daddy's the dirty rascal"; and we had a campfire with all the snacky things kids like. But I just wanted to go back home the entire time.

Something in my body felt wrong. I felt to my core that something about my pregnancy was off, and I felt vulnerable to miscarriage. I wanted to be back in the safe comfort of our home, so I could withstand my looming fear. That weekend I began reliving the trauma and sadness of the miscarriage I never fully processed.

My sisters and mom gave me sympathetic looks and advised that I stay positive, even though it's hard. It didn't help at all. Due to some rain and a sincere lack of enthusiasm, we all bailed on camping before bedtime on the second night. My siblings displayed disappointment about the early dropout, and I felt relieved. I was anxious to get back to the comfort of my own home, so I could sulk the way I needed to without being told to smile.

A couple days later, on Wednesday, I was having a relatively normal day at work. Typing away at my desk, I felt some dampness in my underwear. I briskly shuffled to the bathroom to evaluate the wetness; was it discharge? Did I actually pee myself at work? Or was it the worst…blood? I slowly removed my pants and pulled my underwear down—just discharge, thank God! I went pee, then wiped.

The wipe was a bit too slick, so I looked down, expecting more discharge. The tissue was crimson. I froze for a moment, almost forgetting where I was, then continued to clean myself up. I turned to the toilet and located a lonely, feathered nickel-sized clot resting at the base of the white ceramic bowl. Before flushing, I evaluated the amount of blood present, as blood from the paper ominously turned the toilet water red. *Okay, calm down Rachel, this is a bit worrisome, but we don't know anything yet. Let's not jump to conclusions*

I knew my mother spotted with my younger brother, so she went on bed rest and the pregnancy was sustained. Spotting did not necessarily mean miscarriage. I self-affirmed the baby still grew with every heartbeat, and they clung to me as I hoped I might just need to go on bed rest for a bit. What I knew for sure was that I couldn't spend the rest of the afternoon stressing at work, and I couldn't wait one more week for my ultrasound booking. I flushed the toilet and watched some of my optimism spiral away. As I shakily washed my hands, emotion started to drain from my body, then I robotically gathered my things and left the office.

My mind shifted into crisis-management autopilot: I called the clinic to move my appointment as soon as possible, texted our company human resources manager, texted Wes and asked him to pick up Sebastian, and drove home to snuggle under couch blankets.

My family loudly interrupted my sullen silence when they crashed through the doors, dropping bags on the floor and flicking off shoes. Wes seemed to notice I needed time to myself and did a wonderful job playing with Sebastian, making him dinner, feeding him, bathing him, reading him books, and putting him to bed. They buzzed around the house doing our evening routine as I sat paralyzed on the couch, waiting for the quietness of a sleeping toddler in my husband's arms.

But while I longed for Wes's embrace, he decided he needed to sweat out his tension through ball hockey, something I didn't have the privilege of doing with my body in turmoil. I looked at him with clear disappointment and desperation in my eyes. I'm never one to sugarcoat or leave hints when something is this important. This was one of these moments.

"Are you seriously thinking of leaving me here alone while I'm spotting and scared that another one of our babies is going to die?" I was a basket case and needed my husband to join me. My always-optimistic Wes had chosen yet again to avoid considering possible negative outcomes. Though Wes wasn't as anxious as me, he did choose to stay home with me on the couch and hold me until I fell asleep.

The next morning, I woke up on time to drink the prerequisite liter of water one hour before my appointment. We arrived on time, and I felt extremely uncomfortable. That much water was always way too much for my bladder to hold, especially when a technician pressed down on it with their ultrasound wand. The technician got to work, her lips in a tight line across her face.

Generally, when they find the baby, they stick to a small three-inch area for a bit and type on their keyboard to get some good photos. But she looked all over trying to catch a glimpse of something—right hand scanning, left hand poised above the keyboard. *She can't find my baby.* I could tell by the way she earnestly searched for a heartbeat; her back straight, her hand moving the wand slowly, covering the entirety of my lower abdomen. I breathed shallow and slow, hoping the pressure of her wand wouldn't cause my weak pelvic-floor muscles to give up and release a tidal wave of urine onto the examination table.

"You may go to the bathroom and completely empty your bladder now for the internal exam."

I sighed, relieved I could finally release the tension.

She wiped the jelly off my distended belly, and I rolled my maternity pants over my bump and pulled my shirt down. I slid off the table slowly and carefully, as not to induce early urination, waddled tenderly to the bathroom, then raced to get on the toilet before I released onto the floor. Oh, peeing feels so good after depriving your strained bladder from doing so for so long. TW:M//Upon wiping, there was a tiny bit of dark blood on the tissue. I turned to look at the toilet and I saw my body's betrayal. A maroon clot the diameter of a golf ball rested near the toilet's exit. I felt panicked. *What if that's my baby in there?*

I looked around the room for a tool to use but found nothing. So, I reached in the toilet and broke apart the clot, looking for my raspberry-sized baby amidst the congealed blood. I breathed out slowly—nothing. I washed my hands and arm twice, then also used the hand sanitizer. For a moment I paused and looked in the bathroom mirror—I looked like a train ran over me. I took one last long look at the toilet bowl, then flushed what I was almost certain was not my baby and returned to the room.

"Umm, I just had a blood clot come out when peeing. Should we still do the internal ultrasound?" I asked the technician hesitantly. She said, "Oh, yes, there's no problem continuing."

I took her words as comfort, but I should have realized she meant that continuing was futile. I went to the small changing stall and pulled the curtain shut. I gently removed my pants and pad-lined underwear before folding them strategically to conceal my delicates. I shrugged the light cotton gown onto my shoulders and carefully tied up the two back laces to be as modest as possible. I then re-entered the exam room and gingerly positioned myself on the sterile strip of white paper, feet together, knees splayed apart.

The technician reminded of "gentle touch" and the probe entered slowly. During the internal ultrasound, I felt an abnormal amount of wetness down below. I reasoned the technician most likely went a little heavy on the lube. After less than twenty minutes, the technician slowly slid the probe out of my vagina and said, "I got everything I need, you may go clean yourself up now."

I slid off the bed carefully, feeling self-conscious about the wetness. I looked back down at the bed to see if I had left any discharge or lube behind, and what I saw made me catch my breath. The white paper liner was so drenched in blood that it had disintegrated. Dark red was smeared along the tan leather edges and sides where my butt slid off the bed.

My throat began to constrict as my eyes shifted back to the technician. She caught my glance and said easily, "Don't worry about it, I'll clean it up." *I wasn't worried about cleaning up*. I was worried about something much more grave than a stained examination table. *My baby is definitely dead. There's no way the baby was still alive after I lost that much blood.*

I quickly left the room, grabbed my clothes from the changing stall, and went right into the bathroom. I had quite the cleanup job. I carefully removed my cotton tie-up gown, white with baby-blue dots but splattered red, trying not to get blood all over myself or the floor. I rolled it up strategically, making sure the dry cloth wrapped around the wet cloth so the basket of used gowns wouldn't look like a crime scene.

A little reservoir of blood hung out in my butt crack. I sat on the toilet with my maternity shirt pulled up over my stomach and my socks on the cold tile floor and tried to process what was happening. I went pee and filled the toilet with a crimson tone and darker hints of clots. I wiped, cleaned, and carefully rose, staring at the different tones of red circled by the splotched toilet seat.

A bit disassociated, I wiped the toilet seat down with a damp wad of toilet paper and threw it in the garbage. I left the toilet unflushed for a bit longer while I began to get myself together. I evaluated my stained body and got to work with a couple sheets of brown paper towel and sink water. Blood caked my inner thighs, butt, and lower back. I mechanically cleaned and patted myself dry before slipping my maternity pants back on.

Fully dressed and cleaned up, I reluctantly moved toward the toilet again. I peered in the bowl and wondered if my baby was in there. I was not going to search this time though, so I reached for the silver handle and ever so slowly flushed, watching as parts of my insides and what could have been my baby spiraled loudly down the toilet and disappeared. Gone without a trace.//TW:M

I picked up my purse and the wadded-up gown and left the bathroom, dropping the gown in the basket as I walked down the hallway toward the waiting room. My husband looked up from his Blackberry.

"Did you see the heartbeat?" I gestured for him to walk along with me as I spoke.

"No, she never showed me the screen and I never asked. She seemed focused." We headed down the hallway toward the stairwell.

"So, the baby's fine?"

"I am definitely miscarrying," I responded with certainty as we reached the stairwell door.

"Are you sure, honey?" I should have gotten him to help me clean up in there.

"There was blood everywhere, Wes. There's no way the baby is alive. Can you quickly go check and see if we can get a photo printed?"

Wes jogged back to reception as I leaned against the dusty beige walls in the fluorescent hallway. He returned moments later, saying he'd asked the receptionist for a photo, who'd asked the technician, but there was no photo to take home. No memento, no solid proof that our baby was more than a process my body went through.

We reached the bottom of the stairs and began walking outside toward the parking lot. "I'm sure everything's fine," he said, trying to console me. He had no clue what I'd just gone through. He was not getting it! "So, do you want me to drop you off at home and we can come pick the other car up later?"

"Are you seriously thinking of going back to work while I go home and miscarry our child all by myself?" I asked incredulously.

He grasped my tone of voice. "Okay, I'll just go inside and tell Ross that I won't be in today." Wes parked the car outside the hospital administration building and jogged inside. I looked down at my phone and texted two of my cousins that I was miscarrying and asked them to come over. I needed some more support than my husband currently offered. Anissa responded that she would drive over as soon as she could get the family van, and Edwin drove down right after his ten-hour work shift that evening.

When Wes returned to the car, we drove home in near-silence. I was in despair and severe discomfort, and

Wes sat seemingly unaffected. My husband held my hand and helped me out of the car, up the front stairs, and into the house. I immediately went to the bathroom and lined a diaper with overnight pads, removed my pants and underwear, and pulled on my miscarriage gear.

I laid a towel on my corner couch cushion before sitting down. Wes fetched me my heating pad as my cramps began to ramp up. Anissa arrived shortly after and hung out with me while I reclined in my diaper under a fleece blanket.

TW:M//As the day progressed, I occasionally felt a large clot slither into my diaper. I would then waddle to the bathroom, pull down my diaper, and search the clot for my baby. I would empty the clot into the toilet, change my pad, and bring Wes back to look at what was happening. I wanted something to shake him into my reality, my pain, but nothing clicked.//TW:M

I figured he was dealing with this event through distraction and denial. I barely saw him the entire day, but I sporadically heard him doing dishes in the kitchen or a load of laundry downstairs. Later that evening, when Edwin arrived, we ordered pho, then Wes asked if he could go play hockey. I felt abandoned. I needed the supportive partner my husband had been throughout our relationship. Where was he?

As Wes put our son down to sleep, Edwin reasoned with me that Wes needed to process this stress in his own way, which maybe meant playing hockey.

"Well, that's nice for him," I said, bitterly. "He can leave and escape this reality while I'm here sitting on the couch bleeding our dead baby into a diaper *all by myself.* This is a partnership; he should be here in the trenches with me."

When Wes came back into the room from putting

Sebastian to sleep, I caught a look of despair on his face, and I decided to put him first. "Go to hockey," I said with the airiest voice I could muster, "I'll be fine, I'm all set up here." Within thirty minutes, all the members of my support group had left, heading for their relief from the emotional day, while I sat stranded on the couch with my heating pad and towel. Alone in the dark.

Weeks later, when I wrote this journal entry, I read it out loud to Wes so we could talk about how I had felt so alone during that time. I expected him to confirm what Edwin had suggested about him needing to sweat out his emotions. Instead, my husband surprised me with the confession that he had never acknowledged the pregnancy at all. In an effort to protect himself from experiencing a similar pain to our first los,s he decided to not emotionally invest in the pregnancy until much later. *What a distinctive male privilege.*

I guess I was as alone as I felt. Miscarriage number two was a pain uniquely my own. A solitude of sadness.

i felt you

I knew you were there
on a cellular level
before the lines turned pink
before you had a name
you began to change me.
My whole body responded to your presence
and I loved you right away.
I dreamed of you,
I hoped for you,
I willed for you to remain;
to live in me until
you were ready to breathe on your own.

The Bees

Eight weeks was all it took
for you to be my child
to carve a permanent place
inside my heart.
I didn't plan it this way—
you weren't meant to come
so soon after I lost your sibling,
and so you left me
before I could beg you to stay.
I sensed you leaving early
so I rushed as much as I could
just to get a photo.
You were gone before I had the chance
to listen to your heartbeat.

I wasn't ready for you to leave
I searched for you
In the toilet bowl
bloodied and red—
I couldn't give up without seeing you first.
Without having concrete evidence
you were more than just
a feeling;
more than my imagination;
more than a hope.
I needed to know you were
real.

I just wanted to hold you,
to see you on the technician's screen,
to hear you kick the Doppler wand.
I wanted more time with you.
I wanted more time
with you.

In the weeks that followed my second miscarriage in five months, my body went through a severe hormonal shift alongside a mental dive. I began to spiral in a way I never had before. I was not suicidal or showing any obvious signs of depression. Instead I experienced symptoms I couldn't place: I was irritable, hyperaware of my surroundings, and I had trouble sleeping—*something I am a professional at when I become depressed.*

I had trouble concentrating at work and became triggered by job-related jargon and project names that reminded me of my previous relationship. Episodes that had been dormant for so long began to cloud my focus and haunt my days, and nightmares began to fill my nights. Bad memories would make it hard for me to focus on work.

Later I realized I was experiencing PTSD (post-traumatic stress disorder) triggered by a traumatic event: the solitude of my second miscarriage. After a few weeks of these symptoms, I felt ill-equipped to pull myself out of this funk, so I began researching therapists. I interviewed three female therapists and counselors and chose to go with one who reminded me of a good friend who was very comforting and a constant cheerleader in my life.

After the first session it was clear to me that this woman was in over her head with the amount of trauma I brought to the table. I was looking for some tools and some cognitive behavioral therapy that could help me reframe my mind around events and memories so I could control my behavior surrounding them. My mistake was that I mistook my emotional reactions as a behavior I could somehow control. Her mistake was allowing me to pour out my heart and then seeing me as too vulnerable to receive constructive tools.

I went to two more sessions before I conceded that she was not the right fit. She was a wonderful, empathetic listener, which was nice, but I didn't have time to delve into my pain and sit in it as it ruminated around me. I had a child who needed me whole, and a husband who needed me functioning. I couldn't waste time exploring feelings. I needed someone to fix this shit and zip it back up, so I could be a better in my roles.

I began a new search and looked for effective therapists and quick therapies. I learned about EMDR (eye-movement desensitization and reprocessing) working well for people who had PTSD from abuse and rape. I chose to find a male therapist since I find them to be more solution-focused. After a few emails and calls, I decided to go with a registered psychologist who specialized in EMDR for trauma—especially with women who had been raped by men. His practice was conveniently located blocks from my home in downtown Kitchener. But he was inconveniently priced at $175 for fifty minutes.

In our first session, I asked Dr. Derbert to complete some forms that would allow me to shorten my work week to four days. I wanted to cover some difficult topics, and I didn't think I could squeeze a session into a lunch break and then return to work as a functioning employee. My request was to have Wednesday as my recovery day each week, and I requested to have my desk turned around so people no longer approached me from behind as they addressed me.

The company I worked for during that time has been the best company I have ever worked for. They accommodated me at every turn and did so with empathy and understanding, not reluctance or impatience. The project-manager side of me planned a path to healing and normalcy. During the next two months things did *not* get better—they got worse.

Chapter 9 - It Gets Worse

I sat there still and silently sobbing as I held my sleepless Sebastian, stifling a howl of sorrow, my face contorted with grief. I hadn't cried like this in weeks, *so why now?* Grief doesn't always give warning or have the best timing. I tried to monitor my breathing between shudders so my child wouldn't notice my twisted face and waves of tears as he tried to let sleep overtake him. Earlier that day my close friends got married, my sister planned a vacation with her complete family of five, and I shopped for Willow Tree Angels to remember my dead babies.

Tissues began to pile up as I continued to wait for my toddler to drift to sleep in the bed we all shared. I stared at the empty single bed three feet away and lamented that if just one of my babies had lived, it wouldn't be empty. Through grief and fear we kept him between us at night, trying to soak up as much littleness as we could.

We used to dream of many moments with toddlers and babies: little feet pattering up and down the hall as our children chased each other around, kids piled on the couch fighting for a seat on Mommy's lap, and crowded bathtubs with fought-over toys and bubble-beards. But the more we stumbled and fell the less we were able to dream of the lovely noise a full house could bring. The more we lost, the more it hurt to hope. So we tried to soak in the one bit of sweet innocence we had because we feared he might be our only.

Sebastian finally fell asleep, starfish style, so I slunk out from under the covers and tip-toed out of our room. When I found myself at the top of the stairs in the kitchen, I allowed myself to wail with sobs, shaking and dripping, evidence of my sorrow pooling near my toes. With an assist from the noise of the washing machine, I released my pain into the cold kitchen air, crying into the quiet night. My body heaved until it didn't. I then began to wash dishes on autopilot, my feet cold and bare on the shifted laminate floor.

My husband texted, informing me that he was on his way home from ball hockey. I stopped my cleaning and mom-swayed while I waited for him to arrive. I wanted him to hold me before I went back to bed. To warm my chilled, aching bones and to kiss my tear-stained cheeks. He knew. And he would join me if I needed him to, but most likely he would just hold me until my back no longer ached and my heart would let me sleep.

I stood shivering by the oven light, wearing one of my dad's old T-shirts and a pad-lined diaper. The first three days of my period were much heavier at night. Diapers, I had learned, helped me avoid stained panties and waking up to a similar scene from *The Godfather*, minus the horse head. *If you know you know.*

I looked up as Wes approached our front door, and I walked to meet him there and unlatch the lock. He stepped in from the cold with a look of worry on his face. "What happened?" he asked with concern. I suddenly felt silly.

I started to sheepishly explain about the empty bed sitting in our room, and shopping for angels earlier in the day. "I know, it's stupid," I said before Wes cut me off.

"No, it's not stupid. It's totally understandable."

And with that the flood gates opened again, and I began sobbing as he encircled me with his arms.

"My sister, with her perfectly spaced children, is planning a vacation, and what if we go together, and my other sister comes?" I wailed, my face pressed against his chest as tears flowed.

"They'll both be skinny with their abs and bikinis and I'll be a flubby stretch-marked mom with saggy skin. Will I wear a bikini? Maybe, but every minute will be so hard! Just going to the beach—they will have to sunscreen multiple children, and we'll just have one. Will I be pregnant by then? Or will I be recovering from yet another miscarriage? Or will we be still trying, for a third year in a row?"

"Rachel, Rachel. Rachel. Then why would we go with them? If it's going to be so horrible, why go? Why don't we just book our own vacation?" I pulled away from Wes and started heading for the fridge.

"Because then it'll be us and Sebastian, and we won't have any dinners as a couple, because we won't have babysitters," I explained as I took out a container of leftover aguachile and tortillas. "We'll never have a break from parenting, and Sebastian won't have anyone his age to play with. I want him to make memories and have fun with his cousins."

"Well, maybe now just isn't the right time for that. You've been through a lot this year, and you need to give yourself a break." I tossed two tortillas in the microwave and added thirty seconds to the timer. Wes stepped in for another embrace, and I strengthened my posture, stiffened my upper lip, and made a sarcastic joke.

He laughed. "Well, I'm glad you can always find humor in anything," he said as he smiled adoringly at me. I broke a smile as I grabbed the warm tortillas from the microwave. We dug into the Glasslock container, each making wraps and talking about ball hockey and the less dramatic events of the day.

Wes went to shower off his hockey sweat, and I kissed him before heading to bed with Sebastian. I was exhausted and barely stayed awake until Wes came down to bed and kissed me good night.

Back at therapy, we talked about my miscarriages and yearning to be a mom four times over. Dr. Derbert related my pain from pregnancy loss to his pain when he broke up with a high school girlfriend. *This guy does not get it*, I thought. *Let's keep going, though—this has to be helpful at some point!*

TW:PTSD//I stood in the apartment, steeped in a monochromatic palette of browns at the top of the stairs with a crowd of people who weren't strangers, but none of whom I could directly recognize. Light swept in at the foot of the stairs as men roughly forced two teenage girls up into the apartment. The air thickened with heavy fear so palpable that I began to feel like I was suffocating, choking, gasping for a breath.

The blond with long brown roots had a torn lip and a bruise on her midsection, and the younger brunette had a black eye. They were both dressed as any teenage girl would be at a midsummer dance trying to catch the eye of their crush, but the men who brought them into the building were much older. My chest filled with rocks as I faded to the back of the room to avoid the men's attention.

"Everyone, follow me!" one man powerfully directed as he effortlessly forced the thin girl into the bathroom. The crowded room filtered through the door as directed. I quietly started slinking toward the top of the stairs before catching a glimpse of one girl being bent over with her pants down and a man choking another in the tub.

Fear spiked in my heart and I started fumbling down the steps as fast as I could. The steps seemed to grow longer and longer, stretching into infinity before me until I finally reached the bottom. As I approached the bright door, I heard a man say, "Now let me show you the way to get a Britney Spears to behave." I could *feel* him unbuckle his belt as I momentarily froze at the door.

If I didn't run, I could be next. I felt it in my gut that the girls would be raped, and I viscerally remembered the feeling. I heard movement and started running down a sidewalk that led to an unknown landscape. How many of those nameless men in that room would join in? RUN. Would the girls survive the afternoon? RUN. Fear propelled me forward. I wanted to save those girls, but I knew I wouldn't have survived if I stayed, so I ran and ran and ran until…

I woke up.//TW:PTSD

I felt my son sleeping against my back, breathing with a soft snore. I looked up at the clock—one hour before I had to get up for the day. I kept trying to fall back asleep and change my dream, or at least forget it and have a different dream. Instead, my mind began filling with intense memories: flashbacks to a dark cabin, flashbacks to him behind me, flashbacks to trying to survive the night.

I slipped out of bed and numbly went to the

bathroom upstairs. I looked at myself in the mirror; the creases in my forehead did not match the faces of other twenty-seven-year-old women I saw around town. My face looked fatter and whiter, with more pores than usual. My hair in a ponytail begged to be washed, but the idea of a shower irked me in unexplainable ways. Red, puffy eyes stared back at me and implored me to go back to bed and skip work. So, I relented and flicked off the lights before trudging back downstairs. *Some days are just fucked. Try again tomorrow.*

I crawled into the opposite side of the bed and snuggled up behind my husband. Wes grunted, and I whispered that I'd had a nightmare as I put my arms around him. He clasped my hand and leaned into me. We snuggled there until I warmed up, then he turned toward me. We gazed at each other as he checked in on me with his beautiful brown eyes. He started kissing me, and I started forgetting. Then a little head popped up behind him.

"Mama!"

My curious, happy morning toddler peeked over daddy's shoulder as he mused that mommy was on the wrong side of the bed. He quickly tried to climb over daddy and shimmy between us. He snuggled and considered sleeping longer then wanted more space so he crawled up to lay at the top of our pillow with his head resting on dad's head. Wes and I took the opportunity to kiss some more. Sebastian then spotted a book on the night table. He crawled across the bed, picked it up, and brought it back over to us.

"Mommy, read!" he exclaimed. Sebastian was excited, since I was usually gone before he woke up in the morning. I turned on my side to be the little spoon and somewhat absent-mindedly read the story as I flipped from page to page, interrupted on occasion by a perky tot seeing things for the first time on the twentieth read-through. We barely made it to the end of the book before Sebastian slid down the side of the bed and grasped my hand to lead me upstairs.

"Food," he demanded.

I grabbed a frozen piece of zucchini bread. We nuked it in the microwave for twenty seconds, then I handed the warm slice to him as we walked toward the bathroom. I used the toilet then employed some baby wipes to give myself a quick "bath" as my toddler watched. *Who needs privacy?* I arranged my hair so it looked acceptable, then left Sebastian to play as I returned to the basement to get dressed.

Comfy bra, comfy pants, and a comfy-yet-professional top. I grabbed frozen lunches for myself and hubby and an outfit for Sebastian before heading back upstairs. Sebastian and I sat on the living room couch while dad got ready for the day. Then I dressed the little monkey, and we all headed out of the house together—an hour and a half late for work. I got into the office, looking like crap, and no one asked why I was late. Luckily, my puffy face and stuffy nose kept people at a distance, so I didn't have to make any water-cooler talk.

TW:PTSD / All at once the room become pitch black. I couldn't even see the hand I held up in front of my face while I dizzily swayed, disoriented by the sudden darkness. My hair stood on end as I became increasingly aware that the door to the cabin had closed, along with my window of opportunity to return to safety. He existed between me and my only known exit, and I could feel him approaching me from behind. My breath caught in my throat as I anticipated his inevitable touch. *Snap!* I was actually at my desk. I worked to catch my breath; my skin felt like it was unraveling and my insides seemed to be falling out of me. *What the actual fuck.*//TW:PTSD

I needed to divert my attention for a moment so my memories could make their way back into their boxes. I browsed Kijiji, an online platform for selling used items or cheap services similar to Craigslist, for second-hand toys. My go-to distraction noodle had developed into a bit of an addiction. As always, the best selection and prices were in Ottawa, which was a six-hour drive away.

My husband thought I was nonsensical that I was willing to drive that distance to save money. He would chuckle endearingly at my shopper's math: Since this was originally $800 and we bought it for $360, we *saved $440*. We could totally have a weekend away with that money saved. "Nah, honey, he'd say, "we didn't *save* anything we *spent* $360."

Men. Not understanding math. Eyeroll.

Great! Now that those dark things had crawled back into their boxes, I got back to work. Spreadsheets, projects, *workity-work-workeroo. Stay focused on the task in front of you.*

At my next therapy session, Dr. Derbert and I reviewed ways I could recover from flashbacks and intrusive memories so that I could function and be present with my family. We also practiced meditation techniques. I learned to conjure a positive, calm memory of walking on the beach at sunset with the soft water lapping against the shore, and I followed the footsteps of my husband as he held Sebastian on his shoulders . Other grounding tips were to go for a quick walk outside around the building, grab a soothing drink, do breathing techniques, or locate things in my environment with the five senses.

Later that week, sleep evaded me. In bed, I tossed and turned and found it hard relax into the calm of night.

TW:PTSD//As I began to drift, I jumped right into a nightmare: The lights were all off in my house as I headed into the kitchen from the front hall. I could see my husband hiding in the nook of the toy room. He was on his hands and knees and started playfully sprint-crawling to me. It terrified me. Darkness overtook the room.

Wes seemed to have no clue that I was completely frozen in fear. I cornered myself by the wall and the stove and slid my left hand along the tile to the light switch. It didn't work. I tried to scream but my throat caught, and the only sound that escaped was a high-pitched breath of air—like a dog whistle. Wes disappeared.

I pressed my back as far as I could into the corner so no one could come up behind me in my own kitchen. Yet I began to feel someone's breath on the right side of my neck, and a hand touched my shoulder. I tried to scream, but I could not get any air. My throat closed as the hand slid over my shoulder and moved across my chest. He had a solid grip. I tried to alert Wes. I tried to scream as loud as I could, but only a high-pitched whistle escaped my throat.

Then I woke up in bed. *Breathe.*//TW:PTSD

I felt my son sleeping warmly against my back as I opened my eyes to the red light of the alarm clock: two thirty-six a.m. I considered waking up Wes and telling him about my nightmare, but decided not to, because he was up late working and had another long day ahead. I knew I should try and sleep, yet my mind was so awake. I was in fight-or-flight mode and couldn't turn down my alertness. I tossed and turned the rest of the night, fighting to fall asleep, until I looked at the clock and it was one minute before my alarm. I lay there for a bit longer before I got up and showered.

As I dried off, I walked into the dark of the

bedroom and gazed at my sleeping husband and child. I considered crawling into bed and telling Wes I'd had another nightmare, but instead I kissed his cheek and rubbed his hair. I took my time getting my clothes together and periodically walked back into the bedroom to check on them. I wanted Wes to sense that I needed him. I wanted him to tell me that we should just stay home and snuggle, or go on a road trip and burn that cabin down. Still, he slept, and I pushed myself to leave the house and go to work, even though I didn't want to.

Later that afternoon, I was back in my therapist's office, sitting on his couch with a pillow on my lap. We were talking about my nightmares, and somehow he segued into gushing about his daughter. *How is this helpful? Every session he expresses that I remind him of his daughter, then tells cute stories about her. Is the late afternoon a bad time for me to see him? Is he just burnt out of care by the time he gets to my appointment at the end of the day?*

I needed him to dig down deep as much as he asked me to do. I couldn't go into my darkest corners of fear and shame if he was going to move the conversation so casually to light topics that I literally DID NOT GIVE A FUCK ABOUT. *Like, I am here to fix my shit so I can live a better life. I am paying $175 for fifty minutes.* I thought I might need to get another therapist. Is it the therapist, though? Or was this a pattern with me?

All I knew was that I needed this guy to invest in me emotionally. I couldn't entertain his monologues. He was supposed to be helping me. There was a barrier preventing me from opening up to him, probably because he talked about my trauma nonchalantly, like we were chatting over tea. So, on the way home I began to write him an email, to hopefully help him understand why I needed a change.

Dear Friend,

The next chapter, The Cabin, is the email I sent to Dr. Derbert so he could understand what it meant to be a woman who'd been sexually assaulted by a man. This is a hard chapter to read but also an important one. It marks the turning point of this story, so please do not give up. See you on the other side.

Love of love,
Rachel

The Bees

Chapter 10 – The Cabin

Trigger Warning:
This chapter contains sexual assault (pages 155-156), kidnapping (pages 158-159), emotional abuse (pages 163-165) and suicidal ideation (page 169) Please be kind to yourself and respect your personal limits. If you would like to forgo these triggering scenes you may read a summary on page 323.

Laughter and excitement filled the car as my sisters and I headed eastbound for a weekend of fun. We were on an adventure and headed into the woods just outside of Ottawa. One of my siblings drove quite distractedly, picking at a scab on her ear and looking in the rear-view mirror at her progress. The road wound through trees and hills, and she didn't seem interested in the "driving" aspect of being the driver. My other sister and I exchanged worried glances as we occasionally drifted into the oncoming lane.

"PAY ATTENTION TO THE ROAD!" we'd both say.

"I am!" she said defensively.

"No, really, both hands on the wheel, and stop looking in the mirror and at us. We don't need to see your eyes when you're talking!"

By the time we reached the park, we were glad to be out of the car. We quickly registered at the front gate and were directed to where we could set up our campsite. We drove up and started unpacking. Eventually, my sisters' partners and my older brother arrived, and we all organized our things before checking out the beach, playground, fire pit, showers, bathrooms, and the mess hall.

We had planned this weekend of white-water rafting for months. The farther we got on the seven-hour drive from London to Ottawa, the more distance I felt from my relationship struggles. After more than three years of dating, Andrew and I had broken up weeks earlier for the second time. It was the summer of 2012.

On this trip I purposely tried to forget about my failed relationship. I wanted to escape reality without dwelling on boys all weekend. And by the time we got to the secluded rafting place there was little to no cell signal—perfect!

The campground filled with young rafting instructors and young campers ready to party. I threw caution to the wind and bought a few beers from the shanty-bar.

Soon I joined a beer-pong game in the pavilion and bummed a few beers off the young male rafting instructors. My teammate was a tall and handsome young man named Chaz. He had dark hair and tanned skin, and gorgeous arm muscles that both my hands could barely wrap around. He was attractive and easy to flirt with.

The more I drank and played beer pong, the more touchy-feely I got with Chaz. Soon we were falling all over the place like drunken frisky fools and headed to a dark place for some privacy. We made our way to the beach and started messing around in the play center. We kissed and started tugging at each other's clothes. Chaz made his way kissing toward my stomach and began undoing my shorts, when we heard someone walking by us.

I could tell by his breath and his low muttering that it was my older brother out searching for me. I was mortified. Chaz and I froze in silence until he moved far enough away for us to make a run for it. I buttoned my shorts and Chaz took my hand as we scampered to the boathouse. Once inside, we didn't waste much time before we started kissing again.

Moments later a fellow instructor came to see who was in the equipment space. Chaz and the instructor had a brief chat before he returned and suggested we take the back path to his cabin. I was in. This was going to be my first one-night stand ever. I felt excited and intrigued to see what all the fuss was about and if one-night stands were really as exhilarating as the media and movies implied.

Chaz held my hand as we took a path to the instructor's cabin area. We giggled and kissed every few steps. He squeezed my boob and I pinched his butt. Every once in a while, we did a few running steps, or maybe it was drunken stumbles. Either way, I was excited to get to the cabin and show off my moves.

Once the door shut, we got right down to business for about two minutes. *Two minutes in heaven is better than no minutes in heaven, am I right? #flightoftheconcords.* Before we could get our clothes off, someone knocked at the door. Chaz answered it. Holy embarrassing! My siblings stood there asking to speak with me.

The next five minutes I spent fending off their chastising tones and insinuations of sluttiness. I assured them I was making an informed decision and not being pressured. They tried to get me to leave with them. I wasn't interested.

At this point I felt committed to follow through with my plan— not Chaz's sake, but because I wanted freedom and exhilaration. I was embarrassed and hoped Chaz wasn't too turned off by this dramatic familial imposition. Eventually, my judgmental siblings left, and I re-entered the cabin, dismayed.

Chaz comforted me and we began kissing each other again while undressing each other on our way to the bed. We didn't waste much time with foreplay, then he didn't waste much time finishing. Hmm.

That was quick. And not as satisfying as I had hoped. He fell asleep snoring, and I lay there feeling empty. *Maybe this whole one-night-stand thing isn't really for me.* Or maybe it's just not for women in general.

I lay there thinking about how I had treated my siblings for this quick, orgasm-less fling. I felt like they were only there to judge me, but years later I realized they had been genuinely worried about me. I treated the weekend as a solo escape instead of time to bond with family, and I snuck off without letting them know I was okay. I interpreted them through my own lens of Catholic shame and behaved very inconsiderately. In other words, I acted very twenty-one.

I eventually dozed off, enjoying sleeping on a mattress in a cabin rather than a crappy tent. I woke up before everyone else—sans hangover—and enjoyed a quiet shower as I got ready for the day. Even though the previous evening was not as satisfying as I had hoped, I still found myself ogling Chaz during the day and hoping to catch his stare. I wanted a redo. His arms were something to marvel, but I was in another rafting crew, so I shifted my focus to enjoying the tour.

The water still ran cold from the winter runoff into spring, so falling in or jumping out was not on any sane person's agenda. But in order to stay *in* the boat, you needed to focus and pay attention to your grip, balance, and paddle. Attention deficit disorder runs stronger in some people in my family than others (*I can say that because I have it—that's how it works right?*), and one of my distracted sisters somersaulted right out of the boat when we hit a wave on one side. The look on her face was hilarious! She found it funny so we all were able to enjoy the humor. Highlight of the trip. She rode the rapids a little farther before we circled back to pick her up.

Rafting lasted about an hour and a half, which tuckered us all out a bit. After relaxing in the afternoon, the evening was party time again. I wanted to meet up with Chaz, because I enjoyed the attention he gave me the night before. He was nowhere to be found, so I sat by the campfire and had some great conversations with other campers. At one point the guy I was talking to got up to get me a drink, and one of the rafting instructors came up to chat with me and handed me a beer.

He was one of the smaller men in the crew—short and scrawny. His curly hair was deep red and freckles covered his cheeks and nose. He had a thick Irish accent and all the other instructors called him "Irish." He seemed pleasant enough, so I carried the conversation with him and showed polite interest in his mildly engaging stories of traveling and kayaking rapids as I periodically glanced up, looking for either Chaz or the gentleman fetching me a drink.

Soon Irish asked if I would like to watch some of his kayaking competition videos. I didn't see why not; I was low-key skeptical how this sport was a real thing and wondered how points were scored. Instead of pulling out his phone he said they were on his laptop in the instructor's pavilion. I felt rude changing my mind, and I figured it would be quick and I could continue my conversation with the man I was with earlier in ten minutes or so.

So, we moved away from the crowd up to the instructor's cabin area while Irish told me about his girlfriend of five years back home. We walked, keeping a safe distance from each other; no flirting, no touching. I wasn't interested in Irish. I intended on bumping into Chaz again.

When we got to the empty kitchen pavilion, I sat at the picnic table while Irish brought over his laptop. He started showing me videos and explaining what moves he was doing in his kayak. He effortlessly scaled and paddled through impressively sized rapids. After five or ten minutes I felt I had sufficiently placated Irish's interests, shown polite attention, and felt ready to head back to the fire. Irish remembered I was in architecture school and suggested he show me his cabin.

Naive as I was, I trusted him and didn't feel scared or intimidated. He was smaller, he hadn't tried to make a move on me, and he was a regular employee of the rafting company. He wasn't just some college kid with a summer job. He was also in a long-term relationship with a woman he loved. I was actually interested in seeing his cabin (*I know, hard to believe*), because I wanted some precedents for temporary living spaces and compact living accommodations that worked in real life. Yes, I am that much of an architecture nerd. So, I went with him to his cabin. *Buildings are like puppies to me; I would get in an unmarked van to walk through an interesting building.*

I don't remember exactly how we got from the kitchen pavilion to the cabin. I am not sure if it's because I was suddenly so inebriated, or because what happened next was so traumatizing that my mind has blocked it out. I remember him saying, "This is it," before gesturing to his cabin. The rest of my memory comes back in pieces.

TW:SA// All at once the room became pitch black. I couldn't even see the hand I held up in from of my face while I swayed, disoriented by the sudden darkness. My hair stood on end as I became increasingly aware that the door to the cabin had closed along with my window of opportunity to return to safety. He existed between me and my only known exit, and I could feel him approaching me from behind. My breath caught in my throat as I anticipated his inevitable touch.

I'm naked. How did I get here? I look up and I remember how. My eyes adjusted and I could see vague outlines of his slim figure. I moved to find my clothes, but he swiftly caught my fumbling motion in his hand and pinned me down with ease. I underestimated the strength of a scrawny man versus an inebriated woman. I quickly realized I had no chance in hell of getting away from him, and if I fought, I would likely be injured or even killed.

I always thought that if I found myself in this situation, I would be able to get out. I would yell and make a scene, I would fight and win. I was athletic, I was a national wrestler who regularly beat the men on my team. I failed to note that wrestling had rules: no punching, no pulling hair, no raping. I froze out. I blacked out. I came to.

His penis invaded my mouth and I struggled to breathe. *No teeth—I need to live. No vomiting—I need to live.* He ran his fingers through my hair lovingly as if this was the most consensual thing he had ever done. I tried to pull back, and his fingers curled into a grip. He forced himself deeper, making me gag. *Don't throw up, you need to live.* His hands remained clenched in my hair as he thrust over and over against the back of my throat. *Watch your teeth, don't throw up,* I repeated as tears stained my cheeks. *I need to live.*

Irish thrusted inside me as I lay on my back groggily coming into consciousness. How long was this going to last? I did not feel drunk or disoriented anymore, but I could not see my rapist because my eyes stayed shut in self-defense. I kept repeating in my head, *Someone come save me,* as if a genie would appear and grant me my wish if I squeezed my eyes tightly enough. I had trouble disassociating, so I continued my mantra, *Someone come save me.*

Then something in my mind switched to autopilot. I'd been here before a hundred times with Andrew. I suddenly knew how to get through this and how to make him get off me faster. I did as my ex conditioned me to do for the previous three years: I moaned and I gasped, I talked dirty and told him how amazing he made me feel, and I faked orgasm with shudders and toe curls, eyes clenched shut. All in an effort to get through the night, to make him finish, to survive his dominance.

Then he asked me a question that has haunted me since: "Can I come on you?"

"No," I quietly replied.

He smirked and came all over my stomach, aiming for my chest. I felt bewildered. Why did he even ask if he didn't care how I answered? Then it dawned on me: He was asserting his power. Maybe he didn't like my fake enjoyment or auto-participation. Maybe he preferred dominance over a scared woman. He was making a point that I truly had no choice in the matter. I was his.//*TW:SA*

Then he stretched out on the bed between me and the exit before drifting into a snore. I found his shirt and wiped myself off, then pressed my body along the opposite edge of the bed and the cabin wall. I contemplated trying to crawl over him and find the door, but where were my clothes? I peered into the blackness of the cabin, wishing I could evolve into a different creature with night vision. No matter how I strained to adjust my eyes, I couldn't see much farther than the edge of the bed. My clothes were nowhere in sight.

How did I get to this cabin? He led me here, stumbling, and I naively followed, not even pondering if I was safe or if he was trustworthy. I was not sure how to get back to my campsite and the others. *Would there be space for me in the tent? Would my siblings even allow me to join them? They probably thought I was slutting around.* So, I wrapped my shivering body in blankets and found peace in a vertigo-induced slumber in bed with my rapist.

Morning came faster than I thought it would. Sunbeams filtered into the cabin windows, birds chirped beautifully, and the room seemed light through my closed eyelids. I listened to him shuffling about, dressing as I pretended to sleep. He stood at the door for a bit before leaving, and I felt his stare on my body. I feared his thoughts as he gazed at my vulnerable soul, stripped of dignity.

The sound of the door opening one cabin over cued Irish to leave. I could hear him chuckling with a buddy about last night, no doubt bragging about his conquest—his latest "kill." I lay completely still under the blanket against the wall and strained my ear to follow their voices as they trailed off to a safe distance. I opened my eyes and snapped up to a sitting position in the bed to evaluate the cabin. One desk, one chair, and one bed against the wall.

I searched the room for my clothes, quickly putting on my cute short shorts and tank top. I did a bit of research in his room to learn out more about him. I didn't find much other than some clothes, kayaking gear, and a tin by his desk that contained a bunch of loose pills and some cash. I took the money just so I could take something from him. Looking back, I wonder if those loose pills were what made me black out. I'd only had one beer, maybe two.

TW:K//I needed to leave, to get to a safe place again. I walked over to the door and tugged. It was stuck! I pushed; no movement. I pulled and pushed, and it didn't budge. *What the fuck was going on?* This door was rudimentary, with no latch or deadbolt – just a wooden handle. I stepped back and evaluated my exit. The hinges suggested the door opened *in* to the cabin. The heavy wood door was too much for me to lift or bust through, and I could not take the hinges apart.

I noticed my rapist-turned-kidnapper's kayak paddle leaning against the wall and took it into my hands. I wedged the paddle between the door and the frame and tried to pry the door open. It didn't move more than an inch. My abuser was gone for now, presumably eating breakfast at the pavilion, and I wasn't sure how soon he might come back. What became very clear was that he expected me to still be there upon his return, because he had done something to the door to keep me locked inside his rape cabin.

Oh, fuck. *Focus.* There were three windows in the cabin: one over top of his bed, which was screened and nailed shut; one by the door, which was glass and nailed shut; and one by the desk, which was screened and nailed shut. NAILED SHUT! Okay, the best bet was to break through a screened window—*but which one?* The one by the bed had a massive beehive, and the one by the desk had a smaller beehive and a small tear. I chose the latter.

With no time to spare I grabbed the paddle and jammed it into the screen. The bees came through the hole into the cabin, swarming. I backed away quickly, gathered my wits and jammed the paddle into the screen again before ducking away from the bees. One more swing of the paddle created a hole big enough to fit through. *Fuck, I'm terrified of bees.*

I turtled in a ball beside the desk to avoid the swarm defending their hive. *Breathe in. Breathe out. Oh, fuckin fuck, I have to climb through that window right by a pissed-off bee nest. How long do I wait for the bees to calm down? How long do I have before he comes back? Breathe in. Breathe out. You can do this.* I crouched on the floor and moved the chair right under the shoulder-height window.

Squatting by the wall I gave myself a pep talk. *You can do this! You got through last night— you can do anything. A bee sting is not that bad. You need to get out of here or you will get so much worse than a bee sting. Breathe in—go!* Without a second thought I was up on the chair and lifting myself through the window. I landed on the soft grass below and bolted to the gravel road to escape the bees. I didn't even get stung.//TW:K

I did it! I survived!

I escaped the bees! I escaped the cabin! I survived the night! The rush of relief and adrenaline pumped through my body like a full-on high. My body heaved as I breathed the crisp morning air and the freedom of nature. I spread my arms and fingers to the sky and grinned to the morning sun. I'm alive! I'm free! I'm a strong woman who escaped the bees! Then my eyes locked on the cabin. *Why the fuck wouldn't that door open?*

To my horror, I saw a thick wood plank locking the cabin door shut from the outside. There was no way in hell I could have opened that door from the inside. *What the fuck?!* How long would he have kept me? Was he hoping for a romantic breakfast? Or round two? *You know what, I don't have time for this*, and I turned to leave. But then I didn't. Instead, I did the most fucked-up and inexplicable thing of my life. I opened the door and walked back in. I took a pen and a piece of paper and wrote him a note that said, "Thanks for the wonderful night," and signed it with a little heart and my name.

Why would I do that? In retrospect I think I did it for two reasons: It was my last effort to take control and rewrite the narrative of that evening, and it was a big *Fuck you I escaped your rape cabin!* to him. Or maybe I just had such low self-esteem and self-worth that I even wanted *my rapist* to like me. *Ugh, barf.* I stuck the paper in the door latch then ran along the gravel to a fork in the road. I recognized the location from the drive into the park site, so I doubled back and ran along the road to my family campsite.

As I rose over the crest of the hill, I could hear my family singing "Happy Birthday" to my sister. *Crap, I'm late!* I approached the campsite in a run and a wild look of freedom on my face. My family scowled at me. They were beyond pissed. I was out slutting about AGAIN last night, and then I was late to ring in my sister's birthday. What a disgusting human I was. My elation of freedom disintegrated and my adrenaline high took a nosedive. I didn't even want to shower anymore; I deserved to have his disgusting residue on my body.

No one would speak to me. My siblings fought with each other about who had to drive with me on the six-hour ride home, and all considered just leaving me there. I felt sick. I felt incredibly guilty. I felt stupid. I felt responsible for my own rape. Was it even rape, though? I mean, I left him a note. *I moaned.* I bet his neighbor buddy heard my moans and knew I was just a slutty slut. Who would believe me in these short shorts? Who would believe the girl who had a one-night stand the night before? I walked away from the crowd with him—what did I expect?

Numb, I silently followed my siblings to the pavilion for breakfast. I spent the time there keeping a lookout for two people: the man I had crushed on earlier that weekend, and the one who raped me. For some reason, I wanted to apologize to Chaz. I'm sure he had already heard about my sluttiness, and he probably felt dirty for falling for my lies, but he didn't.

He truly was my first one-night stand. He was my first taste of freedom from a repressive, controlling, abusive three-year relationship. But who would believe me? My long blond hair and eyeliner said everything people needed to know: She wanted it. I made eye contact with Chaz, and his sad eyes quickly looked away. He knew. So, I stood up and trudged back up the hill to beg my way home with my loving siblings.

My brother ended up relenting and allowing me in his vehicle while the other four left separately. The mostly silent six-hour ride home was drenched with disappointment and disgust. The only relief was his rock music—the stations my sisters detested, but which I had grown to enjoy during the years he coached my soccer team and we bonded. We briefly spoke when we went through a drive-through for food. I half-expected him to ignore my presence and deny me food, so I graciously and thankfully accepted and appreciated that he allowed me to order a meal. *Pretty pathetic, eh?*

I don't recall if my brother dropped me off at my aunt and uncle's in Toronto, or if we drove to my parents' house together. I presume I was brought to Toronto, as I had to work the following day. I don't remember the rest of that evening or when I eventually showered, but I do remember the numbness that followed my trauma. The shock and disbelief that yes, it really could happen to me, and in fact, it just did. I felt guilt and self-doubt as to whether it was indeed rape or if I was just being "dramatic," as my family always said.

The next day back at work, I spoke with my coworkers and acquaintances about their weekends. Soon someone asked me how the highly anticipated white-water-rafting adventure went. I almost blurted out that it was great, other than the fact I was raped. But instead, I simply said, "It was really fun."

Each night in the week following my rape I spent almost an hour in the tub soaking after work. The warmth soothed the rips and bruises on my labia, and I felt better the "cleaner" I could get. The solitude of the bathroom allowed me to avoid interactions with my extended family, because I was stunned to silence. My trauma forbade me to speak. I was unable to talk about what happened or to pretend everything was normal. Facing people seemed impossible.

The next weekend I told one of my sisters what happened. She worked at the Sexual Assault Support Centre in Kitchener, and she said she believed me. She brought me a hospital to allow me to receive any treatment I deemed necessary. They wanted to do a physical exam, but I was too sensitive and scared to be exposed to a stranger so soon. They wanted me to tell them all the details, like they were fact-checking me. I couldn't handle it.

My big sister cut in and said I did not need to tell them anything I wasn't ready to talk about. Though my sister requested the nurses follow sexual assault procedures they refused to do a physical exam if they didn't get the story first. This suited me just fine because I didn't feel ready – I wasn't ready for five years. So, I asked if I could have gotten a sexually transmitted disease in my throat.

They said that wasn't likely, but that they would take a look. The tongue depressor and flashlight almost had me in a panic. *Calm down.*

"You have some extensive bruising. That's likely what's caused the discomfort. You don't have an STD." I couldn't look at my sister. Now she knew he had raped me *that way* as well. The hospital visit had me feeling revictimized again. I felt beaten down and invalidated by the medical system.

TW:EA//I received mixed reactions as my family scrutinized the weekend. Someone told me I shouldn't have drank so much. A few people completely stonewalled me. Some deemed me a slutty liar.//TW:EA

Though I was in pain that summer, I was still wrong in many of the ways I. *People don't get free passes to be assholes just because they're struggling.* I was off-kilter from my breakup with Andrew, then swirling from confusion when I realized how abnormal some of his behaviors were, and I spiraled downward as my family got more and more frustrated with me.

I completely disregarded how my actions left collateral damage to my loved ones. I embarrassed and hurt them that weekend, and I was reckless with my words. I lived in my own storm and only saw my own pain. A lot of my direct memories of those months have been lost to PTSD, so I don't know how I may have hurt others beyond what I've mentioned here.

My mind played tricks on me as I gaslighted myself. *You're telling me you walked to a cabin alone with a boy in the dark and you didn't think he wanted sex?* But then I'd tell myself, *No, he had a girlfriend. It's doesn't make sense. I thought I was safe.*

Then the other voice took over again. *You didn't fight that hard though; you could have thrown a punch or two—aren't you a wrestler?*

Wrestlers don't punch, and I was scared he would hurt me. He was way stronger.

He didn't look that strong, he was kind of scrawny.

Well, he was strong to me that night. I was drunk

Are you sure it was rape? You were drunk. Maybe you just don't remember the parts where you told him you wanted it. Or where he asked and you said yes.

Consent doesn't lock you in a cabin!

You wrote him a note.

He bruised my throat, he tore and battered my labia, and when he asked me a question I said no and he did not listen.

I reminded myself of the tangible facts. *I had to fucking escape!*

I had seen enough *Law & Order SVU* to know I would have lost this battle in court. Still, I fought my internal dialogue and refused to become a woman who blamed herself for the rape that a man committed. I would defeat those fucking voices and the doubt of anyone else, because *I was only a victim that night.* I would not let him ruin my whole life.

TW:SI//Whenever I had intrusive memories or flashbacks of Irish raping me or the blinding pitch-black of the cabin, I would readjust my mind to focus on my escape. I had a note written and saved in my phone saying, "You are strong. You came back into the light. You escaped the bees!" Those words are how I survived that summer, barely keeping myself from stabbing my stomach with steak knives in the kitchen. I shakily resisted the urge to rip off the skin he came on and cut out the body he invaded.//*TW:SI*

TW:EA//I assume people avoided talking to me because they didn't know what to say, and they were frustrated with my behavior that summer. At the time, I took this as them not being able to stand being near me, because they felt I was a disgusting slut who got what she deserved. During a hard conversation with my mom, she suggested I needed to apologize for my behavior, but since no one spoke to me, I hid in my room and wrote anguished apologies on fancy cards. At some point I stopped, because I had nothing left to give. I battled too many internal demons of shame, guilt, depression, and suicidal ideation to have the energy to mend relationships. Relationships that I now felt banished from forever.//TW:EA

My mother was so stressed and worried about me, she asked my brother to always be in the room with me when she couldn't. She knew I was suicidal. She also didn't know what to do, what to say, or how to help. She chewed her lips and cheeks so much she resembled Frankenstein or Billy from *Hocus Pocus* with broken scabs and gaunt eyes.

I can presume that much of my family felt the same way: worried, helpless, and unsure how to express their love. This left me feeling unloved and abandoned. And that's how I landed back in Andrew's arms again at the end of the summer—because I thought he was the only person I had left who loved me.

"Let me tell you something you already know. The world ain't all sunshine and rainbows. It's a very mean and nasty place, and I don't care how tough you are, it will beat you to your knees and keep you there permanently if you let it. You, me, or nobody is gonna hit as hard as life. But it ain't about how hard ya hit. It's about how hard you can get hit and keep moving forward. How much you can take and keep moving forward. That's how winning is done!"

- Sylvester Stallone, <u>Rocky Balboa</u>

This is the turning point in the story. The slow rise and forward movement after a decade of beatdowns. You have made it past the trauma met with resilience, and now we can begin the healing process.

Dear Friend,

If you have someone in your life who is experiencing pain like I was, TALK TO THEM! Give them space to tell their story, and believe them. Let them unload their pain on the kitchen table and then say "I will take some of this if you will let me. I want to carry your pain so that you are not carrying it alone." Don't let your fear or discomfort get in the way of loving them the way they need it.

With love,
Rachel

Chapter 11 – Calming

The rape I just described in the last chapter was the first time I've ever written about it. I wrote it because I needed my therapist to understand my trauma. Dr. Derbert had four to eight appointments per day. He didn't seem to have the emotional bandwidth to invest in my history and emotions, but I needed him to. I couldn't just be another just another trauma bucket that he sorted through and fixed. I needed to be able to trust him with my vulnerability, and to achieve that, I needed him to be vulnerable as well and to feel at least some of my trauma.

Since I couldn't bring myself to read my account of the rape out loud, I asked Dr. Derbert to read it to himself at my next appointment. I needed to see his reaction. He covered his mouth, took off his glasses, wiped his eyes, and cursed. He was starting to get it. Maybe now we could get somewhere.

Dr. Derbert and I agreed to start some EMDR to lessen the memories of Irish raping me. Even though I felt we'd had a breakthrough at the previous session, I was still acutely aware of how many oxygen molecules existed between myself and the door, and the amount Dr. Derbert displaced with his body between. So I suggested we start with something less traumatic so I could understand and warm up to the process.

During our first session, we began with calming techniques and meditation in lieu of EMDR, so I could employ these tools when I had an intrusive memory or moment of panic.

The next week, I came prepared to discuss my relationship with Andrew. I'd recognized that I'd experienced as verbal and emotional abuse but had minimized any sexual coercion. I thought Andrew was an easier topic to broach than Irish. We sat facing each other, Dr. Derbert and in his desk chair and me on the couch. He explained to me the process of EMDR and I honestly felt very skeptical of this voodoo magic.

He asked me to conjure a memory in my own mind while rhythmically tapping my knees back and forth. The theory of EMDR is that bilateral movement from hand tapping or eye movement during a relived memory helps the brain process the trauma quickly and file it into long-term memory without retaining the emotional impact. The goal at the end of a session was for the memory of an event to lose its power and stop fucking up my dreams. *Cool beans; I would try anything for that.*

I understood and consented to the tapping, because it felt less awkward than moving my eyes back and forth. I chose to close my eyes because I thought it might help my concentration, but when we started our first session, my body and mind completely shut down. I couldn't remember anything about my relationship with Andrew—good nor bad. Dr. Derbert used the term "emotional blockage," which he described as my extreme emotion and fear attached to those memories causing my thoughts to shut down.

I couldn't remember anything: my child's birthday, what I did the day before, or what I had for lunch a couple of hours earlier. Memory loss was one major symptom of PTSD that I'd struggled with and continue to encounter. Recent studies have shown that acute trauma or trauma from prolonged periods of stress can rewire your brain away from retaining short-term memory. The primary stress hormone, cortisol, redirects neurotransmitters away from the medial prefrontal cortex and hippocampus (the areas of the brain that problem-solve and retain memory and sends them toward the insular cortex and amygdala (the areas of the brain that perceive the environment and generate emotion). This chemical response to a perceived threat allows us to react in a way to survive.

When the perceived threat leaves and our body gets stuck in a loop of trauma, cortisol continues to affect the brain, causing PTSD. Cortisol levels also affect many other systems. People who experience PTSD have higher levels of immune disorders, difficulty losing weight, fertility struggles, thyroid complications, cardiovascular health problems, and Alzheimer's. *Lovely.*

While experiencing symptoms, I had to write everything down in the moment, especially at work. During the months of intrusive thoughts, I had trouble remembering much of anything. My brain felt like a sieve. However, when I had an intrusive memory, nightmare, or flashback, I could remember the way the air in the room felt, how my shirt landed on my back, and every intimate detail and sensation. Worst. Combo. Ever.

I found my rapist on Facebook. I couldn't focus on work, so I thought, *Fine, let's just get it out of my system.* I also found the rafting company he worked for so I could find photos of it, which ended with me scrolling past a photo that hit me right in the gut. I froze and stared at the screen. *That's him.*

I scrolled further and found an album called "Meet Your Tour Guides." His photo was the first one: Stephen. He was tagged in the photo. I followed the link to his profile page. He still worked there—six years later. I started looking through his photos: raft-kayaking in Norway fjords, off a bridge in Ireland, and in the French and Italian Alps. *Wow, he's really living the life, ain't he?* He'd traipsed freely all over the world while I'd been laden with pain for the previous six years. Pain I could not seem to unlock and release. Pain that created a hint of sadness that may never leave the shadow of my eyes. *How is that fair?*

He'd probably forgotten that night. I was sure it was one of many where he smiled as he manipulated a woman's soul and left his mark of fear. I wondered how many he'd caged and with pain and left with the key around his neck. Did he even know he was a rapist? Was he one of those guys who felt so entitled that sex, with or without consent, was owed to them? Or was he a person who intentionally lured and enjoyed the fear and power?

For the first time in six years, I wished I'd filed charges against him. I had never blamed myself for not reporting him; I knew the statistics and the likelihood of a trial and a conviction. Haven't you seen *Law & Order SVU*? I understood the judicial system and how I would be victimized and scrutinized at trial. I never blamed myself for trying to heal and survive rather than prosecute, and I still don't. I only wish he could have received some of what he gave. I wanted him caged with pain instead of living so freely. I wanted to give him the heavy weight I had been lugging around for years. *I wanted to be the free one.*

Stephen Bonnet from Galway, Ireland: you have ruined so many things for me. You ruined Irish accents and one-night stands. You ruined partying and feeling safe in the dark. You ruined haunted houses and trusting new men.

You ruined my sleep and my dreams, you interrupted my workday, and you emptied my bank account while I paid hundreds for therapy. All because you put me on edge and made me hollow. Six years later, I was struck with PTSD and you still worked and lived a fun and fancy free. *Fuck you, you piece of shit.*

My brain shut down, and I felt like I was outside my body. I stared at his photos and flicked through his smile-filled adventures around the world. Nothing. I looked at his job experience at the same rafting place from where he hurt me. Nothing. I numbly walked to the kitchen for a glass of water, then headed to the dining room and kissed my husband good night as he typed away on his laptop. Then I went to bed to sleep off the dissociation.

With all my flashbacks and intrusive memories, my Kijiji toy addiction began to flourish. I convinced Wes that driving to Ottawa for a big haul was only logical. He was willing to let me try anything so I could heal. So, I messaged all the sellers and booked pickup dates, locations, and times with each person. I bought from three sellers in Ottawa and two on the way home.

I planned on driving there after work one day, sleeping in my car overnight, and completing the transactions the following day. Wes convinced me to book a cheap Airbnb. I was reluctant at first, because it *ate into our profits*—shopping math. But Wes's thinking was, *This crazy trip is costing me five hundred bucks, so what's another sixty to avoid any possibility of new trauma for Rachel.* Touché, husband.

Here's the thing though: Irish raped me in Ottawa. I hadn't been back there since, and I felt my body winding into knots in the days and weeks leading up to my trip. My back and shoulders became a solid brick of muscle, and my neck was so tense I thought my head might pop off. Wes knew I was nervous, while I tried to remain cool, calm, and totally ready to do this, because it was six years ago and it happened in the woods, not the city. Clearly, I was lying to myself. Wes knew better, good for him, *pat on the back, babe.* (But really, I'm glad he approved of my maniacal need to purchase all the toys!")

The trip felt amazing. I know I know, you expected some drama—*stahp*! I've had enough for a lifetime. On the drive into Ottawa, I enjoyed the luxury of silence and solitude without the responsibility of parenting, or having to act in front of Wes that I was doing better than I actually was, or worry about being a burden at work. I was just able to be me—buying a carful of toys. I bought dinner at a drive-through and drove to Ottawa from Kitchener in one shot.

The Airbnb was easy; I didn't even have to speak to another human. Perfect set up for this kind of trip. I used the lock box and triple bolted the door once inside. In the morning I met one rich white lady before her hot-yoga class and took her kid's gently used Calico Critters, picked up breakfast from a nearby café, then went across town and met two different dads in a parking lot for more Calico Critters and Polly Pockets—*vintage* ones.

After stowing all my toys in the car, I sat and ate. Friends, it was hands-down the best breakfast sandwich I have ever had—and likely will ever have. House-made tomato jam, spiced napa cabbage, creamy goat cheese with pepper-spinach frittata-style eggs on an English muffin. It was *divine.* Even though I had a schedule for the day, I doubled-back to get two more of those scrumptious things.

As I drove down the highway back toward home, I felt the tension begin to release from my muscles. With a great experience and delicious food, I felt a calm come over me. I went to Ottawa, and nothing bad happened! I didn't see the man who raped me. I didn't have crazy dreams or flashbacks. I didn't run down the streets naked howling at the moon. *It was fine. I'm fine. Hope returned. I was going to be okay.*

I had gone dark and twisty for so long that I didn't feel confident I would ever come out of it or be in control of my mind again. On the way home I picked up some snowsuits for Sebastian and felt the urge to get home as soon as I could and exclaim to Wes, "I'm healed!" I'm glad I didn't, because it probably would have woken up Sebastian, but also *that's not how PTSD works.*

PTSD felt like I was alone in the eye of a tornado. No matter which way I turned, how much strength I used, or how hard I ran, I couldn't break through to the other side. Instead, I would get whipped back into the eye by the relentless winds of painful memory. "Fate whispers to the warrior, 'You cannot withstand the storm.' The warrior whispered back, 'I am the storm.'"

I felt like shouting back, "I AM the storm, MOTHERFUCKER!" And I refused to stop battling.

I'm having trouble focusing at work this morning—again. Yesterday, it was because I had a dream about my ex-fiance. Today, it's because I am exhausted from infertility: not being able to get pregnant when I desperately want to and losing the baby when I finally get pregnant. I thought I'd be on maternity leave by now. I greatly looked forward to having a newborn. I wanted to be home with my infant in the mornings, then have my rambunctious two-year-old break the silence of the day by bringing noise back home from morning preschool.

I desperately wanted those afternoons with my boy. Afternoons of joy, jumping over the cracks in the sidewalk, picking up rocks and putting them where they really belonged, and cantilevering him over the river's edge so he could feel like a duck. I wanted to be exhausted from parenting at the end of the day and have my wonderful husband take over while I cooked a delicious meal.

I wanted to use our double stroller on family walks—and for it to be full. I wanted to fall asleep at night with a newborn abreast—but not really sleep all night, because I had a newborn abreast. I wanted a chance to enjoy the first months of a child, because this time I'd know better. I'd know what to expect, I'd understand the crying, I'd have the patience, and I'd be ready after waiting so long.

I was sick of my meticulously organized infant items gathering dust in their plastic-wrapped totes on shelves in the garage. I never thought they would be sitting unopened for so long. I organized every stage of childhood my son passed so it would be easy to resume with the next child: clothes, diapers, toys, bottles, blankets, and breast pump.

I dreamed of my children playing together: sharing hobbies and fighting over toys; sharing friends and squabbling over the TV; sharing study groups and arguing over the car; sharing playdates and claiming their babysitters. The longer it took for my son to get a sibling, the more I mourned the closeness they would have shared. The more Sebastian was alone, the more I feared he noticed.

Upon my return from my emotional journey to Ottawa, I did a whole bunch of things: I quit my therapist, I put in notice for my job, and I began fertility treatments. I wanted to refocus on what mattered most: my family. I wanted to squeeze every drop I could out of Sebastian's childhood, because he might have been the only child I got to squeeze. I also wanted to take better care of our house and my temple (your temple is your body for you non-raised-catholic folks). I had gained forty pounds over the course of my two miscarriages and struggle with PTSD. In order to play soccer the way I wanted and beat my kid when we raced across the lawn, I needed to get my shit together.

At that point when I played soccer, I felt like an old puppet with ripped limbs being directed by a puppeteer who had ADD. Nothing was going in the same direction and I felt flabby and disjointed. I peed when I lunged, I peed when I stopped too fast, and I peed if I sprinted. If I forgot to wear my spandex, the extra skin on my stomach would audibly slap against my legs as I ran. I felt embarrassed, and at most games I left to "go pee" at least once, which was code for me going to the changing room to cry about how unathletic I had become. I didn't recognize my body at all.

I tried to remind myself of the battles my body went through while losing two babies within five months and experiencing the tides of hormones that had crashed over me. I tried to recognize the strength and bravery it took to put myself back on the field and try to regain my health, but those words didn't sink in. I had gained many pounds and chins and comfort ate often due to my pervasive nightmares and flashbacks. Yet I continued soccer to get out of the house and socialize in a healthy manner.

After soccer, I would talk for hours in the cold outside the dome with one of my best friends. We both struggled with PTSD, and he was a wonderful person to connect with and share our pain. I would hang out until I felt like there was ice forming in my bone marrow. In order to warm up when I got home, I would have to take a thirty-minute hot shower. Parents of young children know that they're lucky if they can get five minutes for a shower. Thirty was an eternity.

Wes and I could afford to live on his income, so I pulled Sebastian from daycare and started spending quality time with him while beginning the process to expand our family. I got all the blood tests (twenty-one vials!) and pry-your-vagina-open-for-a-sample tests. Turned out I had plenty of good eggs in my baskets, but also a lot of cysts. The doctor diagnosed me with Polycystic Ovarian Syndrome. Add it to the list!

The plan was to begin my first fertility cycle when I got my next period—but it never came. We waited through December and January. The fertility clinic wanted to take things slow. They wanted to watch the first cycle without any interventions. Which was annoying and did not fit my timeline. So, I bought Clomid off Kijiji from some guy in Toronto. Turns out Clomid was not only used to pump out eggs, but also as weight-lifting steroids. *Who woulda thunk?* This side effect benefitted me, because there were so many meatheads that wanted 'roids, I could get Clomid like it fell off the back of a pharmaceutical truck—in original pop-out packs.

An acquaintance was a registered nurse who was in the process of becoming a nurse practitioner, and she had conceived her first child using Clomid. She understood the process and gave me guidance. I would have never done this solely from online searches.

Right before our triple family trip to the Bahamas with my sisters, the fertility clinic started me on a drug to induce a period. They took blood tests first to ensure I was not pregnant and gave me the green light. So, I popped my pills and waited for the red river of pain. Nothing happened.

We were in the Bahamas and I had no way to

contact the fertility clinic. I felt nauseated and generally unwell, so I figured I was ovulating really hard and getting symptoms. My sister advised not to take the Clomid without a period first, because if I was somehow pregnant, it could have negative effects on the baby. Instead, Wes and I had sex as much as we could so his strong Ukranian sperm could inseminate those eggs real good. Still, I waited for my menstrual cycle to start.

During the entire vacation with my sisters and their families, I felt too woozy to enjoy the free unlimited alcohol. I figured it was the low-quality water or the subpar buffet. I very much looked forward to returning to Canada and eating familiar home-cooked meals. To my dismay, or delight, my nausea persisted back in Kitchener. I thought, *This can not be.* There was no way I was pregnant! Less than two weeks earlier, I'd gotten a blood test that came back negative.

During Sebastian's nap, I took a pregnancy test. Two glorious pink lines. I just about jumped out of my skin and peed my pants in the process. I called Wes and told him right away, no "Big Brother" shirt for Sebastian and later surprise for daddy. This time, my husband got the wonderful news along with me. Next, I called my mother, then the fertility clinic. They were…confused. They called me in to get a blood test the next morning, and I joyfully let them stick me with all the needles. My HCG levels were more elevated than an early pregnancy should be. So, the next day I had a dating ultrasound. I was seven weeks pregnant!

And I didn't even need to use the back-alley Clomid pack. *How the hell did that happen?* Turns out I was five-and-a-half weeks pregnant before the Bahamas. The only explanation I could come up with was a mix-up at the fertility clinic. The doctor immediately started me on

Progesterone suppositories as an extra precaution to sustain the pregnancy. *That shit was nasty.* I had to insert this gel capsule in my vaginal canal. I gagged and dry-heaved almost every time. It was a disgusting, slippery two months walking around with squishy gel messing up my underwear. But it did the trick in thickening my lining to help prevent miscarriage! Silver (uterine) linings!

When I settled into the fact I was pregnant for the fourth time I felt slightly concerned about another miscarriage, something deep inside me knew this baby would live. My whole being calmed. Still, I went to my doctor to line up some ultrasound appointments to give me peace of mind during the first trimester.

I booked the twelve-week screening, but I also wanted one at nine-and-a-half weeks to manage my anxiety. My doctor vehemently disagreed, saying that if the baby was going to die, the number of ultrasounds wouldn't change anything. *I knew that*, I just wanted reassurance along the way that the baby was still there. He rambled on, telling me that one in four pregnancies miscarries—it's not a big deal. NOT A BIG DEAL?! Well, it was a big deal to me! *Everyone dies one day, and it's still devastating to lose a loved one.* I would never tell someone who was in pain that one hundred percent of people die eventually, so they should chill out.

Sebastian was in the room and sensed the tone and tension. He walked right up to the doctor and put his hand out in a stop motion and said loud and firm, "Stop! You no talk to my mommy!" The doctor (adorably) acted surprised and said, "Boy this child protects his mama!" And I smiled and snuggled Sebastian, comforting him from adult topics. The doctor relented and agreed to give me another script for an ultrasound.

Isn't it wild that the doctor only listened once my

two-year-old son put him in his place? Another reminder of the pervasive sexism in the medical system. I gave sound mental health arguments for an extra ultrasound for my pregnancy and the doctor rebuffed me and belittled my emotional needs. Some may think it's a stretch to call this particular moment sexist, but when it's a pattern, it's hard not to see it this way. According to the National Library of Medicine, forty-five percent of women report traumatic birth. It takes, on average, a woman four more years than a man with the same symptoms to be diagnosed. *Four more years*—and that's just sexism. We hadn't even touched on racism. As reported by the CDC, women of color are three times more likely to die in childbirth. Hell, Serena Williams is the GOAT of tennis and the story of her childbirth and aftercare is harrowing.

Comparing notes with my female friends and relatives, the stories have been consistent across the board: unnecessary episiotomies, being left without a doctor until the situation became an emergency c-section, medical coercion for additional procedures, obstetrical violence, being ignored until the pain landed them in ICU for liver failure, being told their symptoms were due to their weight until one day they almost died from pulmonary embolisms, and the list goes on. At this point, I don't book an appointment unless I think I'm dying—it's not worth the run around and random tests that don't resolve anything. Women and people of color deserve so much better from the medical system.

Wouldn't it be wonderful if doctors were trained to trust what patients tell them? That's what I hope for my children. I hope my daughter doesn't need to police her body for unnecessary interventions during labor, or fight doctors for years to be diagnosed with something her brother is diagnosed with in weeks. Let's vote and hope for that. Until then, I will be a fierce advocate for my children and loved ones to receive the care they deserve, even if it ruffles feathers.

Chapter 12 – Rebirth

Trigger Warning:
This chapter contains: sexual assault, physical and emotional abuse (page 183-184) and post-traumatic stress disorder (page 186). Please be kind to yourself and respect your personal limits. If you would like to forgo these triggering scenes you may read a summary on pages 323-324.

The first-trimester symptoms with Emersyn felt stronger than my previous three pregnancies. I was practically couch-bound most of the day and moved slowly when I was up. I survived off soda crackers, ginger bites, water, and tea. Sebastian would play all over me with his cars and often took out his doctor's kit to give me a checkup. He offered me his sippy cup of water and fetched my puke bucket. At the same time, he imitated me when I dry-heaved or vomited, thinking it was the funniest sound ever. So kind and comedic.

Once my morning sickness dissipated, Sebastian and I started doing all the fun things. Except for March break, that is, when the flu hit the entire extended family. We slept at my parens' house for the week, enjoying time with cousins, when a wave came over me. Wes was in bed with a sick Sebastian, and I was on the opposite side of my parents' six-thousand-square-foot house, vomiting in a garbage can as I sat on the toilet. My body was sweating and shaking so much, I left a puddle on the floor and truly thought I could die. I had trouble breathing between heaves and couldn't call out to anyone. (Spoiler alert: I survived.)

I threw up until two a.m., then stayed still like a dead whale on the couch until morning, fluctuating between hot sweats and chills. Boy, do I feel empathy for women who experience hyperemesis gravidarum (uncontrollable vomiting during pregnancy). It took days to recover my strength and energy, and I began having a repeated intrusive memory invaded my brain and played on repeat until I wrote it down:

Andrew showed me into the sun-streaked living room. "So this is the living room," he grinned as he started the tour of his first student house. I looked around: brown couch against the opposite wall and a mattress on the floor, against the couch. We continued through the house as I held my breath in disgust. "I don't think these kitchen floors have ever been washed," I muttered, a bit shocked. We'd come that weekend to clean and paint.

The main-floor bathroom, which would be shared by Andrew's two roommates, looked somewhat clean and updated. The basement had a second fridge, living space, a cramped bathroom beneath the stairs, and three small bedrooms. Andrew's bedroom was the first on the right. The only way his furniture fit was with the double bed against the left wall and his desk against the right, with less than three feet between the two. This was student living at its cheapest and close to campus.

First, we were giddy with excitement to christen the place before any of Andrew's house mates arrived to move in. We laid down together on the mattress on the living-room floor and had sex in the same sort of mechanical way I had become accustomed to: blowjob for him, one position, second position, he's gratified with orgasm, I'm not. As we lay side-by-side on our backs, Andrew looked over at me with disappointment, "You didn't come, did you?"

"No, but that's okay." Andrew's face changed to something I didn't recognize.

"Let's try a bit more," he said. TW:SA, PA, EA//

"Oh, don't bother, it's okay."

Andrew leaned with his arm across my stomach facing my feet and got to work. His long, bony fingers began to search for my clitoris and explore my vulva. I felt nervous and scared. He'd done this before, and it only ended in pain. I jerked as he passed over my most sensitive spot. I could sense his grin as he passed back over it, delighted he'd made my body jerk. He found it again but now he stayed there and began rubbing repeatedly with increasing pressure. I started to panic. *This doesn't feel good.* He was being too rough.

"Andrew, please stop."

He ignored my strained voice. I tried to sit up and get away, but he surprised me with his strength as he kept me pinned down using his arm and shoulder. Seconds felt like minutes as I tried to manage my pain and emotion.

"Andrew, I'm too sensitive. It doesn't feel good."

"No, you're just scared to come. You need to just let go," he coaxed. My voice caught in my throat, and I clenched my fists and straightened my legs, trying to squeeze my thighs together.

"Andrew, please stop," I begged through tears. "I'm not going to come, you're hurting me." In one swift movement, he stood up and angrily walked out of the room. //TW:SA, PA, EA

And I lay there, paralyzed, feeling broken. Feeling not enough of a woman, because I couldn't orgasm for him. Feeling inadequate as a girlfriend, because I couldn't give Andrew what he wanted. Feeling guilty for hurting him and making him upset. If I could just reach orgasm, he wouldn't ignore my pleas and get so frustrated.

I went to the bathroom and washed up before getting dressed. I felt an overwhelming need to make it up to Andrew, so he wouldn't leave me for a better woman. I set up a warm bucket of water with some soap and brush. I could hear him rustling around in the basement – probably setting up his bedroom. I started scrubbing the kitchen floor on my hands and knees.

I scoured for hours turning brown tile to ivory tile with aching knees and gritted teeth until his roommates began to filter in. With people around, we immediately went back to couple-of-the-year mode. Andrew exclaimed, "Oh, that's what you were doing up here?! Oh, honey, you didn't need to do all that work for us—I thought you were resting!"

Bullshit. But I glowed back anyways, responding with a cheerful, "But doesn't it look so much better now?"

"Yes, thank you so much, honey. Take a break and come hang out with us."

There's something about the vulnerability a woman feels during pregnancy that heightens her senses: Her smell is acute, her hearing is almost canine, and her physical sensations are highly attuned. Emotionally, I have always been more susceptible to the echoes of trauma during the revelatory time of growing a baby. A disturbing, intrusive memory would replay in my mind until I could release it, normally through writing. The previous memory had been completely locked up in a hidden corner of my brain.

I had never thought about this incident, not even right after it occurred. I just survived and moved on. Now that I processed this memory for the first time during my pregnancy, I was surprised I'd never considered this sexual assault. Looking back now, the incident seemed so clearly wrong, yet I hadn't considered that previously. *I felt guilty. I felt responsible.*

He was the one who deserved pleasure and happiness, not I. *Where was my head?*

For the ten months I was a stay-at-home parent with Sebastian, before Emersyn was born, we rolled into a harmonious routine together. We paired up for gymnastics class and swam at the local indoor pool, we enjoyed playing at the local parks and splash pads, and we went on mommy-son adventures to the aquarium, zoo, museum, and more.

My boy and I had lazy afternoons with an hour of quiet time reading books and playing, followed by an hour of educational TV. Then we played in the yard and slurped Popsicles on the front-porch stoop until daddy got home. I would head inside and make dinner while Daddy increased the pace, keeping Sebastian busy with extra outdoor time or some indoor wrestle-mania.

We split weekends between sleepovers at Grandma and Grandpa's with cousins, and tinkering around our house batch-baking, cleaning, or visiting with friends. We often walked down to the Portuguese coffee shop for cappuccino and *natas*, chatted with the ladies who worked there, and enjoyed the shaded patio before walking home.

As we walked back from the cafe toward our house, I noticed a woman approaching us from about a block away. As always in downtown Kitchener, I assessed her intoxication level and mental health to ensure we moved for her to pass us with ease and without confrontation.

When we got closer, I sensed body language I had seen before. She was slightly hunched over, holding her stomach, and gasping slightly. To me she exhibited physical pain, and I recognized her facial expression as someone who had just survived trauma and was still in shock.

TW:PTSD//The arch of her hunched back and the waddling shuffle made me think that something terrible just happened to her and that that something was rape. *I know, it's quite the leap just to see someone in passing on the street and to jump to this conclusion.* I immediately thought of my similar symptoms years earlier, symptoms that came from trauma and a battered vulva.

My husband quickly caught up to us, toting our caffeinated beverages. I said to him, "Did you see that lady?"

"Yeah."

"Something about her made me feel like something terrible happened to her. She's walking like she just got raped."

'She's probably just high. There's plenty of people downtown that are high at this time of morning."

We continued to walk and talk, but about a block later, I started feeling odd. I needed to sit down right there. My chest felt heavy, and I had trouble breathing. Walking was laborsome. I chalked it up to being pregnant, sore, and out of shape, and I pushed myself to just make it back to the house, which was less than a block away. After crossing the street, I stepped onto the sidewalk and realized my fluttering heart and inability to breathe was panic from remembering my rape and seeing it as a part of another woman's life.//TW:PTSD

I immediately began to employ my therapy tools to try and calm myself as I gripped the stroller and trudged forward. I took deep breaths in…and out…breathe in…breathe out…. Go to your happy pace—the memory that your therapist said to conjure at times like these. *You're safe* I told myself, *You're walking with your husband and child on the street.* Breathe in…breathe out…. *It's a beautiful day, look at how the morning sun shines through the trees….* Breathe slowly in…breathe slowly out…. *This could be a pleasant memory to conjure, a morning walk with my child and husband…. It's okay….* Breathe in slowly…breathe out slowly…

Wes kept chattering along beside me, oblivious to my labored and controlled breathing, my change in posture, physical discomfort, and sudden silence. As I walked up our driveway incline, my breathing deepened. At the top, Wes stood behind the stroller to prevent it rolling back as I unbuckled and removed our son from the seat. It was time to go to gymnastics class. I asked Wes to put the stroller in the garage as I took my latte from him.

Amplified emotions swirled within me, and my latte seemed lighter than usual— too much foam, not enough liquid. I felt irrationally upset about this and acted cranky toward Wes when he returned from the garage and said he needed to change his shoes before gymnastics. We were going to be late. As Wes headed inside, I felt too out of breath and anxious to get our child in his car seat. So, I waited.

My cheery husband skipped down the steps within a minute and explained to Sebastian that Mommy was grumpy while he buckled him into his seat and handed him a book. I rolled my eyes as I walked around the car to get into the passenger seat, but Wes had parked too close to the curb, which blocked the door shut. I told Wes he would have to back up so I could get in and then I walked to the sidewalk to wait.

On the way to gymnastics, Wes said, "We are definitely not having a third kid," insinuating that my hormones were ridiculous and too much for even him to handle. I immediately said, "I'm not grumpy or hormonal. You're not paying attention. I'm triggered. Did you not notice my anxiety attack when we were walking home?"

"No."

"When we were walking home, that lady triggered me. You didn't notice my breathing and that I was upset?"

"No, and you don't know that she was raped."

'I know, but honestly if you think about it, every woman that lives on the street has most likely been raped at least once."

"You're probably right."

Throughout the nine-plus months of pregnancy with Emersyn, I learned from past mistakes: I stayed active and healthy so my body could handle the strength giving birth required, and I took time to mentally and emotionally prepare for the stress of labor and fourth trimester with a toddler by my side. I took long walks and did prenatal yoga. I reads blogs and books about birth and pain-management techniques, and Wes and I took a pain-management course. We also did a therapy session to address our concerns and fears leading into labor and parenthood 2.0.

I was determined to have a positive birth experience, yet when I thought about postpartum, I couldn't fathom surviving months of colic again or putting my family through another round of depression. Wes was scared of another traumatic birth experience. We discussed our fears with the therapist and came up with plans to survive the worst. I organized two days a week with helpers coming, preschool and gymnastics for Sebastian, and a list of warning signs for postpartum depression. The plan made me feel prepared to manage any outcome.

My calm and heathy pregnancy with Emersyn healed my entire being. I craved salads and ate so clean that I got leaner. I took care of my body and went to regular chiropractor and massage appointments. I had very little pain and moved gingerly about right until I gave birth, which gave me the ability to play and enjoy every last moment I had left with just one child.

The trauma of my miscarriages seemed to dissipate after I passed the twenty-four-week mark. I was going to have my rainbow baby girl, and the hole in my heart didn't sear with sadness the way it had for months as I watched my Willow Tree Angels up on the windowsill. This time, I was older and wiser and ready. I appreciated morning sickness and heartburn, because I loved having the privilege of bringing a baby to term after losing two.

I fiercely advocated for my health and mental well-being and went to three different midwives before deciding which one suited my approach. I happily drove twenty minutes to my appointments, bringing snacks of banana bread and chocolates to celebrate each milestone. I relished in every kick and roll, taking videos of my belly jumping through tears of joy. My fourth pregnancy went so smoothly, it eclipsed my previous torturesome PUPPP experience. The moments of positivity began to balance out the negative memories, and I felt a healing power.

During the summer months, I organized weekly cousins playdates. The host, which rotated each week, provided the food, snacks, and activities while the parents tried to enjoy a warm coffee while watching our kids play, fight, and bond.

When fall came, I helped transition Sebastian to two mornings each per week for preschool and solo gymnastics. I knew it was important for him to be active with peers, and it gave me some alone time with Emersyn. It took Sebastian two weeks before he stopped crying at goodbyes.

Emersyn was due on October 2, 2019, and I think it's fair to say that September 2019 lasted about three years. I coped by treating myself; I'd have a chocolate-and-red-raspberry leaf tea and receive a shoulder massage from Wes every night. It was my sorry-you-didn't-give-birth-today consolation prize. And every morning, I had tea and biscotti as a sorry-you-didn't-wake-up-at-two-a.m.-in-labor-last-night treat.

I took the time to mentally prepare for birth: I painted a spiritual creation to visualize calm beauty in womanhood and manifest positivity; I created a mantra banner for my day of labor and took time to delicately decorate it; and I spent time reading and learning about pain-management techniques throughout the stages of delivery. I would not make the same mistake I'd made with my first labor experience. This time, I was going in prepared and with a plan, and there was no chance in hell I would give up control over my body by getting an epidural.

I envisioned a waterbirth at home in my living room with my midwife, husband, child, mother, and cousins there with me. I imagined my crew would be helping, fetching me pad thai, and playing with Sebastian. *Lofty dreams to eat during labor, I know.* I prepared my son with watching child-appropriate at-home water-birth videos. They were beautiful. Sebastian acted excited and ready to have a role in this special day. He told me multiple times he wanted to bring me a towel as I labored in the pool and bring the baby their blanket.

My due date came and went, and my midwife appointments became more frequent and accompanied by stress-tests and ultrasounds. Between ultrasounds, I lost fifty percent of my waters. When? Probably when I peed, because I never noticed or wet the bed. I needed to be induced the next morning, October 16. at the hospital, due to risk. My home-birth dreams went out the window, but I didn't have time to be devastated.

I had more-important things to focus on if I wanted this birth experience to remain positive. I had to reenvision my birth plan. I had to reorient my mind to the new risks and possibilities of being put on a Pitocin drip. My desire for no needles was not an option. The idea of Sebastian milling in and out of the room was not going to happen. Rather, he was going to have a special day with his godfather.

I called up my crew and informed them of the new situation and plan. Then I packed a bag and tried to get as much rest as possible, because the next day was *the* day. We tried to make the best of the new situation. Wes brought a whole bag of tricks: protein bars, Gatorade, my painting, my mantra banner, my playlist and speakers, and battery-lit candles. The midwife was able to get the corner suite, which was the biggest labor room. It even had a tub if I wanted to use it.

In the morning, we rock-'n'-rolled, listening to upbeat music as we laughed, talked, and joked. When the midwife inserted the IV, she did a wonderful job and got it on the first try; a much smoother process than with birth number one. She knew I had thin, valvey veins, and she was prepared. But I felt nauseated and hot, and began sweating profusely. I fought with all my might not to pass out from the IV, and I won. A wet cloth found its way onto my head, and I breathed myself away from unconsciousness.

The midwife covered my arm with a towel, and for

over an hour I couldn't bear to wiggle my fingers or move my arm an inch on that side. *I know, right? Huge eye roll. This is my drama-queen moment.* The midwife added Pitocin to my IV right before Sebastian dropped by for a visit with his uncle Edwin. Within two hours, cramps ramped up into real contractions, so it was time to switch gears. Sebastian went back home for dinner and bed, and the room quieted down. Anissa fixed my hair in a warrior braid, as I stood and began to sway with contractions. The lights were dimmed and candles were lit. Wes switched my playlist from fun, upbeat, empowering female vocalists to soft songs of love.

I focused on my mantras and stared at my painting. I slow-danced with Wes, and he gave me shoulder rubs. Whenever I started to go blind with pain, my tribe of women felt it, and one would softly say empowering words like, "You're so strong, Rachel" or "I'm so proud of you, you're doing great." I moved from slow-dancing to sitting on a ball rolling my hips in circles to help my baby girl spiral down my canal. *I am opening like a flower.*

All at once I felt the need to lie down. I made my way to the bed, then had a five-minute contraction. In my mind, this was what I would be doing for the next ten hours or so. With Sebastian's birth, I had long and overlapping contractions for fifteen hours. I was just at the beginning. I needed to push my feet against something. The doula offered herself for me to push against. I shook my head, knowing she would get knocked over if I did that. *Oh my god, I need to shit. BAD.* I rolled off the bed and ran toward the bathroom when the doula stopped me and blocked my way.

"Rachel, you're giving birth."

"No, I have to poop. I have a massive poop, and I don't want to do it on the floor."

The midwife knelt down behind me to check my dilation and I cringed trying to clench that giant shit back into my intestine.

"Rachel, that pressure you're feeling is the baby, it's not a stool."

That was unbelievable, because as far as I knew, babies didn't explode out of your ass. Also, I was just getting started, I was not ready yet. This was too fast. My body became lead-solid, and I couldn't seem to move my legs or hold myself up anymore. The doula and my mom took my weight and guided me toward the gurney, which I couldn't get on. My body was stuck giving birth standing.

Contractions disappeared, and all that remained was my body splitting in half and burning. Burning so fucking much. Didn't Johnny Cash write a song about this? I lost control and began screaming like a banshee in alarming agony. I almost bit off the finger of my doula. Her hand was too close to my mouth, and *I swear I still shrink with embarrassment every time I remember doing that*. Like, what was I doing?

A nurse popped her head in the room wondering, what was happening. My cousin ran back from her coffee break and started taking photos, and I exploded in fear and pain. My mind left my body and floated in pieces untethered around the room. The midwife touched me softly from behind and grounded me by saying, "Rachel, if you don't breathe the baby out, you will tear."

All the particles of my dissociated mind snapped back into place. *Okay. I'm back and in control. Man, that was kwazy cupcakes for a hot minute there.* I focused on breathing and tried to release and relax my muscles as much as possible to allow the baby to naturally flow out. *Let yourself melt and become soft. No pushing, just calm and collected breathing, trusting my body to do the work.*

Do you know how hard it is to not tense up your muscles when experiencing the height of all human pain? I felt every millimeter of Emersyn evacuate my vulva. And when the midwife caught her, she carefully placed her on the bed in front of me, umbilical cord still joining us.

I looked her over her beauty in wonder and questioned how she could possibly be so small and tiny when she felt like giant beach ball on her way out. Emersyn Maria Suhonos, eight pounds, one ounce; twenty-one inches long; was born on Wednesday, October 16, 2019, at 6:07 p.m.

After a few moments of taking in my daughter's gorgeous face and perfect cry, she was taken to be cleaned and weighed, and three adults assisted me into bed. I shook in shock and rattled the hospital bed. Excuse me? Push out the placenta now? *But I don't want to.* I felt like my vagina had been turned inside out. Even the air felt like sandpaper.

"You need to Rachel. You can do this. Just one push."

Okay, one push, *fuuuuuuuuuuuuuuuuuuck.* My mother relished in holding the baby first, then my husband snuggled her to the song he had picked out ("Happy Birthday," by John Legend and Kygo). Cousin Anissa held her goddaughter, and I trembled under a thin white sheet. The midwife informed me that she needed to check if I needed stitches. She said she would first rub on numbing cream, then check my labia, and do any stitching needed. I mustered the strength to get through the last bit of pain— only one stich needed.

As I was being checked, in came Sebastian. His uncle Edwin stopped at the door and, exhausted from the day, opted to head home. Sebastian seemed confused and intrigued. Our wonderful midwife showed him all her tools as he watched, rapt, feeling like a grownup. Then he had a turn holding his baby sister.

Then someone brought Emersyn to my chest, and as exhausted as I was, I was ready to hold her after three long years of waiting. She calmed, knowing she was back home. And as she warmed my heart, the song I picked just happened to come on the speakers: "Light," by Sleeping at Last—lyrics below. (Actually, my husband just told me as I was editing this that he turned it on, because he's a perfect human who remembered I told him I wanted this song days prior.)

May these words be the first
To find your ears
The world is brighter than the sun
Now that you're here
Though your eyes will need some time to adjust
To the overwhelming light surrounding us
I'll give you everything I have
I'll teach you everything I know
I promise I'll do better
I will always hold you close
But I will learn to let you go
I promise I'll do better
I will soften every edge
I'll hold the world to it's best
And I'll do better
With every heartbeat I have left
I will defend your every breath
And I'll do better
'Cause you are loved
You are loved more than you know
I hereby pledge all of my days
To prove it so
Though your heart is far too young to realize

The unimaginable light you hold inside
I'll give you everything I have
I'll teach you everything I know
I promise I'll do better
I will always hold you close
But I will learn to let you go
I promise I'll do better
I will rearrange the stars
Pull 'em down to where you are
I promise I'll do better
With every heartbeat I have left
I'll defend your every breath
I promise I'll do better
I will soften every edge
Hold the world to it's best
I promise I'll do better
With every heartbeat I have left
I'll defend your every breath.

– Sleeping At Last

This was a beautiful and perfect birth experience. Better than I could have imagined.

My mom brought Sebastian back to our house and put him to bed while we finished up at the hospital. Within three hours of giving birth, I walked to the toilet, then to the shower, and Wes gently washed, dried, and dressed me. Anissa rocked Emersyn and dressed her in her going-home outfit. The midwife cleaned up the room and helped pack our things. Less than four hours after giving birth, Wes, Emersyn, and I walked through the door of our home. Amazing. Our family felt complete.

Chapter 13 – A Breath of Silence

Trigger Warning:
This chapter contains: post-traumatic stress disorder (page 202).
Please be kind to yourself and respect your personal limits. If you would like to
forgo these triggering scenes you may read a summary on page 324.

All night I fed Emersyn on demand and slept when she slept. In the morning I wanted to normalize things for Sebastian, so I brought him to preschool. Looking back, that was a little absurd, but I was on a high. I had adrenaline and copious amounts of unabashed happiness. I gave birth standing up! I was a warrior mom capable of anything! I had the most beautiful redeeming birth experience, and I was so incredibly grateful and happy.

Sebastian, however, seemed slightly despondent when he returned home from school. And that's when I realized he had hopes and dreams for this birth that never materialized. He didn't get to see his sister arrive in the world, and he seemed skeptical that this baby truly did come from Mommy. Anissa came by later and showed us all the photos she had taken during the birth. Sebastian's entire focus was on the phone as Anissa swiped from slow-dancing to ball-bouncing to giving birth, graphically capturing Emersyn as she emerged from between my legs.

This is what he needed to see. She moved on to photos of the baby held by the monitor, being cleaned, and finally being held by Sebastian. "That's my sister," Sebastian said with certainty now that he'd viewed those photos. His whole being illuminated as his smile widened with happiness and recognition. It was settled. Emersyn was indeed his sister. My heart grew four sizes that day.

From that point forth, Sebastian was the epitome of a helpful, loving brother. He enjoyed holding and kissing Emersyn and perked up to the sound of any fussing or cries.

I felt superhuman in the first month of motherhood with Emersyn and Sebastian together. Two days after giving birth, we drove down to my parents' house for Thanksgiving. The following weekend at my younger brother's stag and stag, I won the beer-holding contest where, against other women, I had to hold a twelve-pack parallel to the ground. I literally had to use Lamaze to get through to the end. All my aunts and uncles commented on how quickly I'd recovered from pregnancy and labor with the flip of a coin. My body had not recovered, but my mind soared with elation.

My months of planning and preparation for a successful, beautiful birth experience paid off. I didn't need big medical interventions, and my crew treated me with love and kindness throughout my labor. I felt grateful for my support tribe of women (and husband) and was surprised by my own strength. The rush of emotion made me feel like I'd escaped the bees all over again.

Wes stayed home for the first week postpartum, and then I was on my own to resume life and try and attain normalcy for Sebastian. He wanted to still go to school and gymnastics to get social interaction and get all tuckered out—all things I needed him to do. If he missed his activities, he got all cooped up. So off I went, toting a car seat filled with a baby girl, and my hand grasping that of my marvelous boy.

I had a routine for each day of madness: How we got dressed, how we got in the car together, and how we got into school and gymnastics while my body recovered and I lugged bags and children. I had my cousins lined up to come help me two days a week in a plan to eliminate any possibility of postpartum depression—or worse, to save Sebastian from a colicky, crying-filled house. Luckily, Emersyn did not have colic and was a very calm baby.

Initially, my cousins were a source of fun and adventure for Sebastian, but several months later, in an effort to reconnect with him, I started letting others care for Emersyn for short periods. For the fourth trimester, I was not interested in sharing Emersyn with anyone other than Wes and Sebastian. I had suffered infertility and miscarriages for three years to get my beautiful rainbow baby. I earned the right to be greedy. I unapologetically kept her to myself and said no to people who offered to help by babysitting her. (No thanks, but you can help by taking out the garbage or grabbing me a plate of food while I breastfeed!)

I offended my mother the most with this attitude, so she just went around me to get Emersyn from Wes. Whatever. I knew clinging to our newborn wasn't healthy for me or my relationship with Wes, or Emersyn's relationship with her daddy, so I forced myself to let Wes watch her as often as possible. But my reluctance to be without her was not because I felt anxious or obsessed. It was because I was head-over-heels in a movie kind of way in love. I never got sick of holding her. I never felt like I needed a break. This was a complete one-eighty from my previous mothering experience.

And I often felt guilty and worried about that. That my struggle with Sebastian and my ease with Emersyn would translate in my children down the road. Would it appear that I loved one more? Would it hurt them? Had I damaged Sebastian with my postpartum depression? Had I spoiled Emersyn with my easygoing calm? The way I mothered each child during the first six months was with complete, attentive tenderness —but I'm sure they felt the difference. I half-blame my depression for Sebastian's colic; maybe he knew I felt nothing. Maybe he was crying out for a better mom.

I loved my kids equally, and I wished I could have been the mom with Sebastian that I was with Emersyn. I also wished I had the time with Emersyn that Sebastian received. With two children, my heart grew to accommodate and love both endlessly, but my time only divided. A mother can love infinitely, but the length of day finite. *I worry there's not enough time to give.*

The First Two Months of Motherhood Are:

> Back at home and all alone,
> Exhausted body to the bone,
> Crying all night and through the day,
> Wondering if we'll be okay.
>
> Achy nipples, swollen breasts,
> Sleeping baby on my chest,
> Husband snores, I'm wide awake,
> Baby snuggles without a break.

The Bees

Wearing clothes that never match,
Baby learning how to latch,
Pile of dishes in the sink,
Barely time to fetch a drink.

Heaps of diapers by the door,
Food scraps on the kitchen floor,
Soaking onesies in a pail,
Counter piled up with mail.

Baby wipes and Penaten cream,
Frantic diaper-changing screams,
Self-doubt, drowning, overwhelmed,
Modern village nowhere found.

Under-eye circles and matted hair,
Sprawled on couch in underwear,
Baby blankets smelling sweet,
Tiny hands and tiny feet.

Saggy breasts and stomach flap,
Leaky nipples and tired back,
Rosy cheeks with little sighs,
Perfect smiles and twinkling eyes.

Smiling at you with delight,
Cooing in the morning light,
All my fears have gone away,
Loving you these monthlong days.

Nuzzling wispy baby hair,
Rocking with you in a chair,
Soaking in your littleness,
Softest skin I love to kiss.

Surviving through month two and one,
Future brighter when it's done,
Soaking in the morning sun,
Tiny fingers gripping one.

I woke up not quite sure what morning it was. That week had seemed so long and vast that I felt like a buoy bobbing in the ocean of time. Endless hours of endless days with no sense of how long I float before I could regain my legs on land the weekend. *Oh, right, it's finally Friday.* Six forty-five a.m. and lying beside my sleeping two-month-old daughter as my husband got ready for work and my three-year-old son stirred in his sleep.

TW:PTSD//I had just spent the last half-hour in an intense memory. I was back at that night in the cabin, remembering all that happened. I wondered about my memory lapses: Were they blackouts, or could I just not remember because they were traumatic? How did I get from standing in the dark to being unclothed and raped? Maybe he drugged me! Remember those pills I found in his cabin?

I always just assumed I'd drank too much, but thinking back, I'd only had a few beers, no hard alcohol, and not even enough for a slight hangover the next morning. Maybe I always told myself I had too much alcohol so I could blame myself. Give myself a little skin in the game. Maybe if I hadn't drank so much...

But if he drugged me, this changed the whole dynamic. If he drugged me, he raped me. There was no way to prove anything now, but it was an interesting thought. //TW:PTSD

I saw my son's head pop up on the opposite side of the bed. It was too early; he usually slept until seven-thirty. I didn't want him to be cranky. "You taking a video of me?" he asked as I put my phone down after I finished sending an email. "No, baby, I was just typing an email. Are you okay?"

Wes walked into the room from his shower and took over a little. "Honey, it's not wake-up time yet. Do you want to sleep in your bed or with Mommy and Emersyn?" Sebastian wanted to sleep with Daddy. "Sorry, bud, I have to go to work." So, he climbed up into my bed and cuddled under the blanket. Everyone got a kiss from Daddy as he said his goodbyes and left the room to finish getting ready. *Today could be a long day* I mused as I gazed across at my two sleeping children.

It's here. The darkness that has been lingering around the fringes of my mind. No longer is it idling beneath and threatening my mental health. No, now the darkness has emerged with a purpose. To shake my soul. To take me down. To bury me in a hole so deep that I have to claw my way up before sunlight warms my face again. What stirred this darkness in my soul? What tapped on its door and summoned it forth? A song. *A simple song on the radio.*

She sang about his enjoyment of her pain and how he crushed her self-esteem. It was simple. It was beautiful. It was her breaking her silence about a man she once loved. A man no one knew was so dark and manipulative. I understood. Her words hit me at a visceral level.

The song stuck in my head for two weeks, tugging on a loose thread and unraveling what I had tucked away in the back of my memory. *"You promised the world, and I fell for it. I put you first, and you adored it.... Set fire to my purpose, and I let it burn. You got off on the hurtin' when it wasn't yours,"* sang *Selena Gomez.*

The darkness crept up on me and seeped out of its hiding place. I barely noticed, until I became melancholy on a day of doing one of my favorite things: baking. The next morning I was a whirlwind of anger and irritation. "*I needed to hate you to love me."* A squabble with Wes about coffee triggered me and sent me flying out the front door and shutting it a little too loudly. During my drive to run pre-party errands I realized my emotions were amplified, because I felt like I was trapped with my ex again.

Though I was getting better and faster at recognizing my triggers, I still had incidents where I didn't catch myself in time. I immediately pulled over and texted Wes to apologize and explain what had triggered me, explaining that it wasn't his fault. But this was not his first rodeo.

"I think I know what initially triggered you: that song." My husband had heard the song on his way to work they day before. I was dumbfounded. He was right. The timeline added up. "How could something so simple, so stupid, leave me completely shattered?" I wondered. I discovered a woman who I could completely understand and relate to from a place of knowing. But unfortunately, she wasn't someone I could actually talk to.

The day continued as we prepared for our annual Christmas tree party. My cousin Edwin and his girlfriend came early and helped set up food and drinks. When people started arriving, I took a page from my sister-in-law's baby playbook and strapped Emersyn into a baby carrier. *No one asks to "help" you or demands to hold a baby sleeping in a carrier on mommy's chest.* The strategy worked wonders; you're welcome to anyone reading this book who needed this little cheat sheet.

It was hard to say no all day to people who meant well and just wanted to love on our child, but my responsibility was to our baby first, who had no interest in being the object in a game of hot potato. She was a fully formed human who deserved to be treated as more than a source of entertainment. We invited people to visit individually if they wanted to hold Emersyn and bond, but not at a party of forty people.

Christmas was a goddamn dream. Sebastian fully understood the concept of Christmas, and everything sparkled with pure magic. Our family was whole. A year prior, I had just emerged from the fog of PTSD; the year before that, I was about to miscarry; and the year before that, I struggled with postpartum depression. It was about damn time we had a wonderful Christmas.

We all had matching pajamas and enjoyed our easy morning by the tree lights, sipping tea and eating croissants. Sebastian was elated with each festive miracle, from finding Santa's footprints to discovering the toys that came alive Christmas Eve, to pillaging his stocking and opening his presents.

Toys that come alive at Christmas? Yes! This was the best suggestion for traditions we had received. One of my best friends and I were talking one day when I asked for suggestions as Wes and I started our own family traditions. Her parents had set up all the toys late Christmas Eve, the story being that they only came alive while the kids slept, and that when they awoke, they froze in place. Her parents would station dolls, animals, and army men getting into all kinds of mischief and causing debacles. We loved the idea and used it for our family. It was a hit! Sebastian talked about his toys' silly adventures for months and looked forward to the same magic the next year.

When it came to Christmas, Wes and I liked to focus on spending special time with family and magical traditions. Presents were minimal and meant to be secondary. We bought the children a big shared gift (one year, it was dress-up trunk with clothes, another was a big fire station with two trucks, and this upcoming year will be a balance beam and rock wall—all under $250 combined and second-hand). They also received a stocking from Santa, which was mostly candies and dollar-store toys, as well as tickets to an event, like the aquarium, Cirque du Soleil, or a monster-truck show.

Everyone says that once the kids get older, we'll change our ways and begin to buy into the commercial side of Christmas. I guess we'll just have to wait and see!

Once we finished up our festive Christmas lunch, we drove to my parents' house for a fun sleepover with cousins. We awakened to Grandma and Grandpa's special Christmas-Boxing Day, with all the traditions from when I grew up: a king's breakfast, reading the Christmas story, singing carols, opening gifts, a smorgasbord of snacks, a long family walk, and a turkey dinner. The kids were off the wall with excitement and fun, and I mostly kept Emersyn, my little hot-potato, in a baby-carrier.

But it couldn't always be sunshine and rainbows. After the Christmas season ended, I found my happiness begin to slip a little. I still bled from giving birth to Emersyn, and the lack of sleep was really catching up to me. Emersyn breastfed every ninety minutes, and she *only* breastfed.

We tried fresh-pumped breastmilk, frozen breastmilk, and all kinds of formula at numerous temperatures. We spent way too much money trying different bottle brands and different nipple types and textures that had different rates of flow. She wasn't having any of it. Which left all feedings to me.

As much as I didn't mind, my body was asking for more sleep. I needed a mindset-check, so I wrote a bit of gratitude to remind myself of my beautiful life. *I am incredibly lucky to have my life, yet sometimes I lose sight of the good. When I find myself feeling down for no reason, I challenge myself to turn to positive language.* What was I thankful for that day?

What was bothering me or overwhelming me, and how could I turn that into gratitude? There have been studies that suggest practicing daily gratitude can help a person be more positive.

Power of Gratitude, January 2020 – three -m.o. baby
I get to

- stay home with my beautiful children
- breastfeed my daughter and fully soothe and nourish her while bonding.
- make my son healthy meals.
- sleep snuggled up with my baby, who is healthy. read books with my son, because we are privileged to have time and money to do so. And I get to answer all his curious questions, because he is so bright and inquisitive and loves learning.
- hold my daughter throughout the day, because I can soothe her so well.
- have long days at home so that time stretches longer and memories are built stronger in these fleeting years of littleness with my children.
- pay our bills with ease.
- plan our schedule, because my husband supports me.
- go grocery shopping and don't have to mentally tally our bill as I shop like I had to in college. I get to buy as much healthy food as I want.
- go out every once in a while and enjoy a meal without cooking or cleaning.
- do laundry using a machine with easy access to clean water.
- spend quality time with my son, watching him grow and learn.

The winter felt long, with days spent cooped inside as tiny Emersyn was too sensitive for the cold. Any chance I had, I went outside with Sebastian, who seemed much happier on those days. Preschool and gymnastics were my saving grace. We also tried to frequent a local indoor playground. I would walk around breastfeeding or holding a sleeping babe while Sebastian enthusiastically ran from activity to activity. If he did active play for a certain amount of time, I would let him indulge in three arcade games.

Anissa still visited on Mondays, and I began to feel ready to let her hold and care for Emersyn so I could focus some individual time with Sebastian. We were really getting into a routine, and I was settling into this two-kids and two-hands deal.

The first two years of motherhood is...

Arms stretched high with baby yawns
Days begin before the dawn
Spit up, vomit, sucking thumbs
Wiping tiny baby bums

Breastfeeding, bottles, sippy cups of milk
Skin smelling sweet, hair soft as silk
Baby growing up too fast
Trying to make these memories last

Pacing the halls during witching hour
Peek-a-boo as you try to shower
Learn to wave and clap high-five
Cutest kids ever alive

The Bees

Babbles and cooing smiles so bright
Starting to notice everything in sight
Sitting, crawling, learning how to walk
Clapping, singing, dancing, talk

Cheerios, arrowroot, and pureed jars
Playing with stackables and dinky cars
Bath time, singing songs, bubbles on your head
Nighttime stories have you jumping on the bed

Highchair playing with your food
Generally in a happy mood
Tossing food down from the sky
Watching if they'll fall or fly

Need to sweep after every meal
Tickling as you giggle and squeal
Popsicles on the front porch stoop
Toddler watching while you poop

Calling Mommy from the bed
After-nap cheeks rosy red
Buried head against my neck
Not ready to wake up yet

Cutting teeth, bonking your head
Making sure every book is read
Clear the shelves and cover the floor
Practice opening and closing doors

Exersaucer, jolly-jumper, swing, and mat
Chubby cheeks, rolly legs and baby fat
Milestones quickly passing by
Making mommy want to cry

Elevator arms reaching past
Tipping over my water glass
Baby gates are my saving grace
'Cause once you walk you start to race

First time sitting in the grass
Your little personality showing sass
Biting stages for both of you
Making me wonder what to do

Smiles for mom just entering a room
Eyes sparkling looking at you
Tongue poking out to the side
Slobbery kisses mouth open-wide

Nighttime nursing dwindles away
In our bed babe wants to stay
So we continue to co-sleep
Midnight kisses oh so sweet
Feet on face then face on feet
Family snuggles with little sleep

Days were long
And the nights were longer
Memories together
Made me love you stronger

Baby to toddler year two and one
Gosh we had a lot of fun
Stories told in bittersweet light
Some of the best years of my life

Chapter 14 – Pandemic

Trigger Warning:
This chapter contains: post-traumatic stress disorder and sexual assault (pages
215-217). Please be kind to yourself and respect your personal limits. If you
would like to forgo these triggering scenes you may read a summary on page 324.

One mid-February night, Wes started talking to me about what had been happening in China. He showed me videos of people being sprayed down with sanitizer by workers in hazmat suits as they left planes, he showed me hot spots on maps where some theorized mass graves existed, and he showed me reports of apartment buildings being welded shut after government officials walked around with thermometers. "It's coming to Canada. I've already told my boss we need to get everyone set up to work from home. He doesn't seem to agree, but I'm going to start planning for it, anyway."

I felt mildly alarmed and wanted to hoard all the food, but I decided to be rational. One month later, coronavirus ruined March break and cancelled weddings. Life flipped on its head, and we were in lockdown.

When the Ontario provincial state of emergency

was put in place in March 2020, we had no idea how long the restrictions would last. A strict quarantine for a few weeks was the logical consensus among my family members who worked in biomedical engineering and healthcare.

We all abided by the rules and took the lockdown very seriously, ordering groceries to be delivered to our doorstep and sanitizing everything that came into the house. We stayed inside if our neighbors were out front playing, and we kept our social distance when we went for our morning family walks. We had a daily Zoom call with my parents and siblings where we mostly talked about the case numbers and government press conferences.

After two weeks of this, we bubbled with my parents. For our sanity and theirs, we knew it was the right thing to do. We anticipated having to settle into this lifestyle, because lockdowns were likely to come in waves for years to come. With global warming and new diseases coming from the permafrost and rising temperatures, we thought that rolling pandemics and quarantines might be the future. If you looked at the housing market and the surge to vacate concrete cities, it seemed many people felt the same way.

For many people. the pandemic was a magnet for hardship and a catalyst for pain, but for others, it was a revelation. Silence and isolation meant learning to take care of one's mental health and seeing toxic relationships for what they were. Bad friendships, marriages, and relationships family members were ended.

The pandemic had a way of peeling back our daily lives until we saw our roots again. Which relationships had a shaky foundation? Who stuck around and who disappeared from our lives? Who took this time to reach out and check on others, and who cocooned inward and shut out the world? Everyone's way of managing this life-changing event affected their loved ones.

Some hoarded toilet paper and spoke to loved ones through the internet or their front window. Some coped by denying reality and turning to solutions on YouTube, where influencers gave them a sense of control with half-baked conspiracy theories. Some made bread and others made silly TikTok videos. And some fell to despair, loneliness, and depression. *Everyone coped in the best way they knew with the tools they had access to.*

The pandemic greatened the divide between the haves and the have-nots. Some people prospered and bought their first home or moved up financially, while others lost their jobs and were rendered homeless. The divide grew between people who had a firsthand account of Covid by losing loved ones or working in the ICUs, and those who vehemently denied its potency and questioned statistical analysis done by professionals.

For me, the pandemic enlightened many relationships and allowed for healing and growth. From October, when I gave birth to Emersyn, to mid-March, when the lockdown started, I continued to bleed—*yes from my vagina.* Or more accurately, from the plate-sized wound left by the placenta that never fully healed. The blood would dry up for a day or two, and then it would start up again. I was trying my best to be the best mom to both of my children, which meant not resting enough and working far harder than when I had one child. *I swear the workload with two kids doesn't double; it just infinitely increases.*

At the beginning of lockdown, Wes was forced to work from home, and was laid off ten days later. He was around to help more, and I was keeping the kids home. After three years of physical and emotional turmoil, my body finally had the chance to renew itself.

I like to always be busy, so this inactivity was mind-numbingly boring. We implemented a routine that we thought we could enjoy as a family. In the mornings, Wes and I made each other caffeinated drinks and bundled up the children to go for a family walk, which eventually extended to about an hour. We did this to help us with our health, to get the children out of the house, and to have a nice refreshing start to the day. After about a month I was ready to finally start getting back into shape!

I was *really* unfit and my body felt sluggish; all I could do on my first day of training was jog for fifteen seconds. So that's what I started with: I jogged for fifteen seconds, then walked for forty-five seconds, and I that ten times. I did intervals like this with Wes and the kids during our family walks for a while before I began running on my own. I would run as long as I could before taking a one-to-two-minute walk break, until I got to the point where I could run for thirty minutes straight.

On weekends we would drive an hour and a half to my parents' house to change the scenery and pace. I always planned to cook or bake something special: funnel cake, charcuterie board, tiramisu, deep-fried wontons, and the list goes on. Part of what helped Wes and I stay positive was doing things to make others happy—cooking and treating my parents on the weekend was one of many. We also sent anonymous craft beer to friends, made activity baskets and dropped them off to neighbors, nieces, and nephews. We made special mugs for Wes's mom and my two cousins, batch-cooked dips to bring to my siblings, and brought baked goods to friends. Positivity breeds positivity. Random acts of kindness were the way we spent our extra money.

Wes was out of work for two months. We put his severance into a savings account and tried not to touch it until my maternity leave ran out. We could live frugally, because there was nowhere to go.

For weeks we only saw my siblings and nieces and nephews through Zoom. Sebastian had no one his age to play with, and I could see it affecting him greatly. It was terrible feeling helpless as a parent to give him what he needed. As much as we played with him, baked with him, and tried to make days interesting, we were never going to be able to fill that void left by his peers. I struggled with my own happiness when my son's was clearly lacking, so my sister took him for two nights so he could play with his cousins. He was *so* incredibly happy and relieved. He walked to her car and got in with barely a good-bye. *He was ready*. And when he returned, so had the light in his eyes.

Two weeks later, on my mother's birthday, eight weeks after the lockdown began, my sisters finally felt comfortable visiting my parents and extending their bubble. Though the eight weeks in which I had my parents all to myself were a wonderful way to calmly reconnect, it also came with some hard conversations about where I had needed them in the past.

TW:PTSD,SA//"No one would let someone rape them! They wouldn't just lie there, they would fight them tooth and nail. That's why they drugged those children— so they wouldn't have to deal with them fighting back every time." We were talking about Jeffrey Epstein, and my mom said words that enraged me. *Remember, Epstein did not kill himself.*

"You need to educate yourself," I replied. "Most people don't fight back when they're being raped, because they are just trying to survive. They know they will be beaten— possibly to death—if they fight."

My mom was aghast. I could have gone deeper and shamed her and shook her, but instead I dropped it. I could have said, *Maybe when it happens you learn quickly not to move an inch. Because when you try, he corrects you with violence. When you swing, you find out how easily he can restrain you with one hand. One clenched and powerful grip. He shows you with ease how well he controls your movement.*

Your brain calculates that fight and flight are no longer viable options, so you freeze. You freeze within an inch of consciousness. You freeze, and you don't move an inch. You don't move as he rapes you. You don't move as he sleeps between you and the door. You don't flutter your eye as he wakes and dresses. You don't move a bit when you hear him leave the cabin. You don't exhale until his footsteps and voice have faded in the distance.

When he's safely gone you open your eyes. Eyes that squeezed tight the previous night while his possessed your body. Eyes that feigned sleep as his assessed his conquest. You look around the cabin and focus. You slowly move off the bed as you see the space for the first time in the light. Numb, you move silently, searching for your clothes—the clothes he rid you of as he stripped you of your dignity—strewn on the floor and furniture.

You collect your items and dress quickly, finding relief in being clothed. You investigate the room to find out more about this person. In a tin of loose pills, you take a five-dollar bill, just so you could take something from him. It wasn't much. It wasn't enough.

When you head for the door, you certainly didn't think it would be locked. You check the windows and they are nailed shut. Freezing may have been the only way to let him think he could leave in the morning for breakfast. Freezing may have been why you had the chance to escape. Freezing was the only way to make it to this point, this place where you could fight.

Now was the time for fight. You assessed the hinges on the door and used a paddle to try and pry it open. It barely budged. You assessed the windows, the drop below, and the forest beyond. You jammed the paddle and broke through the window, used the furniture to climb up and out the window to land on soft long grass.//TW:PTSD,SA

Then flight, as you ran faster than you ever previously had. Away from his cabin. Toward the safety of your siblings.

I froze, I fought, and I flew. Because my life depended on it. I always knew those were my only options at the time. I am so glad I never had someone tell me what a "proper response" would have been.

When people hear the statistics by the National Sexual Violence Resource Centre that eighty-one percent of women have experienced sexual harassment or assault and one in five women have experienced attempted or completed rape, they immediately jump to asking how they save our daughters and sisters. My response is that *you can't.* If someone has decided they are going to rape someone they will. He could be your daughter's friend, boyfriend, or a complete stranger. But, according to RAINN, ninety-two percent of rapes are committed by an acquaintance, family member, or friend. Your daughter's not likely expecting that person to behave in that manner. By trying to teach girls and women how to avoid being raped, it teaches them it's their responsibility, and indirectly tells them it's their fault if it happens. Which is complete bullshit.

Women will protect themselves till the end of time. We know we are walking around in a world of predatory men. We will avoid running at night, we keep our keys between our knuckles as we go to our car, we keep our drinks nearby and covered, we wear spandex under our dress when we go out, and we check the back seat before getting in. We take a whole bunch of safety precautions to help ourselves, but if someone has decided they are going to rape us, we can't win.

Here's what I want you to shift your focus to: the percentage of boys and men who commit rape. We know from the Department of Justice Violence Against Women

Report that ninety-nine percent of *rapists* are men, but what does that mean? What *percentage* of men have committed assault or rape? We all like to think that it's no one we know, but if you look at the number of women who are raped, who do you think is doing it? Do you think it's tree gremlins?

It's your brother, it's your dad, it's your best friend, and it's your teammate. Let's place the responsibility where it belongs: on boys and men. Don't talk to women like that. Don't talk about girls and women based on their appearance. Don't make jokes about rape vans and that "no means yes." Squash the adage that boys will be boys. Squash locker room talk. And let's squash toxic masculinity. Boys are not entitled to an orgasm from a woman, they are only entitled to an orgasm from themselves. That's it. All these men thinking women owe them sexual pleasure is what is fucking wrong.

Let's make a point to teach our boys not to be rapists. Let's teach about affirmative consent and the reciprocity of pleasure, tenderness, and attention. Boys and men should learn how to pay attention to detail and nuance—it's not just a female thing to notice cues. Instead of only expecting women to be intuitive and empathetic, let's expect everyone to be sensitive to sound and nonverbal cues. If both parties are not enthusiastically involved, check in with them. Their stomach has started to hurt? Take a break and get them a glass of water. They're suddenly self-conscious? Compliment them and help them feel comfortable. They've gone silent? Ask them if they are okay, and tell them it's okay to stop.

When I received feedback on my manuscript from my focus group, one of the men asked why I sometimes write with such anger and sound like I hate men. This passage in particular was brought up, so please let me clarify: Every woman you know has experienced or has a friend who has experienced abuse or assault at the hands of a man and is affected by it. Whether it is someone going up her skirt at a dance bar or someone drugging her drink, an acquaintance not listening to her saying no or a boyfriend who put his needs before her comfort. Whatever it was, every woman has multiple stories. So, it's not about you personally or women hating men. It's about the female experience.

The way we move through the world is so vastly different than how men do. We still the fear being prey. We battle with the internal dialogue between paranoia and gut instinct. We don't know if we're safe alone in the house with the plumber. We don't know if we're safe walking to our car at night. We lock the doors when we're alone at the house even if it's the middle of the day. We don't know if the person we're going on a date with is going to grope us, charm us until they abuse us, stalk us, or be perfectly wonderful.

Feminists do not hate men. We love men. We love them so much that we want the world to be better for them too, by ending toxic masculinity, which not only leads to the assault of girls and women, but boys as well. We can all help make this world better, and it starts at home. All men grew up exposed to rape culture, but not all men are rapists. There are loads of decent and wonderful men out there— my husband included—and they came from parents who taught them how to respect women. Teach young boys and men as often as you can how to respect other humans. Teach them to be emotionally vulnerable and intuitive so they notice nuance and detail. The more anti-sexist people, the less rape. Boys who have grown into rapists are not an anomaly. We need to make a point to correct this trend starting with our own children.

Welp. That's how trauma reemerges. You're seemingly talking about a pandemic and then...rape. Sorry about that, you must be exhausted! All women are. Take a pause and we will return to the story...where were we? Right, pandemic.

Once our family bubble included some playmates for Sebastian, the struggle became manageable. Wes got a new job while continuing to look for something better. I continued to run and improve my health, and my sisters and I all banded together to create a summer full of happy memories for our children. We spent three days a week getting together, rotating who was in charge, location, and who got to take some time for themselves to work on personal goals. Both my sisters were in school and used their time to work on assignments, and I only used my time half of the time for errands or exercise.

I thoroughly enjoyed spending time with my nieces and nephews and being a fun aunt. On the days I planned, I treated them like summer camp. I bought a rainbow parachute, and we started the day with circle time and singing songs with toy instruments. I organized crafts, baking, and special treats. The kids were amazing. It was adorable watching their faces furrow with focus while creating and light up with pride when they showed me their work or ate food they'd helped prepare. During this time, the kids' ages were four months, eight months, eighteen months, two-and-a-half, three, three-and-a-half, four, and six. Wow, that seems wild looking back! They were a handful and we three moms all understandably needed occasional time alone. But when school started in September, the visits ceased.

Wes and I watched the case counts around the world and how each country managed the pandemic. As we neared our planned trip to Italy in October 2020 we knew our only option was to cancel and recoup as much money as possible. With our savings from our trip, Wes's un-used severance, savings account, and his new income, we paid off our car and scrounged enough for a minimum down payment on a house.

Now I wasn't on board for buying anything until my financially planned projected preparedness in 2022. I wanted my student loan gone and a bigger down payment, and I wanted us to have two incomes to support mortgage payments. Wes was always looking at houses and property on the internet and showing me places *we could not afford*. But one day he suckered me with the most beautiful plot of land at the end of a cul-de-sac where a twenty-kilometer trail began and led to my sister's town. It was located closer to my family and close enough to our sports teams in our current city. And the price was right.

Wes contacted the agent, and we viewed the land at sunset during a picnic with our children. I immediately started dreaming up house designs and how to financially manage everything. Wes started contacting mortgage brokers and getting information. We learned for a plot of land without a house, the bank required a forty percent down payment. My eyes bulged. We didn't have enough cash for that, and after much conversation, we settled on the idea that we needed to buy a house to get into the market and gain equity, and then buy our dream land to build.

In a whirlwind two weeks, we went from "not looking for two more years" *to impulse-buying a fucking house*. And when I say *impulse*, I mean it. We got caught up in the game, man. We viewed twelve different houses and lost bids on five offers before winning the bid on Caradoc Street. I felt like Joey Tribbiani on that episode of *Friends* where he thought he could win a boat by guessing what it was worth—not realizing that it was a silent auction, so he had to pay for it.

We were excited to have finally landed a house, then were immediately like, Oh, fuck, *we just bought a house!* As you can tell, this is a trend in our relationship. Last time was when we said, *Hey let's try for a baby,* and then were like, *Oh, fuck, we're pregnant.... He we are again, folks!*

We called our parents right away and shared the good news. I had kept the house in my hometown a secret, because I had never intended on moving back. I only looked at it because it was the only house in our price range that wasn't riddled with mice, asbestos, and mold. Wes and I had a map of places we were willing to look: within forty-five minutes of Wes's job, thirty-minutes from a city, and fifteen minutes from a grocery store. Strathroy was right on the cusp of an encircled area. When we searched, I didn't include it in our radius, but Wes did. And when he sent me the listing, I gasped as I flicked through the photos; rookie move. Always look at the price and address *first.* I was in love. I looked at the price: great. But then I scrolled down to location: You have got to be kidding me.

But I was in love. So, I booked a showing for the next day. Since Wes had meetings, he couldn't come, but the owners were closing bids at seven o'clock that night, so it was now or never. Walking into the house with ten-foot ceilings, original hardwood floors, twelve-inch baseboards, antique chandeliers, and stained-glass windows, I almost teared up. This was it. I could not believe a house like this existed in our price range. I went home that afternoon and told Wes all about it. He knew it was love, too. So, he gave his blessing to put in an offer, even though he hadn't seen the place.

We made an offer, then called back after dinner and increased it by eleven thousand. I just had a feeling. Three hours after bid closing, we received a call from our realtor—the house was ours! We'd won the bid by only a thousand dollars, all thanks to that last-minute increase.

When I called my parents, who had toured many houses with us located far from theirs, they didn't expect me to say we were buying a home in Strathroy. They, along with me, thought I would be the last of their children to ever move back to our hometown. I asked them to search the address. I could almost feel my mother jump off the couch in her sunroom when she realized it was in Strathroy. They both cheered in shocked happiness. It felt fantastic to have them so excited for us to be close to them, and at the same time I wondered, *Did I just fuck up?*

Throughout my life my family has intermittently been a great source of love and support and also a source of pain and confusion. At times I felt certain of their love, at others I was not sure if they loved me at all. Putting myself an hour and a half away from the community of friends I had built to be next door to uncertainty didn't seem wise. But here we were. We had "won," hadn't we?

On top of all this madness, the owners wanted a quick sale. So, we incentivized them by dangling a two-week close. We were not prepared but pulled off the mightiest Hail Mary of the century. The first week, I called the lawyers and broker and organized all the paperwork. I gave notice to our landlord, ordered labels and boxes to begin packing, and assembled a moving crew of family and friends along with two rental trucks. I printed plans of the house and began planning how we would organize our things and move in so the transition minimally impacted our children by prioritizing their bedroom and toy room. I developed sores on my cheeks and ears from distractedly rubbing them repeatedly in a state of stress. (I learned this is called self-stimulatory behavior, or "stimming," and is common for people with ADHD, like me.)

We organized a house-plus-improvements mortgage meaning we had four months to finish any renovations we wanted tacked on to our mortgage. The day after our house closed, I had contractors, electricians, flooring people, window people, and plumbers lined up to give us quotes. I systemically prepped the new house while packing the old house in an organized fashion, labeling boxes by where they should be placed in the new house. I painted, built shelves, and removed baseboards for floor refinishing. All in a week and a half while parenting two young children.

Once we moved in, Wes and I cleaned all storage cupboards and unpacked and organized all our furniture, clothing, toys, and everything else within forty-eight hours. I was jacked on adrenaline and refused to live among boxes. We had one week at the new house before we headed to my parents' for two weeks while a contractor sanded down and refinished the hundred-and-fifty-year-old floors. During that time, I hosted fifteen tradespeople, compared all quotes, decided with Wes which projects took priority, then booked in the work.

We stayed with my parents for two-and-a-half weeks, because the floors took longer than anticipated. I was so busy during this time that I wasn't as watchful of my children, and one day Emersyn had unicorn rainbow poop as she passed a bunch of tiny beads she had eaten. Another day, she had really grainy poop, because she had eaten two fistfuls of sand. But they were still snuggled and loved as much as always and probably gained some independence. So, I looked at it as a win.

During the weeks at my folks' house, the work didn't stop. We shopped for and purchased laundry machines, couches, chairs, floor tile, backsplash, ceiling tile, crown molding, and light fixtures. We sanded and painted a coffee table and some of our baseboards. And Sebastian started kindergarten, which was an emotional transition for me.

Sebastian decided he wanted to start school that week and not to wait till the following week, and I believe it was because his cousins were already in school, and he wanted to be big like them. I would have waited until we were settled back at our house, but respected his wishes. Sebastian had a rough first week but then really started enjoying it. I started him on half-days during the fall, because he was exhausted and had headaches when we tried full days. I didn't mind him being home more; in fact, I preferred it. I wanted to squeeze out every moment I had with him at this precious age.

I hit the ground running when we moved back into our home. I continued painting, and Wes and I began installing sound-proofing on the dining-room ceiling, followed by the framing of the coffered ceiling I had dreamed of. We had inspectors and workers coming in and out of the house every day. Two weeks later, Wes and I just randomly started demolishing our main-floor bathroom.

We were halfway done when we looked at each other: *Derp*, that wasn't part of the plan! That project was supposed to be done the following year. At this point, we needed to finish what we started, because we now could not use the main-floor washroom. We were also ten grand over budget. I blame it on exhaustion.

A week later I hit a wall—hard. All of a sudden, I felt so tired that I could have fallen over. The prior two months of working to a sweat every day came down on me all at once right before Emersyn's first birthday. I let Wes do the work this time and settled for a last-minute McCain's frozen chocolate cake with no decorations, theme, or activities. I quit working on the house and focused on daily homemaking and caregiving for our children. At night, when the kids went to bed, I flopped on the couch and snacked until I dragged myself up the stairs to sleep and breastfeed the rest of the night. It took me over a month to recover.

As Christmas approached, installers replaced half our windows and built a gas fireplace in the second-level library. Covid cases started to increase, and my family began to feel the familiar stress that comes with reliving trauma. Another lockdown loomed. The Canadian government advised people not to get together for Christmas, but most of us still did, albeit after a fourteen-day quarantine.

The Christmas celebrations were all for the children this year. I faked it and did all the traditions with excitement and zest while feeling hollow inside. The kids felt the magic and glistened with happiness and cheer, because that's what it's all about as a parent. Due to adult stresses of impending Covid regulations, I found it hard to be festive, but I had children and it wasn't about me anymore. So, I rallied and did my best to enjoy the season through Sebastian and Emersyn's wonder.

When the Ontario government confirmed that schools would be moving to virtual learning and that we would be isolated again, I started speaking with my sisters with hopes of working together in support as we had during the summer. They had other plans. They had different life situations and chose to not allow our children to mingle. They left me to myself when they were the only support we had locally.

And since our friends were almost two hours away, we really were on our own this time. As much as I felt hurt and disappointed with the lack of camaraderie, I wouldn't allow myself to stew, because I would be damned if my children felt traumatized or had lasting negative effects from isolation. I was going to turn this shitty pandemic into a bubble of fun and make memories so fucking sweet that they would remember lockdowns as periods of imaginative fun. I got to work and made a plan.

Sebastian would participate in school online, and we would do something special each day. Mondays, we would bake. On Tuesdays, Grandma would come over to Café Sebastian and eat what we had made the day before (Sebastian would serve her and learn about money). Wednesdays would be *wacky*: full-day themed extravaganzas that took a whole week of planning, some money, and a lot of energy. Thursdays were supposed to be craft days, but I was always so tired from Wednesday, we never really did it. Fridays, we turned our living room into a theatre and watched a movie with treats. Saturdays brought visits to Grandma and Grandpa's house, and Sundays were lazy pajama day.

The plan worked! The kids adored Wacky Wednesdays and looked forward to the next one as soon as the day ended. The day would start with discovering a themed set-up of toys and a creative breakfast. After playing with the toys and eating, Sebastian had online school, and then I would have another special activity: obstacle course for Ninja training, Pirate-ship water table, rainbow crafts, or moon-sand with diggers. We would read theme-related books and watch theme-related TV shows. After another period of online school, I often had themed snacks cut into dinosaurs or ninjas wielding nunchucks. Sometimes, the special day lasted until dinner where we had Master Chen noodles or pirate-ship hotdogs.

I splurged and spoiled them with a Kijiji-cheap bouncy castle that fit in our dining room, and I started looking for other people to add to my circle as playmates for my children and support for me. I did not want to depend on my family, as they had never been a solid source of support.

While I was making the second state of emergency a wild and fun-filled adventure for my kids, I began a ride on a roller coaster of my own.

Chapter 15 – Ready for Redemption

Trigger Warning:
This chapter contains emotional abuse (pages 242-245).
Please be kind to yourself and respect your personal limits. If you would like to
forgo these triggering scenes you may read a summary on page 324.

In the months and years that followed my breakup with Andrew, I found myself unable to retrieve any memory of our relationship, positive or negative. No matter how hard I tried, I could only remember that time period if something triggered me. I felt like a hamster trying to dig out of a plastic cage; no matter which way I went, no matter how much fluff I got out of the way, there was always a hard barrier preventing me from digging into my memory. A wall preventing me from escaping PTSD or properly healing. I was not ready yet. I wasn't far enough removed from it yet, and my subconscious knew it. Now, twelve years after our first date and six years after our breakup, I could finally address the dysfunction and abuse in therapy.

Question:

What do you say when you see them again?
After over ten years
When your bodies have aged
And your faces have changed
Your skin creasing with lapsed time
Only memories remain.

What do you say to the people who let you slip
Out of their lives?
Who never checked in?
Who never stayed in touch?
Who never noticed how he slowly isolated you
    from everything you knew?

How do you explain
To their questioning eyes
The reason you did what you did?
The reason you ran away so suddenly and fast?
They all have their own conspiracies
Their own prejudice,
But none of them would ever guess the truth.

How do you carry the burden of a secret
That's lasted ten years
That you never thought would be confronted
At a summer backyard barbeque?
They only have memories of who you were
Not the knowledge of why you are.

So, do you tell them?
If so, how?
How do you tell them
That your ex-boyfriend, their classmate,

Their student, their friend - a person who seemed
Meek, and unthreatening
The gangly geek who played trombone and skipped ahead in
   math
Was actually your worst nightmare?
Your captor, your abuser,
The reason you have PTSD.

How do you withstand
Their doubt
Their disbelief
Their barrage of questions
Interrogating your pain
Questioning your trauma?

Or do you just avoid the topic?
Allow them to keep their conspiracies
Their judgement of your actions
Their opinion of your character
Only knowing how quickly you left
That you ran
Not knowing what you were running from
The life you were escaping
The strength it took.

Is redemption worth the risk
Of trudging up memories?
Is removing the veil of innocence
From the guilty partner
And exposing him to his community even
Safe?
Is this the last bit of strength needed
To completely free you from your past?

Answer:
Maybe you need to eclipse this discomfort and fear
In order to be completely unburdened and free
Knowing you no longer feel compelled
To keep his reputation clean.

You survived.
You escaped
You evolved.

He will never own you again.
Celebrate in that
And others will see the truth.

In January 2021, I began therapy for the first time since my failed attempt during PTSD in 2018 with Dr. Derbert. I was nervous and scared to go on this journey and work through hard memories. I knew I needed a female therapist who specialized in many areas of trauma, given my myriad experiences. I also knew I needed a therapist who wouldn't cut me off at the fifty-minute-mark and could respond to my needs with empathy and an understanding that only emerged from personal pain and struggle. So, during my emails and initial interviews with my top two picks, I asked if they had personally experienced any one of my struggles. I didn't need to know details or what they had endured; I only needed to know that they would be helping me from a place of *knowing* and not just empty empathy and clinical study.

I ended up choosing a wonderful therapist named Epione. She was very thoughtful and warm, professional and personable, logical and sensitive. Since we met during the second lockdown of the pandemic, we met virtually. I had sessions with her in the comfort and safety of my own home (with Wes on a different floor with the kids), and even though I allowed myself to be completely emotionally exposed, I never felt physically at risk or insecure. Feeling unsafe and resistant to vulnerability was what made me shut down during therapy previously.

During our first few sessions, I existed in a very raw mental space. My tolerance for daily stress was very low, and I found myself fluctuating between completing the day in a numb, robotic state, and then having a seemingly random emotional blowout where I would cry uncontrollably or yell at Wes (something I had never done before). I became emotionally unregulated and responded to painful memory by freezing (numbing, memory loss, autopilot, dissociation, flat, separated) while I cared for the children, and then fighting (overwhelmed, anxiety, emotional outbursts, rage) when I could safely release my emotions to my husband. My chest tightened, breathing felt shallow and painful, and my stomach would bloat and cramp as the day progressed. My body was in turmoil, and I consistently felt the urge to belt out a lioness scream. My trauma had been silenced for so long, and I needed to release my pain.

"As long as you keep secrets and suppress information, you are fundamentally at war with yourself.... The critical issue is allowing yourself to know what you know. That takes an enormous amount of courage." This is a passage from *The Body Keeps the Score*, by Bessel van der Kolk, M.D.

For the first time, I began to open up and speak the secrets of my abusive relationship with Andrew. This felt awkward and, at times, impossible, because I had lied to others and myself by normalizing it all for so long that I'd doubted it was abuse. He never beat me or made me fear for my life. As much as I had come to acknowledge that Andrew sexually assaulted me, I still had not internalized that sentiment. I did not *believe* myself.

Though I had previously given Wes and my family abstract and undetailed tidbits of abusive stories, I had never spoken about Andrew like this before to anyone. In fact, a lot of my traumatic memories were just living in my body without me being able to cognitively identify or remember them. "Traumatized people chronically feel unsafe inside their bodies: The past is alive in the form of gnawing interior discomfort. Their bodies are constantly bombarded by visceral warning signs, and, in an attempt to control these processes, they often become expert at ignoring their gut feelings and in numbing awareness of what is played out inside." Another gem from Dr. van der Kolk.

During our first two therapy sessions, my memories came out in random order and without much context. They emerged from a place of raw remembrance where when I spoke about them my body would disappear and my sight would blur as I faded into the memory I shared with a shaky voice and flowing tears. My body twitched and jerked with trauma and cortisol pumped through my veins. At night I would have stress-seizures where Wes would waken to a shaking bed.

As much as I feared the pain that emerged during therapy, I pushed on, because I knew it was working. The day after my first session I felt lighter in my body. I had begun the journey of processing memories that had been neglected and ignored, and my entire being responded positively to this change. My urge to scream began to subside with each remembrance I released.

During my second session, Epione encouraged me to name all the sensations I felt when memories emerged. From previous therapy experiences, I thought I was very self-aware and able to identify my emotions while logically working through them. But when it came to the strong, unprocessed moments of trauma, feelings flooded my body so intensely that I was unable to sort through or name them. I felt like a riptide had pulled me out from land in a frantic spin; I struggled to figure out which direction to swim for as I tumbled around in a breathless, fear-soaked frenzy.

At the end of our session, Epione gave me the emotions wheel diagram, which was a rainbow-colored wheel of categorized feelings. I found it easier to identify with a description when I read it on the wheel, and then connected it back to a triggered memory. Immediately after our session ended, I took a deep dive into sorting out my feelings.

Initially, I made a broad list of reactions: What did I feel when I dated Andrew? How do I feel looking back on the verbal and emotional abuse in that relationship? How do I feel looking back on the sexual abuse in that relationship? How do I feel about my family's lack of support? How do I feel about my sexual assault? How do I feel about my miscarriages? I asked myself each question, writing down each description from the wheel that I identified with the answer.

Once I answered those questions, I went back and reviewed the emotions I picked out for myself. I felt the need to explain each emotion with an example. So, I got to work. I felt:

- Anxious about my appearance with Andrew, and how he might act when we were in the presence of others. (Would he insult me and laugh?)
- Inferior to Andrew, especially when it came to intelligence and logic. He would say I was bad at math and finance, that I was too emotional, and

that some movies were over my head.
- Desperate for Andrew to love me and for our relationship to last.
- Helpless to the emotional roller coaster I seemed to be on and all the physical symptoms that came with it: stomach ulcers, bloating, digestive issues, weight gain.
- Agitated when we were around my family.
- Hurt by his coldness when he cancelled plans or didn't want to see me, and when he called me names like "Michelin Man," said I looked like a boy, or called me disgusting and greasy.
- Depressed.
- Shameful whenever he scolded me for the way I acted, saying I embarrassed him if I spoke to other men or had too much fun without him.
- Neglected, as he rarely reciprocated my grand gestures of love.
- Isolated and lonely because I had none of my own friends and only Andrew to fill my time.
- Powerless over any life decision, relying on him for basic things like organizing my phone for me and downloading school texts.
- Confused when he would change the narrative or gaslight me.
- Embarrassed whenever he cut me down or made me the butt of the joke in public.
- Guilty when he assaulted me and gaslighted me into thinking it was I who assaulted him.
- Inadequate as a woman for him, because I couldn't reach orgasm with him, and he would call me broken.

So why did I stay?

Well, I also felt infatuated with him and the idea of our relationship checking all the boxes my parents taught me to look for. I was incredibly attracted to his intelligence and wit, and we just clicked early on. He made me feel completely protected and safe from the dangers of the outside world and the opinions of my family.

I felt jubilant when he complimented me, and excited every time I could get him to smile or laugh at my jokes. I felt tender empathy toward his insecurities and understood where his insults came from. He was insecure about his slender frame, which made him want me to be skinnier, so he insulted my weight. He felt his intelligence was his best asset, so he didn't want mine to compare.

He pressured me into sex, because he feared he would be judged by his peers for being celibate. He felt embarrassed that he couldn't bring me to orgasm, so he said I was a broken woman and that "it wasn't his fault I couldn't come." He also tried to force me to orgasm for his own gratification. And he felt insecure when men looked at me, so he joked at my expense to tear down my self-esteem. He didn't want to lose me.

He loved the way I made him feel and the way I made him look. I don't believe he ever loved *me*, because then he would have never insulted me, controlled me, or sexually assaulted me. He loved *the way I made him feel* when I cooked for him, showered him with kisses and attention, cleaned his house, did his laundry, and orchestrated grand gestures of love.

He loved *the way he had conditioned me* into being his pleasure toy. He loved *the way I looked on his arm* with my bleach-blond hair and big boobs. He wanted a trophy wife and even said so. He wanted a broken-down woman who relied on him to control the finances and all the family decisions. He may not have consciously planned out how he was going to bend our relationship to his liking by grooming and abusing me, but that was definitely his underlying and subconscious intention.

After writing down all of my feelings and remembered connections to them, I went over them again a few days later and noticed I had missed the biggest and most predominant emotion that has ruled much of my life: FEAR. *Why did I stay?* I was scared to lose the love of my life, the person I thought was meant for me. I was scared to be alone and never find another person who would love me. I was as broken as Andrew convinced me to be.

I feared my family loved Andrew more than they loved me and that breaking up with him would ruin my relationship with them. I was afraid Andrew would leave me if I didn't comply with his wishes. Scared I wasn't good enough, scared I was destined to be lonely, scared of not being believed, scared of loss, scared of failure, scared …

How did I turn into the woman who molded herself into his desires without being beaten and threatened? He conditioned me for years. I became compliant out of fear he would hurt me or leave me. I was afraid of ridicule and eventually developed a fear of violence for natural womanly occurrences such a healthy discharge, natural lubrication, and menstruation, because he found these things disgusting and repulsive. So, I incessantly cleaned and deodorized, hid my period products, and placated him with oral sex while I struggled with menstrual cramps.

I feared his reaction if I didn't respond the way he wanted during sex and eventually was so traumatized by the pain he caused that I would panic any time I approached orgasm. So, I learned to say the right words to help him finish faster, to dissociate and focus on the ceiling, and to fake an orgasm with moans and twitches so he wouldn't brutalize me while trying to assert his manhood. I cooked his favorite foods to please him, and I cleaned his house and did his laundry. I wore my hair down and kept it long and blond.

During our relationship, I didn't recognize what occurred as sexual abuse. I had been told my entire life by society, school, religion, and my family that my value as a woman hinged on the ways I could please a man. Virginity, beauty, and the traditional housewife were and continue to be prized character traits of a woman.

My sexuality was so repressed and scorned that I never explored my own body before Andrew. My body was meant to please a man, so masturbation never occurred to me. In Catholic school sex education, masturbation was only ever referred to as something males did, and was morally wrong. Talking about female pleasure was, *and still is*, largely taboo. It's why the *Flight of the Concords'* song "Business Time" resonated with so many people. *It's why the porn industry is geared toward gratifying men*.

When Andrew claimed my virginity, he also laid claim to my body, which I let him do, because I thought that's where my worth existed. I wanted him to be pleased so he wouldn't leave me. My sexual pleasure never came into consideration; to me it was a happy extra if it occurred.

I had read article after article in *Cosmopolitan* about the evasiveness of the female orgasm while simultaneously promoting a way to gratify a man: best blowjob techniques or sex moves to make him crazy for you. Statistics from the website Pleasure Best cited female orgasm from penetration as low as 18.4 percent; half of women reach orgasm with penetration and clitoral stimulation; and five to ten percent never achieve orgasm. I had low expectations for pleasure, because I knew it would be a process of getting to know my body and how it responded to touch.

I was in no rush to please myself and was happy for the ability to please Andrew. I sacrificed my sexual growth, comfort, and readiness for sexual intimacy under pressure for the gratification of my boyfriend. It was something I was groomed to do from a young age, listening to my uncles joke about hot dogs and hallways.

As much as I changed to keep Andrew happy, I wasn't a lilting flower who never stood up for herself. I recognized his verbal insults as mean even if I didn't view his sexual aggressiveness as assault or abuse. I would tell him when his words hurt me, and I would expect an apology. There was a pattern of power in our relationship: After Andrew hurt me and before he made amends, I would have the power. But then he'd always take it back.

As much as I was the victim of his abuse, control, and manipulation, I also experienced soaring heights I flew to emerging from pain. Andrew's rare compliments were intoxicating. Pleasing him gave me a feeling that I chased and worked for with every special meal I made or each grand gesture I planned.

After four weeks and a few long therapy sessions, I was approaching my thirtieth birthday. Before the pandemic hit, Wes and I had already discussed how we wanted to celebrate our milestone birthdays: his fortieth and my thirtieth. Wes had his low-key party of lawn games and barbecue with family during the pandemic lull in the summer. And though he was unable to invite all his friends, he was satisfied with how the day went. I, on the other hand, wanted to do a bougie chef-at-home dinner and game-night extravaganza. I wanted to thoroughly celebrate my thirtieth birthday, because I was excited to put my twenties behind me.

But the pandemic ruthlessly squashed my birthday

dreams. I avoided talking about and thinking about my upcoming birthday until three days before, when my therapist encouraged me to reenvision it, because I was only going to turn thirty once. Her words woke me up from my denial, and I decided to heed her advice and really think about what I wanted to do. I chose to have a lazy day at home with my husband and children. I was sick of Zoom calls and was not interested in video chatting with people, because it only reminded me of the party I wasn't able to have.

The day I turned thirty, I slept in and had breakfast in bed, then read a book by the fire. At lunch, Wes brought me charcuterie and wine. After Emersyn's nap I went downstairs to a room full of balloons, a piñata, and a stack of presents. We had our own mini-party where Sebastian and I broke the piñata, the kids helped me open my presents, and we lit candles, sang "Happy Birthday," and ate a cake Sebastian and Wes made together. Wes did all the parenting, and I got to participate when I pleased. Once the kids had fallen asleep, I sipped wine while Wes cooked us a dinner of steak, twice-baked potatoes, and roasted broccoli. And lastly, I shared my birthday sentiment on Facebook:

"Good bye twenties!
Yesterday I spent time appreciating my last day in my twenties and the journey that brought me from a teenager in Undergrad to a home-owning mom and wife. My twenties were exhausting; they contained more valleys than peaks, required a lot of resilience, and changed me into the woman I am proud to be. Through the struggles and triumphs of surviving and excelling, I have experienced the growing pains with gratitude. I am so lucky and

happy to be where I am today.

I am an Architecture and project management graduate.

I am a survivor of assault and domestic abuse.

I am a homeowner of huge renovation project.

I am a mother who endured four difficult pregnancies and adore my two gorgeous children.

I am a wife to a handsome and fantastic husband and parenting partner.

I am a woman who is proud, happy, and very grateful.

I am grateful for the valley leading up to this mountain. I am grateful for silver linings. And I am grateful to be living in a time where therapy is available and progressive.

I hope my thirties allows for healing and calmness. I look forward to watching my children grow and accomplishing more goals alongside my husband. Cheers!"

I thoroughly enjoyed my reimagined birthday. I relished putting myself first and allowing time for self-care. TW:EA//The only issue arose when my family decided to ignore my wishes and put together a surprise Zoom call for my birthday, even though I'd specifically asked that we not do one.

Even though I made sure Wes told them I wouldn't be attending, my siblings got their children to make me crafts and wait for me on Zoom. Unaware of the crafts, I did not attend. Soon after the meeting ended, I received four phone calls from people questioning why I hadn't made an appearance, chastising me for ignoring my nieces and nephews. As much as I pointed out that it was my day and that I had made my wishes clear, they reasoned that it was only ten minutes, and I could have just done it.//TW:EA

This minor incident mirrored the way I have been treated by my family repeatedly. *I was the problem*, and even though it was my birthday, what I wanted wasn't paramount. This conjured unresolved feelings and memories from our wedding in Italy, our engagement, and our pregnancy news. Time and again, when there was cause for celebration my, family put on their shit-colored glasses and saw negativity.

I felt unsupported during times of triumph, and more importantly during times of great struggle. When I left my abusive relationship, I was met with frustration and exasperation. When I suffered from post-]partum depression and later PTSD, they abandoned me and told me to stop dwelling on the past and wallowing in self-pity. The next therapy session largely focused on these difficult feelings with my family.

Since I was a defiant fifteen-year-old, I have felt at odds with my entire family. My siblings and parents somehow demonized me as the source of my parents' cracked relationship. It was six against one, and every time there was hardship, I was the emotional dumping ground and scapegoat.

As much as this was a systemic family problem, I put much of the blame on my mother. I found it hard to realize she was only a human being and not an omniscient deity. While I could logically understand that people made mistakes and could accidentally hurt another, when it was my mother harming or failing to defend and protect me, it felt like much more of an attack on my soul and my worthiness of love.

TW:EA//A recent example followed the birth of my daughter. My mom seemingly dropped off the face of the earth: no nightly calls, no weekly visits, no checking in. I was sure I was imagining things; maybe mom was just busier with work or I expected too much. Four months later, when my sister had her daughter, my mom brought them meals, helped with grocery shopping, checked in, and was available. Hmph. I asked her about the disparity.

"You didn't need me to," she reasoned. I could see her point: I bounced back well from labor, and I had my cousins lined up for helping out two days a week. But at the same time, they were not my mom, and she could have still shown interest and called like she did after Sebastian's birth and all her other grandchildren. And then it came out, "I didn't feel like you needed me. I didn't feel special."

During that conversation, I tried to make her see how wanted and special she was. "You got to be in the room with me during labor," I said. "You held me up as Emersyn came out, and then you got to see her face the same instant as I did. You were the first person to hold her. How much more special can you get?" She responded that there were other people there like my cousin Anissa and the doula. The conversation ended with me feeling confused. Probably because I was gaslighted.

Now, looking back, it still confounds me that she didn't feel special, when she could not have had a more integral role and motherly experience if I had planned it. None of my siblings let her into their labor room when she dearly wanted to be, and at the other end of the spectrum, she found out hours after one of her grandchildren was born. But I didn't make her feel special enough *while I gave birth*, prompting her to not call me or visit for weeks?

I had set up a support system with my cousins, because last time, when my entire family was aware of my crippling postpartum depression, *no one came*. When I experienced PTSD and Wes begged them to help, *no one called*. When I planned my wedding, *no one talked to me*. When I broke up with Andrew, *they shunned me*. When I struggled with abuse, they *blamed me*. And when I was suicidal after being kidnapped and raped, *they ignored me*.

I have had numerous lengthy conversations with my mother about instances big and small where I felt hurt or abandoned by her. In these conversations I searched for empathy, regret, and an apology so that we could heal and have a healthy relationship. She could only tell me that I was the difficult child and that she only ever reacted to me. She felt I planned my wedding in Italy just to hurt her. She remembers how I caused her stress and pain the summer I recovered from rape. She said I was difficult when Andrew abused me, and I lashed out at her.

In her mind, I was not the victim, she was. She would deny past events or manipulate the memory until I questioned my own. My mom was unable to take responsibility for the pain she caused and turned the blame around back onto me. And I apologized. I told myself her inability to acknowledge her mistakes was because she was wrapped up in her own pain.//TW:EA

"Some people will never apologize. And the more serious the harm, the less likely that that apology will ever be forthcoming. In order to apologize a person needs a big sturdy platform of self-worth to stand on. From that higher vantage point, a person can look out at their bad behavior and they can apologize because they can see their mistakes as part of a much bigger picture of who they are as a human being. But some people stand on a small rickety platform of self-worth. They can't let themselves really *see* the hurt that they caused, because to do so would flip them, or threaten to flip them, into an identity of worthlessness and shame. The non-apologiser walks on a tight rope of defensiveness above a huge canyon of low self-esteem."

– Harriet Lerner

These words from Harriet sunk in as I sat in front of my laptop, watching TedX Talks on YouTube.

In a subsequent conversation with my mother, I gently pushed the idea of her attending therapy, given how it had helped me. She'd carried her pain for too long, and I wanted her to feel the same happiness and freedom I was feeling. She told me that the only way she was able to function and enjoy life was to push everything down below the surface, because if she allowed to let herself look at it, she wouldn't be able to survive the despair.

A unique thought came into my mind as I turned into the street leading to my mother's house: she had never been mothered. She'd told me that she was very briefly taken care of as a child before being forced at age twelve by her father to assume a more adult role as her mother struggled with mental health. My mom was never guided through life with the tenderness of a loving mother or father.

Neither her parents nor siblings helped her after she'd had her first, second, or even fifth child. They did not visit and bring comfort during any of her six miscarriages. They didn't call her or send meal trains when her husband lived on the opposite side of the world, leaving her alone to manage the household and five children ages ten to two. She was utterly alone and un-mothered.

I yearned for my mom to take care of me more as an adult. I wanted her to coddle me when I needed comfort; to notice when I needed help and then to give it generously; to help guide me into motherhood. For a long time. I felt bitter about how she seemingly stopped being my tender, loving mom who gave me hugs that fixed everything when I reached high school. I wanted and needed that relationship to continue. But I guess she was depleted after being the mom for forty years and never having a break, never having someone mother her, and not having a modern partnership with her husband. She never felt entitled to self-care, and no one else cared for her.

But in an instant. my perspective changed. And when I walked into her house, dishes from five days earlier untouched on the counter and her focused on her overwhelming job workload, I just started cleaning. I took the time to take care of her the way she needed, the way she was never taken care of before. I made dinner, brought the garbage to the street, set up her coffee for the morning, and wiped down the kitchen.

One of the hardest things for me to do is to let things be messy. I like organizing and categorizing; toy boxes are labeled with photos and words, computer files all follow the same naming convention, storage is organized in coded totes, papers are in binders or accordion files and alphabetized, and cupboards have boxes and baskets to separate based on use, purpose, or type. But people can't always be categorized.

I generally think that people are inherently kind and have good intentions until they display otherwise. Some people can be obviously placed in the demon-spawn category, like Hitler, Trump, and R. Kelly. Some people are clearly more good than bad, like MacKenzie Scott and Oprah. But others are to place.

I typically don't remain friends with people who have crossed a line—like lying about having brain cancer, ghosting me and not inviting me to their wedding after twelve years of friendship, or telling me I'm a narcissist and terrible parent. These are unsalvageable fuck-ups. Naughty list forever. (And yes, I've experienced them all.)

But what about family members? They sometimes can get away with doing and saying things that a friend wouldn't.

In this book I reveal many of the words and ways I have been hurt, abandoned, and disappointed by my family. And reading just those moments may make the relationships seem toxic and unsalvageable and very good reasons for cutting ties. But if you're looking closely enough, you'll see the same people helping with my kids, letting me move in with them during hard times, and bringing me edible arrangements. They taught me, comforted me, and corrected me. With so much complex history, it's nearly impossible to file some of these people into the good or bad category.

I'm learning to cherish the good moments and let the bad ones roll down my back and off my buttcrack. I endeavor to accept certain flaws that will never change and reject any negativity they try to bring into my life. I am beginning to accept the slights that will never be acknowledged with an apology and forgive ignorance that caused me pain. I choose to maintain these relationships. But I don't *need* them to be happy, fulfilled, or to feel love. I am learning to be all that completely on my own, which is freeing and empowering.

I will also put up with a lot of miserable bullshit for the sake of my children. Any ill feelings that a family member may have about me don't extend to them. Sebastian and Emersyn are cherished by their grandparents, celebrated by their cousins, and doted on by their aunts and uncles. My family is a grand source of love, support, and fun for my children. To take that away would require some high-level fuckery that has yet to be reached.

But by God, this is hard to do. Some days I really think things have improved and people are kinder. I think to myself, *I'm past this and I'm over it.* Then someone says something to remind me of past pain, and I realize that nothing has really changed; it's just quieter now. So why am I staying? I want to run away. Cut out the cancer and move on. Remission isn't good enough, I want it out completely. And then within a day or two, I calm down and convince myself that this level of pain is tolerable and worth the positivity that remains.

I have survived so much that I don't think anything could make me end any relationships with family members. If I need to, I will visit my parents with a book to read so I can ignore others, but I will always be there for the joy of my kids. Christmas, Easter, sleepovers, playdates—they deserve to experience these with their grandparents, aunts, uncles, and cousins. Because as easily as I could move to Italy with my husband and be completely fulfilled with new and unburdened adult relationships, there is no replacement for my kids.

I have learned to keep relationships separate and categorized. My parents' relationship with each other does not affect mine with them. And my sometimes-difficult relationship with my siblings will never affect how much I adore their children, nor how I talk about them to mine. Because I want my kids to love their wonderful aunts and uncles. They don't need to inherit my baggage.

I wish more people would take a page from this book. Don't manipulate your kids against your shitty ex— that's an adult issue. Don't victimize yourself to your children. Children aren't meant to be a sounding board, emotional regulators, or attack dogs. Bring some organization into your life and separate people into their roles—a shitty husband may be a phenomenal father, and a wonderful aunt may be a crappy sister.

We're not in a black-or-white, good-or bad-world. Everyone has strengths and flaws. If someone is more pain than gain, it's okay to move on. Just don't forget the strengths when they mess up, because that would be erasing positivity.

Even when I look at my relationship with my ex-fiance, the shittiest one of my life, I can see the good. I feel an acute sense of freedom and happiness from simple things because of him. For almost the first five years of my relationship with Wes, he drove the car maybe five percent of the time. Why? Because Andrew never let me drive and wouldn't always stop the car where or when I asked him to. Without his shittiness, I wouldn't have had five years feeling like the master of asphalt every time I drove.

I thoroughly appreciate the mundane moments of parenting with my husband, because having a calm and respectful relationship where we work as a team is satisfying when I imagine the chaos in a parallel universe parenting with that asshole. I feel grateful when I realize where I am now. I'm not thankful to him for providing that—he gets nothing. Rather I appreciate silver linings that have made me happier.

When you no longer feel like a victim of people or circumstance but a victor over pain, you've grown. And when you can forgive the ones who scorned you, you have evolved. When you can look back on your life and feel like every hardship resulted in growth, you've won. The only way to happiness is living forward.

Chapter 16 Triggered

The Friday after an intense therapy session, I became triggered during sex. Wes touched my bikini area, and I panicked. My heart and lungs grated against my ribs and air moved through my throat in short gasps. I brushed his hand away as I had often done during our years together, but now I called time out. Wes became very sensitive to my aura and gently asked me to tell him about it.

I realized in that moment I had never *really* explained my hand brushes to him. I was certain I had done so years before, but Wes explained to me he just thought I was frustrated he wasn't doing it right and had never considered I was triggered. My soul dropped and I felt terrible that he was under the impression I was brushing *him* away rather than a memory. So, I began to explain why digital stimulation triggered me.

TW:PTSD,PA,SA/ /"Andrew used to hold me

down and overstimulate me with his hands. He would aggressively rub my clitoris to try force me to orgasm, and I would beg him to stop." As the words came tumbling out of my mouth a floodgate of memories burst from a vault deep in my brain and saturated my consciousness. Flashes of Andrew hurting me sped through my mind: me clenching my thighs together to block his hand, a look of determination on his face, me trying to pull his hands away, him grabbing my wrists and pinning them above my head, me begging him to stop, him gently coaxing me to let myself come, him trapping my hands in one of his while the other assaulted me, me having trouble breathing, me trying to push him away with my legs, me crying, a look of frustration on his face.

My memories flashed to us in different beds or bathrooms, and they occurred over a course of two years. And the realization hit me: Andrew did this to me—a lot. So much that I tried many strategies to quell his moves before I successfully placated him. These were the memories I couldn't find when I wondered how I became a woman who faked orgasm to get him off me. I did fight. It just did not work. //TW:PTSD,PA,SA

Before this night, I had only one or two accessible memories of sexual assault by Andrew – the others had remained blocked. With all of these moments of assault climbing out of their hiding places I spent the rest of the night on high alert. My 'lid was flipped' and my amygdala hijacked. I lay in bed from dark until dawn in a state of panic and fear, unable to sleep. I felt intrinsically unsafe.

The following day, I went through the motions and numbly survived by burying myself in my computer and avoiding parenting when possible. My family and I spent the day at my parents' house with my sisters and their families. My children were entertained by their cousins and cared for by my husband, their grandparents, aunts, uncles, and, occasionally, me. I constantly felt under threat of attack. My body and skin felt highly sensitive and I found myself panicking each time I breastfed my daughter. My heart raced and my breath would catch. I had to unlatch her earlier than usual and Wes finished rocking her to sleep.

Once Wes started the kids' nighttime routine, I went straight to the living room and wedged myself behind the couch. I had a wall to my back and my side, and a couch against my other side. I still felt vulnerable to attack from above so I pulled my hood up and tucked my head between my knees and rocked silently. My nerves fired on all cylinders and I operated on vital instincts out of trauma-induced fear. I didn't know how to pull myself together. Primitive survival clogged my brain and left no space for thought or problem-solving.

My executive functioning was offline and I was unable to bring myself back. Soon Wes found me and looked baffled. "I don't feel safe," I said. He sat down on the floor and patiently waited for me to emerge from my cave of fear. Within ten minutes I was able to pull myself out of the corner and into his arms. His touch and voice grounded me back to the present and helped me recognize that I didn't need to fear an attack in this house. I was safe.

The panic dissipated, yet that night sleep was fleeting, and I spent many moments sitting alone in the dark beside my snoring husband. Thinking. Feeling. Processing.

The following day I felt emotionally raw and revictimized; I felt like the assaults had just happened the day before rather than years prior. As these memories came up, I took a good look and saw them for what they were: traumatic instances of sexual abuse. At the time, I never registered them as assault or rape, because I was too concerned with other factors, and honestly, I was in distress.

I never got out of a state of shock, because before it wore off, something new occurred or some other battle needed to be fought. I was often protecting my body or defending my dignity or fighting for love. I felt exhausted from constantly battling anxiety, depression, and suicidal ideation. Andrew trapped me on such a roller coaster that my focus was on simply trying to simply get through each day. Six years later, I could finally face these moments and process them.

Memories of being sexually abused so often by Andrew came as a great surprise to me. How was it possible that I never identified these instances as abuse when they occurred? In retrospect it seemed so glaringly obvious how horrible they were, yet I don't remember bringing it up to Andrew, or even thinking about it the day after. We just moved on.

Wait, now that I think of it, I remember how these abusive episodes typically ended: with me begging Andrew to stop and him flippantly giving up. Instead of feeling violated, I felt guilty and ashamed for not being able to reach orgasm. I didn't bring it up the following day, because the lingering feelings were connected to how I'd disappointed Andrew and not how he hurt me.

TW:PTSD,SA,EA//Memories of assault and rape continued to flood my brain throughout the day. Like the time I woke up in the middle of the night to him kissing me and attempting to penetrate me. How long had he been doing this before I noticed? I turned to him and kissed him back. At this point I knew the only answer was yes, so we finished what he had started.

The next morning, I said, "You know I was asleep

right?" He responded with, "No, *I was* asleep, I can't believe you! I woke up to you having sex with me. I mean it was fine but…'

Bile swirled up my throat. Did I really have sex with him while he was sleeping? *NO, YOU DIDN'T RACHEL. He was just fucking with you. He assaulted* you *in your sleep.* But I believed him and I felt disgusting and terrible. From that point forward, I learned to sleep lighter when we shared a bed, and when he turned to me with an erection in the middle of the night, I snapped awake and ready. And I made sure he looked at me and spoke before anything happened. There was no way I was going to let myself take advantage of him while he slept again. *Vomit.*//TW:PTSD/SA/EA

As you can see, Andrew was a master gaslighter. After he slung an insult at me, he would misdirect my reaction by giggling as if he just said the funniest little quippy tease he had ever heard, and he was delighted it came from his miraculous brain. He had an adorable and infectious laugh, like a young schoolboy. It was hard to look at him in a menacing light with that giggle as a follow-up.

When I'd get upset, he would coo over the phone, "Honey, why don't you just go to bed. You're unreasonably emotional and you know you'll be fine in the morning after you get some sleep." And he was right. I'd hang up, calm myself down, and placate my mind with music or videos until I could sleep. And by the time I woke up, I didn't bother bringing up the fight, because it was much less exhausting to just move on.

If I reacted to an insult, he would say I was hangry and needed a snack—like I was a cranky toddler who couldn't regulate emotion. *That fucker.*

Andrew was financially controlling and mentally,

emotionally, physically, and sexually abusive. There, I said it! Plain as day. He chipped away at me until I became a shell of a person existing only to suit his needs.

TW:EA//The emotional abuse began with subtle jabs towards me—"jokes" that he would follow with a delighted giggle and a condescending comment telling me to lighten up. His easy laughter and demeanor made me question my emotional reaction: Was I taking him too seriously? Should I just lighten up and join the joke? Are his words a big deal?

But eventually, those comments evolved to more striking insults which came from a place of malice.

He would spit out that I looked like the Michelin Man, Stay-Puft Marshmallow Man, or the Pillsbury Doughboy when I wore sweatpants or hoodies. He'd say that I should dress like that sexy woman in the pencil-skirt across the street. I was "disgusting," "greasy," and I needed to shower. I was a dirty slut and his little whore. I didn't need dessert, I was chunky, chubby, fat, and I might as well rest my stomach on the table.

He said I was an immature, embarrassing, illogical, drama queen. That I was too dumb to follow a storyline, and too stupid and incapable to manage my own money or phone. After any public outing or event with friends, he'd list ways I'd embarrassed him, scolding me my while my cheeks grew hot with shame.

He hated when I wore my hair in a ponytail, because he said it made me look bald and like a boy; my hair must be blond, long, and down. He hated when I wore sweatshirts or sweatpants—God forbid I ever wore both at the same time! My clothes must be tight and revealing (even though he insulted my body so much). Andrew did not allow me to drink alcohol. I must visit him. I wasn't allowed to drive.

I never felt comfortable spending time on anything for myself, because free time was meant for him. I gave up sports. He said my architecture school was full of stuck-up, artsy snobs, and that I was different from them and better than them. He said I shouldn't hang out with them, so he refused to hang out with me when I was with them. If I began connecting with a new friend, Andrew said I shouldn't hang out with them because they were dumb, flaky, or immature, and that I was better.

He would withhold affection and break dates with me, which left me completely alone, because he'd made any friendship I had so difficult. He never wanted to visit me, always making me take the bus to visit him and his friends. He refused to visit my school, isolating me from classmates by removing me during the weekend and shaming any relationship I forged.

I'd tell him that he hurt my feelings. I would cry. At first, he seemed empathetic, but then would stay on the phone with me and ignore my tears as he did his homework. By the end, he was distant, unsympathetic. He would say he was sorry with a hollow voice, then force himself to be kind for a week or two.//TW:EA

A few months before the breakup, he stopped even pretending to change or apologize. He even went so far as to admit his plan of isolation and control once he married me. He fantasized out loud how he would control finances, and that I would not be able to purchase unapproved food or clothes. He was going to throw out all my comfy or ugly clothes. He looked forward to having me alone in Seattle, away from my family. *Run, Rachel, RUN!*

It took me a few days to emerge from the fog of emotional exhaustion after reliving my abuse, feeling threatened by it, returning to a place of safety, and processing it. When I broke through to the other side, I felt lighter; the trauma had left my body and I felt a change. The days with my children felt easier as my tolerance for adversity increased. The more trauma I freed from within, the easier everything else felt. This connection of going through pain to heal and free myself made me feel incredibly empowered. I became determined to release the story of Andrew, so I could truly move on.

One day I opened up to my friend Flor over text about the kids and our health regimes. I explained that I had worked out much less during the previous three weeks, because exhaustion flattened me from all the processing I accomplished through therapy. She made a very lovely and thoughtful suggestion to put all my memories and feelings into a box, then have a ceremony to bury it.

I explained that although I appreciated her suggestion, I had already tried to box up my past and hide it from my conscious self. It didn't work. For years, I avoided processing my relationship with Andrew, which left my trauma unchecked and able to resurface when triggered. If forgetting was so easy, I would have done it years ago. I explained to her that I felt largely recovered from the financial, verbal, mental, and emotional abuse. It was the sexual abuse that I still grappled with.

I didn't go into detail about the sexual abuse, but I did share some stories about the verbal abuse. I shared a photo Andrew took of me on a trip to Florida during spring break. In the photo I was walking across the horizon, smiling in the glow of the sunset with the wind blowing my hair and white sand sprinkled all over my feet. The woman in the photo simply glowed.

I explained to Flor that I had chosen to wear a one-piece bathing suit that day, because Andrew had made me feel like I needed to cover my fat body. He then later complained that I looked like a prudish old lady because I wasn't wearing a bikini. She said, "You look skinny and fit," and I agreed with her.

"This photo is a reminder for me to never let anyone make me feel unbeautiful. To love my body no matter what, because one day in the future, I don't want to look back and see a beautiful woman and wish I had loved myself more."

Our conversation left me in a funk. I aimlessly walked around the house unsure of what to do with myself. I resisted the urge to eat comfort food as I had done of late, and instead sat on the front porch listening to traffic. Back inside Wes had just finished the last meeting of his workday and asked me if everything was all right. I indicated Flor and I had been talking about my previous relationship.

"I just feel sad that I went through that, I said. "I want to have some wine and just be sad about my abuse tonight."

Wes was on board. He would get the wine after the kids fell asleep, and we would sulk together on the couch. We ate dinner with the kids, and when they scurried off to play, Wes and I spoke about adult topics.

"I wish there was a step-by-step process that if I followed I would be healed and never be affected by my trauma again." Wes took my lament as a request for help. He then decided to mansplain something he knew nothing about, making me feel like he was frustrated with how I "let" Andrew take up so much of my energy. *Yes, folks, my lovely Wes sometimes makes mistakes too, like everyone.*

I was not having any of it. "Andrew's not taking any of my time and energy. *Healing myself* is taking my time and energy. I spend a lot, if not most, of my time and energy taking care of the kids, the house, you, and all the other people I care about. Me trying to heal from my trauma is spending energy on *me*, not Andrew." He didn't seem to agree, so I explained with a metaphor.

"If someone stabs me and I go to the hospital for help and a doctor stiches me up and gives me antibiotics, which I take every day to prevent infection, and I change the dressings and clean the wound, I'm doing all that work to heal from the stab wound. I'm not doing all that work focusing and wasting my energy on the knife."

"What I'm saying is I think Andrew is more like a tattoo," Wes said.

"What's that supposed to mean? Well, then, I'm getting a tattoo removed."

Wes was essentially saying the same thing my family had said since I started therapy at eighteen years old: Stop wasting your time and energy in a pity party with your past. I don't remember all the words I said, but I took the time to explain to Wes how he made me feel and where he was wrong. I pointed out he had never been raped, had not researched or even thought about recovering from that kind of trauma, and had no place mansplaining how I should "stop letting Andrew take my energy." If I could "drop it" and "move on," I would have done so long ago.

"Do you think I enjoy being triggered?"

"No, of course not. I can see how this is difficult for you."

"So why are you acting like I'm not helping myself? You've just communicated to me that you are not a safe person to be vulnerable with, because you're judging me."

Wes began apologizing, and I challenged him.

"What are you even apologizing for? Have you spent a second thinking about what you just said to me and how it affects me? I'm going upstairs to brush my teeth."

"I'll apologize when you come down."

After I brushed my teeth and changed into some

comfy clothes, I came downstairs, retrieved my laptop from the counter, filled my glass of water, and got into my favorite spot on the couch. Wes sat down beside me.

"I'm sorry, I don't want to be like your family and leave you in this alone," he said. "I want you to be able to come to me and talk to me about these things. I just heard your question and took it literally and tried to give you a solution when I should have just listened. I shouldn't have said that, and I'm sorry."

"It's not about you saying it; now I know what you think. You think that I'm giving my energy to Andrew. You think that you know more than me about my relationship with Andrew, but I've been thinking about this for over twelve years. How long have you been thinking about it?"

"Definitely not twelve years."

"Right, so don't try and explain to me how I should feel and how I should heal unless you've done extensive research, which we both know you haven't."

I felt misunderstood, a feeling I had grappled with since I began dating Andrew. I lived in this alternate reality that no one who surrounded me acknowledged. I was isolated in my trauma with no one who could relate to my experience, let alone handle a conversation where I shared details.

When I dated Andrew, I felt obligated to present a false reality in order to preserve our relationship and the image we conjured about our dynamic. After Andrew, my family silenced me with denial about abuse, and once they finally came around to believing me, they expected me to be "past it." I suppressed my story for the comfort of others. Not only did people not want to hear about it, but I felt that no one could handle the truth.

"1. Our capacity to destroy one another is matched by our capacity to heal one another. Restoring relationships and community is central to restoring well-being; 2. Language gives us the power to change ourselves and others by communicating our experiences, helping us to define what we know, and finding a common sense of meaning. When we ignore these quintessential dimensions of humanity, we deprive people of ways to heal from trauma and restore their autonomy. Being a patient, rather than a participant in one's healing process, separates suffering people from their community and alienates them from an inner sense of self."

—Dr. Bessel van der Kolk

Part of my recovery required me to start having conversations with the people I surrounded myself with and to open up about my experience, so I could feel seen and we could coexist in the same dimension. I found this a very daunting task, so instead I avoided it and began to write the story of my relationship with Andrew. I found writing therapeutic, and it helped me process my memories and emotions.

I tried to write so that my words would conjure in the reader the emotions I was feeling; I needed them to *feel* how *I* felt. I double-processed my past, editing and elaborating. Analyzing my words and my story allowed me to distance myself from my internal struggles and process them objectively as art.

In a roundabout way, I planned on writing a memoir and sharing my story with friends, loved ones, and strangers alike without having to be in the same room as them. This way, I couldn't be interrupted, insulted, denied, or dismissed and told to leave it in the past. If people didn't believe me, they could scoff to themselves in the dim silence of their reading lamp. I could evict a memory from my brain and leave my pain in my writing.

Sometimes I wonder if have lied to myself, purposely forgetting all the good to justify my claims of abuse. I wondered if I'd written with complete honesty or just overemphasized the negative to victimize myself. *I'm sure that's how Andrew would see it.* If he ever read this, he would be shocked. He likely never viewed himself as abusive. He likely never thought about me being trauma-bonded to him or having lasting effects from his words and actions.

Abusers don't look like the villains portrayed in movies and television shows. In reality, they are layered and nuanced, incredibly vulnerable and insecure. Andrew was a wonder with words; a real wordsmith. He had the ability to enter my heart in both good and bad ways. He could bring me to soaring heights with compliments when he was happy or needed to make up for things and shatter me with insecurities when he felt upset or inferior.

In first-year university, I walked by this boutique dress shop in historic Galt Cambridge any time I went to the bus stop or to get a snack at Coffee Cultures. Every time I walked down Main Street, I would slow down my step as I strolled past the boutique and ogle the gorgeous dresses on the window mannequin. But I didn't dare step in the store for weeks. In November, I finally received my Ontario student loan check, and I felt rich so I went into the store to buy a special-occasion dress.

I ended up buying a designer dress: a more conservative but ethereal black dress with gold embellishments. It was ankle length with a deep v-neck, elbow-length sleeves, and empire waist. Gold lace scallops adorned the edge of the skirt, sleeves, waist, and neckline.

The dress made me feel like a Spartan goddess right from the movie *300* and it really made my hazel eyes turn into this light golden-caramel color. I waited for months for an occasion to wear my goddess dress.

Finally, in March I had an excuse: Andrew's musical performance. He had auditioned then practiced all year in the musical, written and run by engineering students. He played trombone in the band and acted in some small roles. My family and I went to Florida for March break, but I had convinced them all to cut the trip a day early, so I could catch his show. My parents even bought tickets and came along.

The day of the play, I had been in the car for eighteen hours, took a short break at my parents' to gussy up, then drove another hour and a half to watch Andrew's performance and support what he had worked on all year. I carefully applied makeup and did my hair, and I wore my goddess dress. I walked into the theatre and quickly met up with Andrew's parents. Soon we found seats and settled in for the show, expecting a clumsy student production.

We were all quite surprised to be laughing throughout the musical performance. By the end we unanimously agreed it was an impressive production. The group of us hung out in the foyer waiting for the prodigal son to appear. Andrew eventually strolled in from side stage and asked us what we thought. We all fawned over him with praise and compliments about the show as he casually agreed and emphasized how he was also so impressed with his group of engineering-student peers. *So humble.*

Once the crowd started to dissipate, we headed to the parking lot. A male student gave me an obvious glance up and down and said to his buddy, "Look at her. Oh, she knows she has those eyes." I smiled inwardly as I anticipated a similar reaction from my boyfriend once we left his parents' earshot. TW:EA//Rather he said disdainfully, "What are you *wearing*?" Then he giggled and said, "You look like a pilgrim. Where did you get that?"

I looked at his feet and said, "Oh, I really liked this dress. I thought it was beautiful." He scoffed at me.

"It's so long, and these sleeves make you look like an old lady."//TW:EA

I had felt beautiful—the best I could look, then with his words I felt like Cinderella with her carefully made dress torn to rags. We walked in the chilly dark of the parking lot now headed to the car.

"Are you coming with us or staying?" my dad asked.

"Come back to my room with me," Andrew said. So, I did. After we got settled into Andrew's dorm room, he informed me that he would leave soon to go a party with the cast members to celebrate their accomplishment.

"Can I come? I haven't really seen you all week, and I just drove eighteen hours to be here." *You asked me to be here.*

"Apparently, it's cast-and-crew only, no one else, not even significant others allowed." My words abandoned me for a moment before I pushed Andrew a little further. But he reiterated his intentions to go without me. He was not going to break the rules to bring me along, nor did he seem to want me to come with him. TW:EA//He made me feel inappropriate for asking, and like a stage-five clinger all at once. *Why did he ask me to come back to his room with him then? So now I'm the needy girlfriend without boundaries, because I expected to see him when he invited me to hang out?*//TW:EA

After Andrew left, his roommate and my friend, Greg, stepped up to entertain me for the evening. He was into the drinking culture of first year and convinced me to try his new party starter: breathe in a hit of weed from his volcano digital vaporizer, then drink a shot of 151-proof rum before exhaling. He egged me into the challenge, and did I it twice. Two hits of pot and two shots was all I needed to have my head spinning off my neck and careening onto the floor.

Less than an hour later I pressed my back into the corner of a dorm, holding myself against the wall so I wouldn't spin out of control and bounce around the room. At some point I rested my hand on Greg's thigh, but other than that I did not remember much about the evening. Andrew returned to find me in the corner and helped me back into his room so I could rest.

The next morning, Andrew acted completely pissed off at me for leaving his room, drinking, doing pot, hanging out with other guys, and, I presume, putting my hand on Greg's thigh. He accused me of being disrespectful to him and trying to seduce Greg. He sent me back to Cambridge on the first bus he could get me on.

TW:EA//For the next four days, he didn't respond to my texts or answer my phone calls. He gave me the silent treatment, which I now know is a form of emotional abuse. I left him multiple messages, saying how sorry I felt and groveling for his love. I even cried while singing our *Cuppycake Song* on his answering machine. *Vomit.* By Wednesday, I felt desperate for him to forgive me so I made a plan to makeup for my perceived indiscretions.

After I had my design-studio critique on Thursday, I took the first bus to Hamilton with bags of food in tow. I brought enough to make him an epic tray of nachos using the dorm floor's kitchen. He barely looked at me and spoke in short sentences, clearly annoyed. But then he was nice enough in front of Greg as they both enjoyed the nachos I carefully crafted. Andrew seemed as if he had come around and forgave me.

When Greg left, we started fooling around and ended up going to the bathroom for privacy in case Greg came back. In my mind, we were having some passionate makeup sex, but after we finished Andrew spat out that he was still completely pissed at me.

I felt betrayed. I felt like he pretended to be something just so he could get laid. I told him I thought he had forgiven me and was over it. He made it clear what we just had was angry sex and he had not absolved me. My gut churned from deception. How long did I need to grovel? I cried for an hour as we sat on the shower floor letting the water rain down on us. He finally spoke to me kindly imploring if I'd learned my lesson. I did.//TW:EA

I remembered that day with such hurt, pain, and embarrassment. Years later he remembered that shower with fondness and spoke of how he felt so close to me. He spent days breaking me down to a heap of sadness on the dirty dorm shower floor. His triumph of control started a downward spiral into an abusive relationship. He smiled as I cried.

The fragmented mind

Defiance
Betrayal
A hit to the face
Smiling
Stroking
Held in your embrace

The Bees

Your words
Melting my heart and soul
Your words
Breaking me in pieces

As I fall to the floor
Your empty eyes seem to roll
Empathy gone
I know I'm truly alone
Until you hold me again
And kiss me up and down my body
Then pin my hands against the pillow
As moans turn into cries
The only wetness seeps from my eyes
I beg you to stop causing me pain
Your off me and at the door
Angry I couldn't give you more
My fear turns into guilt and shame
I apologize and whisper your name

Your back stiffens as you walk away
I know I should leave, but only want you to stay
Beside me
In our tangled embrace

Call me fat
Call me a whore
Treat me like dirt
And then ask me for more

I'll give you my heart
I'll gift you my body
I'll lose my mind for you
And then

The Bees

You'll get bored

You'll find new adventures
And leave me behind
Then beckon me when it gets hard
And I'll jump back in your car

I'll forgive you endlessly
With unconditional love
Clean for you, cook for you
Dress how you want
Say the right words
Be the blonde you can flaunt

You'll take and you'll take
Until I have nothing left to give
You'll deplete my self-worth
Doing what it takes just to live
I'll cling to your compliments
Every time my body hurts.

You'll tell me I'm broken
And there's no one else
Who will put up with me
And my crazy emotions
You love me
And I'll believe you

You'll say I'm illogical
Make me doubt what occurred
Make me question my feelings
My sanity, my worth.

So I'll get help to get fixed
Find a doctor who deals with brokenness
Bend to your pleasure
Because we're soulmates you said.

Pills and therapy
Curb nothing of our insanity
Because nothing could fix
The pain you kept causing me

I'll ask you to stop and
Explain why it hurts
You'll apologize and kiss me
Make me feel like the luckiest on earth
Until
You hurt
Me
Again

And that's how we lived
For six years
It's been seven since
Memories haunt me
Coming back in fragments

Is this how you wanted me
The first time we kissed?

Remembering these moments years later while in a
healthy relationship with the support of a therapist allowed
me to see them with a different perspective. I had the
ability to locate the abuse and be angry for the way he
mistreated me. I had the distance to decipher his
gaslighting and put blame where it should have always

been. I learned to give myself grace for the person I was during survival mode. The way I behaved as a woman in crisis was completely different from the way I was behaving as a woman in a stable, loving relationship.

Now I'm able to give myself love and empathy for what I endured. I have let go of the shame and guilt and forgiven myself for letting him push my boundaries until he overtook me completely. I was only seventeen when we met. I deserved better. He was only seventeen too. He should have been taught better.

I hope he has grown as much as I have. Now he should *know* better. I hope he treats his wife with all the magic and love she deserves, and that I was the only woman he will abuse. I am healing, which leaves no room for revenge. What I have is love and positivity; I hope he has learned from his mistakes with me. I certainly have learned from my mistakes with him.

The Bees

Chapter 17 Unchained

I just realized my biggest fear: losing myself. Falling back into the shell of a person I was when Andrew abused me. I'm scared of putting my heart in someone's hands and having them poke holes in it, or them dying and obliterating me in the grief of loss.

I was afraid that if I lowered my guard of strength and independence that I'd built, I would expose myself to near-certain, insurmountable world-crushing pain. Whether it would be pain from betrayal, or pain from loss, I did not know if I could survive again.

As I began to settle into the Strathroy area and pandemic restrictions lifted I opened up to the idea of building a community around our family by putting myself out there to create new bonds and friendships. Every once in a while, I would go for a walk with the mother of one of my son's friends.

As therapy exposed my past, I began to feel more able to share with others. This woman I walked with had experienced abuse in a relationship and I felt safe telling her things I had only told my therapist. She could handle real talk, because she had lived through something similar and something worse.

One Sunday during our dewy morning stroll, I opened up to her about the struggles during sex following such a long tenure of unhealthy sexual experiences of coercion, assault, abuse, and rape.

Let me preface by explaining that Wes was an incredibly safe, kind, and generous person. During my pregnancy and after giving birth he was so appreciative and respectful of my body transformation that he never once asked for sex. (So much so I started wondering if he was interested anymore.)

When I brought up our love life, Wes emphatically responded about how attractive he still found me and loved having a physical connection with me. He said he did not require sex to stay faithful and loving, and he did not want to push me during my transitional time, because sex was not a priority. Holding hands, kissing, and dancing in the kitchen was where life was those days. He was a grown man.

Wes had gone longer stretches without sex between relationships and he knew other physical connection could maintain love. I thoroughly appreciated this sentiment and have never felt pressure to do anything with him when I didn't feel in the mood or felt uncomfortable in my body. He was sensitive to my needs and for a long time relied on me to make the first move, because he never wanted to put me in a position of obligatory sex.

I want to emphasize how wonderful my husband was with his attitude surrounding sex. All my negative reactions during sex existed because of previous trauma and abuse that I struggled to keep at bay. For the first six years of our relationship, I fought internal battles against triggers and negative self-talk during eighty percent of our sexual encounters.

The other twenty percent was romping wild fun with no negative intrusive thoughts about my body, no feeling of dread washing over me, and no panic-stricken moments. But during that eighty percent, I would have to internally fight back negative thoughts about my body and appearance, or I would have to internally repeat the mantra, *You are safe, you are with Wes,* whenever I felt panicked or his hands suddenly felt like someone else's.

I told my new friend that the only way I could avoid triggers during sex was when I took complete control. Wes only touched non-triggering spots, and I choose the positions and the pace. It had worked until this point, but I wanted better. I wanted to deepen my connection with my husband and allow him to do things I had denied to him—simple things, like touching my bikini area.

For my entire sexual life, I had either been sexually abused or fending off triggers during sex. Twelve years: five abused and seven with PTSD. What that looked like in my brain was enjoying a moment with my husband, and then suddenly his hands felt like my ex's, or body insults would plague my thoughts, or fear stormed around in my guts like a tornado sucking the air down out of my lungs, spinning my intestines, and twisting my stomach.

Some days, my body suddenly became very sensitive, and anything touching my skin irritated me. Or the air in the room would thin out and move away from me, making me claustrophobic. In these moments, I always worked to ground myself back to the present by repeating a mantra and taking in my surroundings with different senses.

Wes and I felt sex was an important way for us to

connect and enjoy each other. Part of me had a hard time letting go of the idea that if my husband and I didn't physically connect often, he would stray. Once I banished that thought, I still pushed myself to stay intimate even when I had an off week or month. I refused to let triggers ruin sex for life. So, when these moments popped up in the middle of intimacy, I powered through until I returned to the present.

I also wanted the striking fear when I approached orgasm to just *fuck off*. Andrew aggressively tried to *make* me orgasm, and whenever I got close, he doubled-down with pressure and persistence. He got rougher with me and caused me pain. This happened so often that my body associated approaching orgasm with pain and abuse. So much so that I needed to be in control of *everything* in order to not spiral into a panic attack and shut down.

My friend came up with two wonderful suggestions: "Start slowly by holding his hand and moving it around your body so that you are still in control but beginning the process of letting him touch triggering areas." She also said I needed to learn to please myself without Wes in the room. *That's right, she was telling me to masturbate.*

I was a thirty-year-old woman who had never successfully masturbated. I purchased the vibrator she and my mommy blog recommended and I took Latoya for a spin. The first few times, I felt very self-conscious and shameful, even though I was alone. I felt timid to have such strong vibrations and worried about overstimulation and triggers. After about two weeks of learning and getting comfortable with my own body, I noticed a change.

In conjunction with therapy and having numerous big-O moments solo, the fear that made my body coil into the fetal position evaporated. Triggers during sex dissipated, and it has been *months* since I had internal battles or had to repeat my mantra to ground myself in the present. *I am now the master of my own body, and it feels incredible.*

I learned to explore my body and enjoy touch again. Basically, I turned into a horny teenager who had discovered that their body contained a fun toy, and I made up for all the times I endured pleasureless sex. Wes found my sneaking off and "new hobby" quite amusing. He understood and cheered me on. *Yas, Queen! Get your O's!*

The more I mastered-bation the less I understood any person who would pressure a partner for sex. There were so many toy options in this world; *just play with yourself. Love yourself. Your partner does not feel like an orgasm today? Cool. Take care of yourself, no sex needed.*

(Over a year later while editing this book, now on its third draft, I still have not had one trigger. It's like a switch flipped. *Fourth draft, still no triggers during sex!* Let's keep it going. Final draft and still all good!)

During this transitional time, my children were at the age where they fixated on a select few things. My son was completely absorbed with Lego and movie nights had consisted of a rotation of five movies all year: *The Croods*, *Penguins of Madagascar*, *Frozen*, *Frozen II*, and *Moana*. After months and months of these films, *I felt like I was becoming Elsa.*

I would be puttering around the house cleaning as the kids played and would randomly break into song and dance: "Let it go, let it go, can't hold me back anymore." The kids joined me and my one-year-old daughter sang in her tiny voice while my son twirled like a ballerina. *This is my jam.* I felt like I embodied the Queen of Arendelle.

"It's funny how some distance makes everything seem small, and the fear that once controlled me can't get to me at all. It's time to see what I can do to test the limits and break through, no rights nor wrongs no rules for me: I'M FREE!"

After months of no triggers, no intrusive memories, and no nightmares haunting me all day, life felt like a breeze. *This is what it's like to live a trauma-free life. This is what it's like to move forward. Hallelujah!*

"And one thought crystalizes like an icy blast, I'm never going back, the past is in the PASSSSSSSST! Let it go, let it go when I'll rise like the break of dawn.... Here I am, in the light of day."

Driving alone on the highway, I would belt out the lyrics. *It's my freedom song.* Through months of therapy, self-reflection, tenacity, and grit, I had made it through the dark night—finally.

At the beginning of therapy, Epione wanted to try an exercise with me that she thought would help me unlock my trauma in a safe way. She directed me to close my eyes and imagine a room with two doors. She wanted me to allow memories, things, or people to pass through one door and out the other. She imagined I would feel at a safe distance to view my trauma. *Except that I'd put myself into the room.*

What came in was an abstract feeling, a deep, sinister darkness that caused me to press myself into the wall and hold my breath until the memory, thing, or person exited through the other door. This dark was the unknown; my repressed memories. I did not dare release the trauma in my body. Like my mother, who feared what would happen to her and who she may fall into if she opened the door to the room in her head, I also feared my past. Epione thought it was interesting that I put myself in the room, into harm's way, to protect myself.

Not only was *Frozen* phenomenal for its storyline and "Let It Go," but also for the song, "Into the

Unknown". *I know I know, I'm not really Elsa—but hear me
out.* Songs are most successful when they have transferable
meaning that can be held against a multitude of experiences
and trigger a response.

> I can hear you but I won't
> Some look for trouble
> While others don't
> There's a thousand reasons
> I should go about my day
> And ignore your whispers
> Which I wish would go away
> You're not a voice
> You're just ringing in my ear
> And if I heard you, which I don't
> I'm spoken for I fear
> Everyone I've ever loved is here within these
> walls
> I'm sorry, secret siren, but I'm blocking out
> your calls
> I've had my adventure, I don't need something
> new
> I'm afraid of what I'm risking if I follow you
> Into the unknown
> What do you want?
> 'Cause you've been keeping me awake
> Are you here to distract me
> So I make a big mistake?
> Or are you someone out there
> Who's a little bit like me?
> Who knows deep down
> I'm not where I'm meant to be?
> Every day's a little harder
> As I feel my power grow

Don't you know there's part of me
That longs to go
Into the unknown   - Elsa

I feared confronting the unknown memories and trauma; I wanted the dreams, triggers, intrusive memories, and body haunts to just disappear on their own. I did not want to risk the life I had built with Wes and my children to respond to my past. I had gone through enough and did not need any more emotionally difficult years. But the unknown was what would occur if I did confront those unknown memories and trauma.

Yet there was a part of me that deeply wanted to heal and get stronger. Some voice inside me told me that life could get better. My story needed to be released—my lioness scream. *We can't let fear hold us back from peace and resolution, though, can we?*

During my first salon appointment in university after moving away from home, my hairdresser gasped when I walked in as he prodded my head in disbelief. My fried hair was like straw, and riddled with split ends. I had a naturopath, therapists, and doctor trying to figure out the causes of my bloating, ulcers, muscle tension, and severe constipation. I took vitamins and Metamucil, ate all-bran cereal, and waited to get a colonoscopy and gastroscopy two-in-one dream appointment. My whole body screamed, *Help me!*

I looked in the mirror at my gray face with deep under-eye circles and creased forehead with my hair in foils. *Andrew's right; I am ugly without my hair down. To be fair though, all hairdressing studios have the worst light.*

I chattered with my hairdresser about school and boys as he removed the foils and washed out my hair. Then he sat me in the chair and gave me the news. "Your hair is in bad shape. To get to the good stuff, we will have to cut about five inches off the bottom. Once I do that, it'll have a much better chance at having good growth and returning to a better state." I held back tears and agreed, cringing with every snip. I left the appointment that day with my arms grasping over a hundred dollars' worth of hair-treatment shampoos and conditioners. None of which were the solution to the *actual* problem.

Every few months, I had a quarterly appointments day when my husband watched the children and did all of the things in twelve hours. This day, I had a massage appointment, chiropractor appointment, hair appointment, and a trip into the city to return and exchange some cabinetry from IKEA.

At my massage appointment the therapist noted a remarkable difference in my body compared to my last appointment. She even mentioned that I looked brighter and seemed spiritually lighter as I walked to the room. She could sense a change in my entire being. My body had begun to heal, and *I loved it*.

The regular muscle tension my body had changed from the previous thirteen years. Since I started experiencing trauma and abuse at the hands of my ex-boyfriend, my back had always been a solid block of muscle—an impossible challenge to completely massage out in a session. After the last few months of feeling like I'd been able to release my trauma (and having oh so many orgasms) my back had very few issues, and my therapist moved on to my lower body quite quickly.

My legs used to be sore to the touch, but that day she massaged them down through all the muscle layers without any cringing pain. She was able to go through all the layers of muscle in my glutes, which were usually locked out. They felt completely released by the end of the session.

My body had begun to relax. I'd finally exited the fight/flight/freeze response!

The release of the trauma and the heaviness of the load I carried—the burden of sadness—dissipated and left me melting in happiness.

At my hair appointment, my stylist that I had been going to for about three years noticed another improvement in my hair. It felt softer, smoother, and less damaged than it ever had before. She barely needed to cut half an inch off the ends. She also showed me the section at the back of my neck of new growth hair: little wisps of beautiful redemption. My whole body was rejuvenating.

I felt like everything was real. Sort of like the Velveteen Rabbit. So many times, I had doubted if everything that happened was REAL. I doubted my trauma, doubted my memory, doubted my pain. But the way I was healing, growing, and relaxing because I had no one to fight anymore just reassured me that *it was all real.*

I had become so strong that instead of letting my past keep me hard and make me push away love or hurt others in defense of myself, I had learned to be softer, both mentally and physically. (As had the wisps on the back of my neck!)

A wash of happiness moved through me, and I felt intense gratitude that I had the opportunity to face the darkness I was scared to allow into my mind. I felt fortunate to be at a point in life where I felt so secure with my environment that I could look at the scariest, darkest things in my world and not fall into a trap of sadness and pity or pain and isolation. Not everyone gets to survive what I have. *I am so lucky.*

At the end of the day, while I drove home under the cotton-candy sky smiling to myself, I listened to Moana and enjoyed the scenery in the golden light. The wildflowers bloomed with tiny white-and-purple florets from the deep green that only rose midsummer, bumble bees hummed calmly with their work, and feathered grass blew gently in the wind. I felt so privileged to drive on a six-lane highway where the roadside disappeared into a euphoric painting.

> "I have crossed the horizon to find you
> I know your name
> They have stolen the heart from inside you
> But this does not define you
> This is not who you are
> You know who you are"   —Moana

I surpassed my perceived limits to find myself, and now I know who I am. People assaulted, neglected, abused, and abandoned me. The way I survived my pain and acted during my years of abuse does not define me. I am not my trauma. Even if others choose not to see the woman I have grown into, I know who I am. I am a beautiful, strong human.

The Bees

Chapter 18 – Seattle

Trigger Warning:
This chapter contains: sexual and physical abuse (pages 298-299).
Please be kind to yourself and respect your personal limits. If you would like to
forgo these triggering scenes you may read a summary on page 325.

Remember when I told you I started running fifteen seconds at a time? Well, it might not have seemed important at the time, but it is, so let's talk about it.

By the end of our Covid summer, I comfortably ran about four to four-and-a-half kilometers in thirty minutes; not even close to my personal best, but a huge improvement for my physical health. When we bought our house, I stopped running due to the amount of work I was doing in other areas of my life. But after the holidays, I was determined to get back on track when some of those fifty pounds I'd lost started creeping back. *Not cool.*

I was ready to give myself a tangible goal. I had wanted to run a marathon since high school, but things always got in the way: architecture school workload, abuse, being pregnant, and having miscarriages, to name a few. I was finally in a place where I could tackle this goal. Wes was on board to support me.

I sectioned out my goal into race intervals: five kilometers, ten kilometers, half-marathon, and marathon. I chose a six-week program to get me to five kilometers and followed it religiously, tracking my workouts and times. This was during my most strenuous weeks of therapy, and I used my runs to work off the emotions—specifically, anger—that coursed through me. I found myself getting sore and feeling generally unwell. I completed my training set and ran my five-kilometer "race" with the finish line at my parents' driveway, but I had ramped up my training too quickly, putting too much on my joints, as I still carried extra weight.

At this point, I decided to double my training periods. Instead of taking eight weeks to work up to a ten-kilometer race, I took sixteen. And I needed to lower my expectations of speed and recovery—I wasn't a high-schooler anymore, and I wasn't going to run ten kilometers in under sixty minutes. I was an old biddy now, and I needed to roll out muscles and stretch. *These things take time.*

I ran my ten-kilometer "race" with the support of my family at the end of June. My sister and older brother both ran a shorter race, and my younger brother and cousins walked the ten kilometers. I finished in my parents' driveway with my husband taking photos and my cheering children holding a finish tape. Even though the heat and humidity made me run slower than I'd planned, I gave myself a pat on the back for completing the distance.

My next goal was a half-marathon (twenty-one kilometers). With my training program, I figured I would be ready to complete this goal by mid-to-late November. I searched races during that time period and then looked at their locations and course elevations. I wanted a flat, easy course for my first half-marathon and longest race thus far.

Seattle. The city that left a dark spot on the map. The city he owned. The city which only contained memories of intense loneliness and confusion. I mean, *it had a really flat course*, it had a big attendance and lots of hype, and I did love the architecture.

You know what? Fuck it. He doesn't own *that city. That's* my *city, I'm taking it back.* I floated the idea to Wes. He was confused as to why I wanted to go back. Honestly, I was a little, too. Something inside me said it would be constructive. I needed to remove that black spot from the map. I needed to balance out those harsh memories with some good ones.

I wanted to own Seattle, and more than me wanting to own it, I just didn't want Andrew to have anything over me anymore. Not me, not a memory, and definitely not an entire city. I wanted to prove to myself that I had healed, and I had grown so far past Andrew that I could visit his city and be unaffected, untriggered, and unplagued by memories.

I wanted to enjoy Seattle as I wished I had been able to the last time I went. That meant not feeling nervous and anxious the whole time, watching how I ate, obsessing about how I looked, and worrying about how the night would end. I just wanted to *be*. To exist in that city freely. *Does that make sense?*

Some may look at my trip to Seattle and say I was a glutton for misery, or that I had a penchant for pain. But I was just trying to rid myself of another layer of my past. The more trauma I shed, the closer I came to the core of my being.

I trained all summer with great dedication and delight. I felt fit and healthy. Even though I thought I looked the same in the mirror, my pant size had dropped from a size eighteen when I started running to a size ten. I didn't feel like a looked like a size ten. I remember asking a sales clerk, "Is your size ten the same as other stores' size ten? Like if I go to Old Navy, will I realize I'm actually a size fourteen?" She chuckled and said she was a size twelve here *and* at Old Navy. *Liar.*

The reason I went shopping in the first place was for a job interview. That's right, I had to leave my favorite gig of being a stay-at-home parent because: mortgage payments.

I started work at the end of August and spent two months hating that I wasn't home with my kids. I was exhausted and trying to keep up everything I did when I didn't work eight-to-ten-hour days. I woke up two hours before my family and headed to work, came home at noon and worked from home while caring for Emersyn, then picked up Sebastian from school, made dinner and got the kids ready for bed, then felt completely depleted after they went to bed. I'd then wake up a couple times a night due to breastfeed. I had no time or energy to squeeze in a run during the week, training almost exclusively on weekends. Then a bad cold knocked me out for two weeks.

> My flu is gone she thought,
> I'll go for a run,
> tonight she thought,
> better wear a neon vest,
> sixteen-kilometer goal, she thought,
> I'm feeling great,
> a comeback....

> A female runner he saw,
> on a back country road
> after dark.

I should follow her he thought,
and he crept along the street,
headlights glaring from behind,
her heart skipped a couple beats

She looked right at him,
he pulled into a driveway
and waited
a moment or two.
She took out her phone,
her only protection,
husband come get me she said,
then changed her mind,
Stay on the phone with me,
until I get into the light.
No, I'll come and get you,
tonight is not the night
he grabbed bedtime kids into car,
tell me where you are.

Once he was on her road
she pressed hang up,
and as the call left her screen
she screamed.

FUCK THE PATRIARCHY she yelled
over fallen fields of corn,
the black wind whipped her legs
as she continued to mutter in scorn,
expletives kept coming as she ran
to meet the corner
where warm familiar lights met her
as she unfinished her run.

During three consecutive outdoor training sessions, I encountered the shittiness of being men's prey. It made me simultaneously want to give up, hide inside, and carry a bat to beat them with. Being followed, men stopping or pulling over to leer, and people yelling nonsense at me through music-filled headphones. *Fuuuuck offfff!*

"What do you wear when you run?" a coworker asked incredulously, wondering how this could happen three times in a row.

"It's fall! I wear a turtleneck, fanny pack, and running pants, and also, it shouldn't matter what I wear."

They all knew this was true but still thought it was outrageous how often this had been happening lately. Although I was the common denominator, it was not my responsibility or in my control. Needless to say, I took a week off from running.

I was not sure what made me angrier: men behaving that way and being their prey, or always having to keep an eye out for circling predators. Certainly, being on alert felt exhausting and infuriating. Managing my behavior to avoid unwanted attention had been something I'd had a welcome vacation from during the pandemic. Transitioning back to a mostly male construction site for my job and running with the wolves was a depressing reminder.

> Today I am a mood.
> I am becoming.
> Strength pulses through my veins
> Threatening to take over
>
> Shoes hit the pavement
> Rhythmically
> Overtaking the sound of my breath

Punch it
Pick up the pace
Step into your power
Your potential is rumbling
At the edge of the precipice

Breathe yourself in
Harness until the moment
You are free to sprint
Wildly as you were born to be.

You are a force of nature
Living spherically
With righteously earned
Joyous ambition

You can do hard things.
You got this.

With only a week left before the Seattle half-marathon, I radiated heat and steam as I ran down frosted streets. It would be a weekend of reckoning as I returned for the first time to the city I associated with Andrew. Not only would I be accomplishing a goal I worked toward since recovering from my daughter's birth, I'd also be reclaiming a beautiful city under my terms for myself. *I want to throw up.*

My whole body was in turmoil. Sure, this sounded like a brave fucking idea on paper, but what the hell was I thinking? *Oh, I'm making such great strides mentally and recovering from my trauma, so let's go to trigger town! Calm yourself. You can do hard things.*

I was bloated, super constipated, and my hemorrhoids were acting up. I was getting stomach pains, my chest cranked tightly to my back, and I got muscle cramps from my butt down to my feet. I may have thought I could handle more than I should. *Rachel, buck up. Flights are booked, hotel is booked, race is paid for, childcare is planned.*

I had been getting back into shape for nineteen months. *I can face this discomfort and persevere. It will be okay. Wes will be there. The chances of running into Andrew are literally one in 755,936. Well fuck. Now that I'd looked up the population of Seattle those odds feel way too fucking high.* I swallowed the bile that jumped up my throat.

Am I going to implode before I even race? Was I getting myself all worked up for no reason? I had been trying to focus on work, kids, and Christmas. But my body kept screaming at me that danger was approaching. *How do I turn off these blaring sirens? Like got it, I'll file that in the back of my brain. Stop giving me Charlie horses randomly, thanks.*

Our trip was supposed to be about rejuvenation. Indulging in food, sleep, and sex (in that order) with my handsome, funny, kind husband. Oh, and running a half-marathon. But the trip was centered around restaurants. I joked with Wes that my goal was drink, eat, and sex—in other words, be drunk, fat fuckers. It got a chuckle. So whyyyyyyy was my body going into war mode? *Just stahhhhp.*

But this had happened before—when I returned to Ottawa for the first time after being assaulted there. Even though the stress was building as the trip approached, I knew I'd feel ten steps closer to freedom when it was over. *So, cortex, please speak to my amygdala and tell it to kindly calm the fuck down.*

A week and a half later, Wes and I sat on a plane to Seattle. The entire trip through the airport, during the flight, and on the light-rail, Wes was completely thrown by how calm I was. *I was ready.* Ready to take back Seattle.

Ready to complete the goal I'd long trained for. And ready to enjoy this time alone with my husband.

After checking into the hotel, we took a bit of a nap to recover from only sleeping two hours the night before. Then we headed out to explore the city. We walked down to the waterfront and ate dinner at a restaurant on the pier. I wanted to share this place with Wes, because it was a really cool eating experience. The server dumped a bucket of crustaceans on the table, and the customer, with a bib and tiny mallet, would break apart and devour this extremely fresh and delicious seafood.

In a fleeting memory I remembered the exact table I had eaten at, eight years ago, with my ex. I remembered how I felt anxious and tight the entire night and was bloated by the end of it. I remembered carefully picking the smaller portions and feeling judged all along. I shook my head and rattled the memory until it flew out of my ear.

The hostess seated us at our table, and we ordered one of the crab-bucket feasts. It was phenomenal. I relished feeling so calm and free during dinner. I was pleasantly surprised that I wasn't anxious or stressed that I would run into Andrew. I was present, happy, and thoroughly enjoyed the experience, with gratitude of where I existed in time and who I was with. The evening ended with complete delight I felt fully nourished and light, not bloated or twisted inside.

Wes and I walked back to the hotel under the lights of the city, holding hands and enjoying the freedom of a trip without the kids. We were just a young couple in love. The next morning, we easily woke early with the time difference. We showered and walked toward Starbucks Roastery before the crowds. We indulged in a flight of coffees paired with chocolates, as well as breakfast sandwiches. We settled into the secluded library and caught up on work while enjoying our treats.

Some people were surprised at how much work I did on my trip, noting that it was supposed to be a vacation. *Hold on, child.* It *was* a vacation. No cooking. No cleaning. No breastfeeding. No diapers. No tantrums. No chauffeuring to and from school. I got to eat delicious foods and leave the hotel without packing a bag of treats and toys for the kids. Doing work in a café with delicious coffee and pastries—call me crazy, but that was heaven.

I had monthly reports due the day before I got back, so waiting until I got back home was not an option. And with up to two hundred emails a day, no vacation was worth coming home to that much work to catch up on. *I ain't no fool.*

Staying on top of my shit was how I functioned at that level. Yes, I will be cocky for this sentence: I was a parent of two young children, *level-up*; I worked hard and received a title change with a twenty-five-percent salary increase, *level-up*; I bought my own house and renovated it with hubby, *level-up*; I trained toward a marathon, *level-up*; and I wrote a book, *level-up*. To be at that level there was no such thing as slowing down and taking a five-day vacation from everything. I saw where I was as a privilege, and I felt extremely grateful and unwilling to sacrifice anything.

"You have to live spherically—in many directions. To accept yourself for what you are without inhibitions, to be open. Put yourself into life and never lose your openness, your childish enthusiasm throughout the journey that is life, and things will come your way."

- Federico Fellini

I took this sentiment to heart. I mean, my ADHD certainly helped with living spherically…*oh, look, a squirrel! I have never felt freer and more capable than I do today.*

Sometimes I walked around with my Superman chest almost exploding with confidence, and other times I sat so hunched in anxiety and hormonal depression and angst that I practically developed a dowager's hump. But on this trip, with my husband by my side, my only anxiety was with my lack of training leading up to the race.

The night before the race, I felt so off-kilter, I was nauseated. I wrapped the blankets around me in bed and lay there, unable to move a muscle for fear it would induce vomiting. Wes ran around the city getting all the things to make it better. Finally, his manly need to solve the problem came in handy! He bought Tums, antinausea pills, Advil, water, and crackers. An hour after taking the pills, I ate a bagel with cream cheese. Then I took a NyQuil and slept like a teenager. *(Teenagers actually sleep, babies don't.)*

In the morning I arose, feeling calmer than I thought I would. My nausea was gone, and I was able to eat a banana and a bit of a protein bar. Wes had arranged a Lyft, and we arrived at the starting line a half-hour before my wave. We walked around and found a place for me to take my nervous pee. Then we watched the walkers start, the national anthem, and the elite athletes start. My wave was the last to go. I waited to join the corral until the last minute to avoid all the shuffling nervous energy.

The race began before sunrise, in darkness lit by streetlights. I popped in my earbuds and used my strategy of chunking out the race: four songs, sips of Gatorade, four songs, two bites to eat and sips of water, four songs, sips of Gatorade, and so forth. Only having to run for four songs always seemed manageable, so that's what I focused on. Any time my mind wandered to how many kilometers

I had left I would bring myself back to the incentive of Gatorade or treats.

Due to Covid, the course had been changed and was wasn't as flat; the first mile had a twenty-one percent incline. I had to use my inner voice to go easy on myself: Finishing was the goal. No training for two weeks due to illness and running a difficult course. *It's an accomplishment just to finish.* But I got cocky. I felt great for the first fourteen or so kilometers and ran at a faster pace than I had trained for.

I used a running app on my phone to track my progress, and due to a GPS glitch, it indicated I was two kilometers farther than I actually was. So, I pushed myself, my inner voice saying, *Just three more chunks to the finish line, only six kilometers, two kilometers per chunk if you keep up this pace, you got this.* But I didn't *have* this. Because as I pushed myself to finish my third-to-last chunk, I saw a mile-marker that squashed my spirit.

Well, fuck this. I'm walking the rest. I thought I had four kilometers left, but this sign right there says *six* kilometers more. *Not today, Satan!* So I walked for the next four kilometers only running in small bits to catch someone or not let that person over there pass me. When the last two kilometers came, I felt I had it in me to run to the end. To push past my limits and completely deplete myself, risking injury to recoup some time and have a strong finish. I chose not to. I chose to walk along the ridge and enjoy the view. I wanted to soak in every minute of this accomplishment, this moment in life where I was happy and free and reaching personal goals. And I cried, for the second time that race. "Through all this chaos and pain, God built a warrior."

The first time I shed a tear was as I rose over the horizon of the bridge at sunrise. I felt light in my body, as if I floated up the incline rather than ran. The dawn broke across the river behind the city skyline and a smile crested my face at the beauty of it all. My phone dinged, and I looked down to see a supportive text from my cousin. And I began to ugly cry. I did not care what other runners or spectators thought I was living through a moment on that bridge over holy water streaked in the morning light and bathing in the redemption of my inner strength.

Gratitude washed over me as I counted all the blessings that led me to that moment. I felt liberated and new, like I was baptized and born again. I wanted to belt out, "This is my city now, motherfucker!" But I didn't, because *I'm not that crazy, folks.*

I grew up being taught that the height of life occurs before the fall, the precious and fleeting golden innocence was the epitome of freedom and happiness, and that the fall of man happens as trees cried leaves and childhood innocence was lost to time's cruel ticking of the clock.

Now, from this perspective standing on top of the hill I'd climbed to escape the wreckage, I felt like this was my golden moment. Redemption that I fought for and earned was the height of existence, and there was no place or time I would rather be than here, now.

I was so glad for that moment on the bridge, because the finish line could have been the punch line of a joke. I felt extreme gratitude and accomplishment by achieving my goal of racing and reclaiming Seattle with positive memories. Because when I got to the finish line, nothing indicated it was around the corner. There was no thrilling music or pelting screams heard from a kilometer away.

I ran down the finish chute to the sound of my feet hitting the pavement. I heard and saw nothing else, as if the starting gun had triggered an apocalypse. I almost wondered if I had taken a wrong turn and may have slowed to look around if a huge finish sign with the timeclock did not span the road. In his booming radio voice, the announcer said, "Aaaand Rachel Suhonos!" and from ten feet behind the finish, Wes fist-pumped a lone "Woooo!" as I crossed the line.

No crowd cheering, no blaring music, no excitement buzzing in the air. No flurry of people with medals, blankets, and water caring for finishers. No crescendo of adrenaline. *Well, that was a little bit* meh. Wes jumped the fence and gave me an ecstatic hug. It was a funny moment, and a little bit of a letdown.

Wes grabbed me a water bottle from a nearby table, and a volunteer casually turned around and asked if I'd gotten my medal yet, then just tossed a rolled-up one in my bag. Wes was having none of that and placed it with some pageantry around my sweaty neck. My husband expressed more pride and excitement than I felt. *He's the perfect support. I'm lucky to have him.*

After we walked to the waterfront together, I stretched and we took some photos before heading back to the hotel. The next day we visited Bellevue, the Seattle suburb where Andrew lived. It was the ultimate fuck-you to be on his stomping grounds and to feel so whole again. TW:PA,SA//

> White tablecloth and burnt skin
> Twist my wrist
> Because you need to win
>
> Soon it becomes all routine
> Coercion and threats
> Don't you dare make a scene

I know your strength
You don't need to remind me
I'll listen
I'll cower
Don't choke me in the shower

Wes and I ate dinner at that restaurant. The one where I burnt my wrist on the fondue pot then he twisted it when we got back to his place and a chunk of skin came off. I have scar on my right wrist because of it.//TW:PA,SA And you know what? This dinner was fucking amazing. I was exhausted, happy, and calm. We sat one table away from where I sat the last time I was there. And aside from me telling Wes the history of it all, I didn't think of Andrew once.

Wes and I just existed. Existed in a parallel universe where I was never abused, never shamed, and never scared. We drank until we were tipsy, we ate until we were full, and we enjoyed each other's bodies like two old people in love.

The Bees

Chapter 19 – Milestones

I still get nightmares sometimes. They stick to my skin like the mist that sticks to the earth at sunrise. The nighttime is haunted trying to face the dawn; it takes a couple of hours for the sun to burn off the foreboding fog and fear to leave my body. The daylight chasing away the cold, damp dread that has overcome my mind.

> I still question myself as I lie in bed
> Did all of this happen, or is it just in my head
> I remind myself of the tangible things
> The scar on my wrist
> The fear of odd things
> Like the scent of the shower
> Putting me on high alert
> Or the way I would worry
> If picked the right shirt
>
> The way you would watch me as I ate my food
> Never being able to say I'm not in the mood
> Learning to fake it to avoid the pain
> Feeling all frenzied just hearing your name

Flashbacks and nightmares
They're my reaction
From something traumatic
So I know these things happened.

Can't tell me I'm lying
I won't listen
Stop trying
The evidence lives in the past you're denying

As much as I hate what I have endured, I wouldn't change a thing, because I am proud of who I have become. I don't believe I would be this patient and persistent, empathetic and resilient, soft and strong woman today without the pain. I will unapologetically stand up for what is right by calling out racism, sexism, bigotry, and wrongdoings because of my pain, strength and empathy.

"I bet a lot of people who went through what you did   don't ever recover. Now you've built a whole new life for yourself. That takes incredible strength to do that."

—Jack Sheridan, *Virgin River*

Looking out my bedroom window early one morning I watched a raccoon climbing a tree. It strategically navigated his way up the massive trunk headed to a nest I couldn't locate. Where the tree split in three, it chose the middle trunk. It reached a hollow and began climbing in. I wondered how the raccoon could fit in a space that seemed too small for his home. A squirrel scurried around a different trunk and watched its neighbor.

The raccoon reemerged with a tiny baby squirrel in

its mouth. He moseyed to a comfortable place to dine and satisfied his hunger in peaceful bliss as the mother squirrel skirted at a safe distance in a frenzy. The raccoon was easily ten times the size of the squirrel and seemed unafraid of an attack. The squirrel knew she was no match for the raccoon, so she frantically circled and watched while daringly checking on her young in the nest.

When the raccoon finished its meal, it calmly returned to the nest and plucked out another baby to devour. I watched, hoping that the raccoon would slip and fall or it would move on and leave some babies in the nest. The squirrel endured the worst and most traumatizing day of her life. One that would affect her decisions moving forward, making it more careful in building a nest and more alert defending her young. While the squirrel navigated survival, the raccoon casually enjoyed an uneventful meal. A meal to be forgotten among many.

I couldn't look away. I wanted the raccoon to fall and die. I wanted the mother squirrel to scratch out the raccoon's eyes and save her babies. But nature took its course, and I innately related. I saw myself in the squirrel and my rapist in the raccoon. He was too strong to fight off as he casually took what he wanted and left me completely damaged. I was just another meal to him. And he? He orchestrated the worst day of my life. He changed the way I approached the world from that day forward.

The raccoon was the predator of this poor unprepared squirrel family. I can never see a raccoon the same cute way I used to, just like when I was twenty-one and experienced the underlying threat that men are to women.

No matter how much I heal, these thoughts never seem to go away. They come from seemingly unrelated things at random times. The big difference is that I am not haunted by them anymore. My pain is no longer possessing me or guiding my decisions. It's a powerless memory.

I used to think I was destined to live in pain for the rest of my life, because of what I had survived. I figured I would have times where I coped well and barely remembered a thing, and times where I was plagued with memories, and that that was just how traumatized people lived.

Now I know better. Now I know who I am. I am not my pain. I am not the woman I was when I Andrew abused me. That was a version of me trapped in survival mode. I am the strength that brought me here, to this moment, where I have begun healing.

> "Sometimes the world seems against you
> The journey may leave a scar
> But scars can heal and reveal just
> Where you are
> The people you love will change you
> The things you have learned will guide you
> And nothing on Earth can silence
> The quiet voice still inside you
> And when that voice starts to whisper
> Do you know who you are?
> I've delivered us to where we are
> I have journeyed farther
> I am everything I've learned and more
> Still it calls me
> And the call isn't out there at all
> It's inside me."
>
> —Moana

And here I am at the finish line of my story. Even though I have healed so much and I feel so incredibly strong, I will never forget that I lost two babies and that I was abused and raped. These things don't go away when you heal, they just get easier to manage on a daily basis. I'm not trying to squash your dreams of erasing unwanted portions of your life; I'm trying to let you know that trauma doesn't disappear, you just learn to live with it and manage it and conquer it. Every day.

The goal is not to erase or replace. It's being able to lovingly talk with your living children about the ones waiting in heaven. It's having the ability to be vulnerable and able to tell your story without shuddering in tears and walking in a fog for days. It's being able to sleep without nightmares and have sex without being triggered. It's remembering and being reminded of your past without feeling haunted. It's feeling gratitude for life beyond the struggle and embracing the ways it changed you into the resilient human that you are.

> "Vulnerability is being willing to express the truth, no matter what; the truth of who you are, the essence at your core, of what you are feeling in any given moment. It's being able to open up your soul and let it flow so that other people can see their soul in yours."
>
> – Oprah Winfrey

I hope I was vulnerable to Oprah's standard in this book. I hope there were moments where you saw your soul in mine and fell a little bit in love with my character. I hope you saw my pain and how I conquer it every day and love me more for it, and in turn love yourself more for conquering your pain. I hope you have learned from my many mistakes and will take these lessons forward with you in life. And if you have experienced similar pain, I hope that you will now give yourself a little more grace and feel a little more hope.

As I write this, it is a warm, beautiful summer day. The garden I made with the children explodes with the fruits of nature. The children dig in the dirt for worms and pill bugs, giggling and talking in their tiny voices while I gently look through the plants for ripened cherry tomatoes to add to the salad at dinner. The bees bumble about, quietly pollinating like magical fairies nourishing the garden, and the air smells of freshly cut grass. As the sun sets into a golden light, turning my babies' wispy hair into glowing halos, the world slows for a moment. My breath stills with the beauty of it all, and I feel wrapped with warmth and gratitude.

For years the bees symbolized fear and danger, and I needed to escape them. Finally in this moment I don't feel threatened by them anymore; I see them in a new light. They showed me the way, they redirected my traumatic memory from pain to escape, and they were my mantra of triumph for years. The bees saved me.

Afterword

It has been two years since I finished writing this book and lots has changed. My initial trepidation of buying a house in my hometown proved to be accurate, so my husband and I finished our renos and sold for a profit large enough to afford a house back in the city of Kitchener. We moved into a family-sized home in a friendly neighborhood backing onto the park and within walking distance to downtown restaurants and cafes.

In Chapter 15 I said, "I have survived so much that I don't think anything could make me end any relationships with family members." Well, after my family read and responded to my book, I started creating some healthy boundaries, which, it turns out, is incredibly hard and something I am not very good at. I'm still learning to identify certain behaviors as toxic, because they were so ingrained, and sometimes it takes days before I realize that something a family member said was manipulative or rude. I am learning, though, and with practice I will get better at identifying and responding.

I have continued my healing journey to love my body, accept my sexuality, and feel comfortable and safe with sensuality. I joined a pole-dancing class, which turned out to be more about fitness and core body strength than teaching middle-aged women to find their sexy side. It was a ton of fun, and I met a lot of wonderful and supportive women, but it did not help me achieve the goal I had set for myself. So, I moved on to burlesque class.

At my first session, I felt like an awkward, out-of-place teenager in a group of confident, beautiful, badass women. I chose to be on the side of the room where I couldn't catch my reflection in the mirror. I felt embarrassed, especially with facial expressions. I faked my way through all my classes, and it was *hard*. At the end of the ten-week course, I performed with my fellow burlesque beginners in front of a group of strangers.

Early in the afternoon, I went to the salon to get my makeup done, and over the course of the evening, I drank an entire bottle of red wine with a straw. I detached myself from fear as all the ladies danced out the nervous energy in the basement dressing room. Some women took shots of fireball, others had vodka; there was camaraderie during the wait to go on stage. We all felt butterflies about having "good face," remembering all the moves, and stripping down to heels, thong, and pasties.

The fierce drag-queen goddess, Sapphyre Poison, announced all our burlesque names (mine was Mamacita Rica), and we walked on stage taking on personas of confidence. The crowd went wild, hooting and hollering at every sexy swish and screaming as we removed each piece of clothing. The noise of the audience silenced any insecurity, and by the end of our number, every lady strutted off stage shaking their tatas.

When I watched the video days later, I realized I looked stunning, confident, and sexually proud—none of which I felt while I was preforming. So, I joined another class to make the way I looked match the way I felt inside. This time I looked in the mirror while we practiced. I focused on looking confident when I held my chin high, and the way I looked sexy as my hips swirled. While I learned the routine, I tried to unlearn all the verbal abuse I had received and repeated to myself about my body size, stretch marks, cellulite, and saggy wiggles and jiggles. As I danced, I moved to release the sexual trauma trapped in my hips.

Recovering and healing from abuse and trauma takes time, and honestly, it'll probably never go completely away. Most days I walk around as if none of my trauma happened: I'm a normal human worrying about mundane things like work deadlines and my child's nutrition, school bullying and after-school activities, date nights and maintaining relationships with friends.

Still, I will have those days when the darkness seeps in, and I go to that place. I don't necessarily dive into a memory. I get triggered by sexism at work, or I experience harassment, but most of the time I can brush it off. I feel confident and healed. But sometimes, especially after a string of incidents or a really bad week, I feel hopeless and dark. I start to feel like giving up.

I start to feel like I am an apple that is so bruised that the whole thing should just be thrown out. How many bruises before the apple is mush? The pain is so deep, threatening, and present that I want to disappear or go live in a secluded cabin in the woods to devolve alone. Forever. So I don't have to pretend I am okay and function like a proper human when I feel dehumanized and unable to do basic things—like take a shower—without trauma fucking with me.

After so many hard knocks, you'd think I could get a break. *I would love a nice full year without hard knocks.*

"I feel like for the rest of my life, I am just holding my breath waiting," I tell Wes. "Waiting for Emersyn to walk in the door when she's five, or seventeen, or thirty, to tell me someone raped her."

Wes's chest stills as he reaches for me. "You can't think like that."

"I can't *not*. Statistics for child abuse are one in five, and women being assaulted one in four. I will always be watching her. Seeing if something has changed. Noticing red flags. And worrying. I refuse to miss something I should be able to see."

His silence says he understands as he holds me in kitchen. We head back to the living room, and as I look at my sweet children my breath escapes me to flutter in an abyss, fearing the unknown—which I can't save them from.

Am I parenting right? Am I giving them the strength and tools to survive what might come to them? Am I teaching them to be kinder children who understand consent?

So often and for so long, I have searched for how the men who hurt me turned out the way they did. I've looked at my ex's parents, who have a seemingly normal relationship and kind demeanor, and racked my brain about how they taught their son to be an abuser. What mistakes did they make? And how can I avoid that with my own children?

I look at the ways my parents triumphed and failed so I can lay and change blueprints of my own. I'm sure I'll make my own mistakes, but I certainly won't repeat any. One way I ensure I am breaking the generational trauma and toxic parenting cycle in my family is by taking responsibility when I make mistakes, especially with my children. I don't parent with fear, but with calm intention. (Which is very difficult some days!) Boy do I sometimes feel like a complete failure and wonder what mistakes my kids will tell me I've made when they're older. And other days I watch my their emotional intelligence, ability to communicate, and mindfulness, and I believe I am doing at least a few things wonderfully.

Throughout the writing and editing of this book, I have aimed to be ruthlessly honest—vulnerable, even if I look selfish during a pandemic; or unnecessarily harsh on my mansplaining husband (they all do it sometimes!); or like a bratty, ungrateful daughter. I am human. Making mistakes is part of growing and learning. Being able to openly admit them and talk about them comes from the knowledge that I know I am the sum of all my experiences on earth, and I love myself because of all of them. I love myself when I am conquering a marathon, and I love myself when I look back on my lowest points.

I am still learning and growing, and I plan on evolving for the rest of my life. As I sip my coffee while writing this afterword, I am ready for the next stage of healing: altruism. I have mended my heart, and now I have enough positive energy in my bucket to pour into others'. I am choosing to become a surrogate to help others build their family, and I am choosing to publish this book in an effort to positively affect other survivors.

I am choosing to expose my body to pain for the reward of others' joy, and I am choosing to expose my story and trauma at risk of judgment for the reward of giving other survivors camaraderie, a template of ways to begin healing, and hope for peace.

If you have experienced trauma, I hope you also will heal. It's a wonderful place to be. See you on the other side.

With love,
Rachel

The Bees

Dear Reader,

This book was quite the emotional journey to write and then edit; revisiting trauma and moments of pain over and over again left me quite exhausted at times. In fact, after my focus group I didn't look at my book for ten months. In the end I pushed through to bring this to publication for you. For the people who may read this book and feel un-alone, or validated, or empowered.

I hope you finished this book with a sense of accomplishment and feel lighter in yourself. Please share this book by passing it along or recommending it to your friends and acquaintances. The more people this book can reach the more it can hopefully help.

If it is not too much to ask, please leave a review of this book on Goodreads, or Amazon. I will read each comment and hope to learn how this book may have impacted you. I appreciate all constructive feedback and all stories shared.

Thank you for reading my story.

ACKNOWLEDGMENTS

There are many people to thank on this journey of healing to publishing. At the risk of missing someone I want to thank all the people who read my book or listened to me talk about *The Bees* and supported me with encouragement and constructive feedback.

Most importantly thank you to my wonderful life partner, Wes, and my amazing children, Sebastian and Emersyn. You are my best and favorite cheerleaders.

Trigger Definitions:

Alcoholism:
any consumption of alcohol that results in
significant mental or physical health problems.

– Wikipedia

Body Image Issues:
Body dissatisfaction occurs when a person has persistent
negative thoughts and feelings about their body. Body
dissatisfaction is an internal emotional and cognitive
process but is influenced by external factors such as
pressures to meet a certain appearance ideal. Body
dissatisfaction can drive people to engage in
unhealthy weight-control behaviours and can become
fixated on trying to change their body shape, which can
lead to unhealthy practices such as with food, exercise,
or supplements. Over time, these practices do not
achieve desired results and often create a trap leading to
intense feelings of disappointment, shame, guilt.

– National Eating Disorder Center

Emotional Abuse:
any kind of abuse that is emotional rather than physical
in nature. It can include anything from verbal abuse and
constant criticism to more subtle tactics such as
intimidation, manipulation, and refusal to ever be
pleased. This abuse occurs when someone uses words or
actions to try and control the other person, to keep
someone afraid or isolated, or try to break someone's
self-esteem. Three general patterns of abusive behavior
include aggressing, denying/withholding, and
minimizing. Withholding includes refusing to listen,
refusing to communicate, and emotionally withdrawing
as punishment. Blaming, shaming, and name calling are a
few verbally abusive behaviors which can affect a victim

emotionally. The victim's self-worth and emotional well-being are altered and even diminished by the verbal abuse, resulting in an emotionally-abused victim.

– Wikipedia

Obstetrical Violence:

Physical abuse, including routine episiotomies, manually tearing the perineum, painful vaginal exams, vaginal suturing without anaesthesia, forcefully pushing on the client's abdomen, or excessive physical force to pull the baby out. *Non-consented clinical care*, including any procedure done without the client's knowledge or consent, or procedures performed under duress, or threats to the client or the baby. *Non-confidential care*, including obtaining patient information where other patients can hear the answers. *Non-dignified care*, including verbal abuse, humiliation, scolding, blaming or shaming. *Discrimination based on specific patient attributes*, including age, weight, race, ethnicity, marital status, health status, economic or educational status. *Abandonment of care*, including refusal to attend to a client in labour, leaving them alone during labour or birth, or failure to intervene in life-threatening situations. *Detention in facilities*, including keeping a client or baby in the facility until they can pay the bill, or keeping a well baby in the NICU until certain demands are met.

– Birth Trauma Ontario

Physical Abuse:

any physical force that injures you or your health in danger. Physical abuse can include shaking, burning, choking, hair-pulling, hitting, slapping, kicking, and any type of harm with a weapon. It can also include threats to hurt you, your children, your pets, or family members. Physical abuse includes restraining you against your will.

– Wikipedia

Post-Partum Depression:

a type of mood disorder associated after childbirth, which can affect both sexes. Symptoms may include extreme sadness, low energy, anxiety, crying episodes, irritability, and changes in sleeping or eating patterns. While the exact cause of PPD is unclear, the cause is believed to be a combination of physical, emotional, genetic, and social factors. These may include factors such as hormonal changes and sleep deprivation.

– Wikipedia

Post-Traumatic Stress Disorder:

mental and behavioral disorder that can develop because of exposure to a traumatic event, such as sexual assault, warfare, traffic collisions, child abuse, domestic violence, or other threats on a person's life. Symptoms may include disturbing thoughts, feelings, or dreams related to the events, mental physical distress to trauma-related cues, attempts to avoid trauma-related cues, alterations in the way a person thinks and feels, and an increase in the fight-or-flight response. These symptoms last for more than a month after the event.

– Wikipedia

Sexual Coercion:

unwanted sexual activity that happens after being pressured in nonphysical ways that include: being worn down by someone who repeatedly asks for sex, being lied to or being promised things that weren't true to trick you into having sex, having someone threaten to end a relationship or spread rumors about you if you don't have sex with them, having an authority figure use their influence or authority to pressure you into having sex. In a healthy relationship, you never have to have sexual contact when you do not want to. Sexual contact without your consent is assault. Sexual coercion means feeling forced to have sexual contact with someone.

— Women's Health. Gov

Sexual Abuse:

sexual behavior or a sexual act forced upon a person without their consent.

— Wikipedia

Suicidal Ideation:

the thought process of having ideas, or ruminations about the possibility of ending one's own life. It is not a diagnosis but is a symptom of some mental disorders and can also occur in response to adverse events without the presence of a mental disorder. The range of suicidal ideation varies from fleeting thoughts to detailed planning. Passive suicidal ideation is thinking about not wanting to live or imagining being dead. Active suicidal ideation involves preparation to die by suicide or forming a plan to do so.

— Wikipedia

Trigger Warning Summary:

Chapter 1 Awakening

<u>Emotional Abuse</u>: Andrew insults Rachel's body, manipulates her, and gaslights her.

<u>Sexual Coercion</u>: Andrew continually pressures Rachel to have sex even though she does not want to. Eventually Rachel agrees so Andrew will leave her alone, and she disassociates while he rapes her.

Chapter 2 Beginnings

<u>Emotional Abuse</u>: Andrew shames Rachel for her menstrual cycle, degrades her, and threatens her with violence.

Chapter 3 Finding Real Love

<u>Emotional Abuse</u>: Rachel's parent's belittle her and tell her no one else will love her but Andrew.

<u>Alcoholism</u>: Talk of Wes' family struggling with alcoholism and an incident where his mother receives a DUI.

<u>Physical Abuse</u>: Wes' mom slaps him.

Chapter 4 From Woman to Mother

<u>Suicidal Ideation</u>: While suffering from lack of sleep and relentless itch Rachel fantasizes about escaping her life and body and fights the urge to end her life.

Chapter 5 Trauma of Motherhood

Obstetrical Violence: Rachel is forced to leave a comfortable birth position in favor of prioritizing the care provider's desire to stick to usual practices. In order to speed up the delivery the doctor gave Rachel an episiotomy after she said no, and then forcefully pulled on the placenta causing Rachel to tear internally and lose over a liter of blood. Rachel was discharged without proper communication of what occurred or how to care for her wounds.

Post-Partum Depression: Rachel felt despondent in the "fourth trimester" and first months of becoming a mother. She felt emotionless and numb, and sometimes felt like she needed to get the baby away from her.

Chapter 6 The Legacy of a Mother

Body Image: Rachel's mother was often dissatisfied with her own body and would yo-yo diet with the newest fad-diet. Her body issues transferred to her children in different ways. Eventually Rachel's mom went so far as to medically alter her body to lose weight with a lap-band then a gastric sleeve.

Sexual Coercion: A scene from *Big Little Lies* where the abusive husband pressure's the wife to have sex until she gives in resurfaces memories of Rachel being sexually pressured by Andrew until she stopped resisting him.

Chapter 7 Struggle of Fertility

Miscarriage: Rachel and Wes lost their second pregnancy at over fourteen weeks with a D&C one day before fifteen weeks.

Emotional Abuse: Rachel's family withdrew financial contribution and tried to bully and manipulate her into changing her wedding plans. Then they withheld by refusing to communicate about the wedding and refusing to attend.

Chapter 8 Not Again

Miscarriage: Rachel and Wes lost their third pregnancy at eight weeks in a traumatic and messy way for Rachel.

Chapter 9 It Gets Worse

Post-Traumatic Stress Disorder: Nightmares and flashbacks of fear-soaked moments of sexual assault, threats, and darkness plague Rachel.

Chapter 10 The Cabin

Sexual Assault: A man drugged Rachel and assaulted her in his cabin.

Kidnapping: The man who raped Rachel then locked the cabin door from the outside forcing her to find an escape.

Emotional Abuse: Rachel's siblings and parents responded to the rafting trip by withholding and ignoring her and refusing to communicate, and by insulting her or gaslighting her about her experience.

Suicidal Ideation: Rachel fantasized about escaping all her emotional pain.

Chapter 12 Rebirth

Sexual Assault: Andrew touches Rachel against he pleas to stop.

Physical Abuse: Andrew restrains Rachel when she tries to get him off her. Andrew hurts Rachel through physical touch.

Emotional Abuse: Andrew gaslights Rachel saying he

knows better about her feelings than she does. Andrew angrily withdraws from Rachel after he assaults her.

Post-Traumatic Stress Disorder: A women who is homeless trigger's Rachel's memory of rape and sends her into a panic attack.

Chapter 13 Breath of Silence

Post-Traumatic Stress Disorder: Rachel realizes a detail from a resurfaced memory helping her recognize that the man who assaulted her likely drugged her.

Chapter 14 Pandemic

Post-Traumatic Stress Disorder & Sexual Assault: A conversation with Rachel's mom brings her back to the moment of surviving her sexual assault.

Chapter 15 Ready for Redemption

Emotional Abuse: Rachel's family tried to emotionally manipulate her to create feelings of guilt after refusing to listen to her birthday wishes. Rachel describes many instances of emotional abuse by her family withholding, gaslighting, shaming her pain, and minimizing her experiences.

Chapter 16 Triggered

Post-Traumatic Stress Disorder: Throughout this chapter memories of abuse and assault are triggered in Rachel.

Physical Abuse: Andrew restrains Rachel against her will.

Sexual Abuse: Andrew touches Rachel while she begs him to stop.

Emotional Abuse: Andrew gaslit Rachel after he

assaulted her or verbally insulted her and minimized her experience. Andrew withheld by refusing to communicate and emotionally withdrawing. He manipulated Rachel.

Chapter 18 Seattle

Physical and Sexual Abuse: In a poem and explanation Rachel reveals Andrew twisted her wrist ripping off skin and left a scar. He also choked her in the shower a couple of time, but not with his hands.

Worthy

My beautiful broken and put back together soul
Shattered by heartless mother
And absent father
Flattened by a late miscarriage
Then another
Beaten by sisters and brothers
And an abusive lover
Twisted around by that rapist fucker

You are worthy
Of healing
Safe love
and happy endings